A+ Certification
Troubleshooting and Repair
Lab Guide, Third Edition

Gail Sandler

Rozanne Murphy Whalen

A+ Certification Troubleshooting and Repair Lab Guide, Third Edition

Part Number: ACS21141LG
Course Edition: 1.1

ACKNOWLEDGMENTS

Project Team

Curriculum Developer and Technical Writer: Gail Sandler and Rozanne Murphy Whalen • **Development Assistance:** Lorraine Vachon, Nancy Curtis, Judith A. Kling, Andrew LaPage, Taryn Manuele and Sue San Filippo • **Content Manager:** Tina Maria Nelson and Clare Dygert • **Copy Editors:** Angie J. French, Christy D. Johnson, Elizabeth M. Fuller and Laura Telford • **Material Editors:** Lance Anderson and Frank Wosnick • **Print Designer:** Isolina Salgado Toner • **Cover Designer:** Vanessa Boehmke • **Photography:** Greg Gefell • **Project Technical Specialist:** Michael Toscano

NOTICES

A+ CERTIFICATION TROUBLESHOOTING AND REPAIR LAB GUIDE, THIRD EDITION

CHAPTER 1: INTRODUCTION TO COMPUTERS

CHAPTER 2: SETTING UP A PERSONAL COMPUTER

Chapter 3: Installing or Removing Internal Hardware

Chapter 4: Upgrading System Components

CHAPTER 5: SUPPORTING PORTABLE COMPUTING DEVICES

CHAPTER 6: PERFORMING PREVENTATIVE MAINTENANCE

CHAPTER 7: TROUBLESHOOTING DEVICE PROBLEMS

CHAPTER 12: IMPLEMENTING LOCAL SECURITY IN WINDOWS 2000/NT/XP

CHAPTER 13: MANAGING FILE AND PRINT RESOURCES IN WINDOWS 2000/NT/XP

CHAPTER 14: MANAGING FILE AND PRINT RESOURCES IN WINDOWS 9X

CHAPTER 19: PREPARING FOR DISASTER RECOVERY

CHAPTER 20: RECOVERING FROM DISASTER

CHAPTER 21: INSTALLING CLIENT OPERATING SYSTEMS

Chapter 22: Automating Client Operating System Installations

INTRODUCTION

This course is the primary course of study for the CompTIA A+ certification program. The course consists of two different volumes: a textbook, containing all the technical information and reference material you will need during class and for later study and review; and a lab manual, containing all the hands-on and discussion activities you will perform during your study.

You should take this course if your job responsibilities include entry-level computer service technician support duties, or if you support computers running any of the Windows client operating systems, such as Windows 98, Windows 2000 Professional, or Windows XP. In this course, you'll build on your experience as a computer user as you acquire the specific skills required to install, configure, maintain, upgrade, and troubleshoot personal computer hardware components and Windows operating systems.

This course can benefit you in two ways. If you want to prepare for the CompTIA A+ Technician certification examinations, this course will provide you with the information you need. But certification alone does not guarantee professional success. So, this course also provides you with the hands-on skills you need to be successful as an A+ technician.

A+ Certification Troubleshooting and Repair, in combination with A+ Certification Troubleshooting and Repair Lab Guide is an effective and comprehensive tool for those seeking preparation for CompTIA's 2003 A+ certification exams. More importantly, with a uniquely performance-based approach, these tools are designed to be the most effective available in preparing you to support personal computers and their operating systems.

The choice and organization of topics shows the emphasis on results—what you will do as a result of instruction rather than a focus on features and functionality. The content is structured around job-based tasks to enable you to learn most effectively—enabling you to retain the material and transfer the information to the job.

The focused, clear presentation of information and the real-world examples make it easy to use this book as a learning tool and as a reference. Each chapter presents one broad topic or group of related topics. Chapters are arranged in order of increasing proficiency; skills covered in one chapter are used and developed in subsequent chapters. You'll notice a progression in your comprehension, application, and integration of skills throughout the course.

About This Manual

A+ Certification Troubleshooting and Repair Lab Guide, Third Edition is designed to give you the practical experience demonstrating, applying, and integrating the knowledge and skills necessary to repair and troubleshoot personal computers and their operating systems. The over 175 activities include Guided and Discovery Exercises to demonstrate and apply targeted knowledge and skills, and Chapter-level Labs to practice and integrate what you have learned.

- **Guided Exercises** are designed to let you choose the level of support you need. Guided Exercises are formatted with two columns of steps, with each column providing a different level of support. The first column contains the "What You Do" directions for discovery learning, and the second column contains the "How You Do It" support for guided instruction. This two-column format in Guided Exercises enables you to choose the level of support and challenge you need, and enables you to tailor the learning to your level of experience.

- **Discovery Exercises** offer you the opportunity to generalize and internalize skills in a less structured, more challenging environment as you discover for yourself how to complete a task. In a Discovery Exercise, all hands-on steps are presented in a one-column format, displaying only the "What You Do" step, without the guidance of the "How You Do It" steps.

- **Chapter-level Labs** are written to take you to the next level of application or integration for objectives you have already practiced. They are formatted similar to Discovery Exercises. All Practice Labs have an associated solution provided in a separate file, which you can use to check your work.

All Exercises and Labs are designed to keep you actively involved in learning the content and to help you transfer the skills you learn to your own situations. Exercises and Labs are arranged in order of increasing proficiency; skills covered in one chapter are used and developed in subsequent chapters. You'll notice a progression in your comprehension, application, and integration of skills throughout the course.

Features

The following components are designed to aid in your learning success:

- **Objectives:** At the beginning of each Exercise and Lab, you will find the activity objective, which helps you choose and organize what you want to demonstrate and practice.

- **Scenarios:** All activities include a scenario that builds the relevance and business context for the activity, and gives you the big picture of the specific example in the activity. Scenarios present the problem or situation in a realistic job-based manner, and give you all the information that you would have in a similar real-life job situation.

- **Setup:** The Lab Guide provides a list of specific hardware and software requirements, as well as detailed instructions to build the computer environments you will need to perform the Guided and Discovery Exercises. Because of this, you can be confident that the Exercises will run as documented, with no discrepancies between the computer environment you are using and the job situation described in the activity scenario. With this structure, you can demonstrate that you can successfully perform a required job skill in a realistic job situation.

  Some Chapter-level Labs use the same computer setup as the Guided Exercises and Discovery Exercises for the associated chapter; others require a separate setup, which is provided with the lab. In many cases, Chapter-level Labs can be performed using a choice of different computer configurations, giving you the opportunity to fine-tune your skills in diverse hardware and software environments.

When a specific activity requires additional classroom setup or a change in the original classroom setup in order for the activity to work properly, activity-specific setup steps are included. The activity-specific setup might also contain information that pertains to the specific activity example, or background information that, on the job, you would already know prior to being presented with the information in the scenario.

- **Hands-on and Minds-on steps:** All activities, both exercises and labs, include steps for you to perform to achieve the activity objective. Steps can be either hands-on (scripted directions for a tactile exercise) or minds-on (scripted directions for a mental exercise). These steps provide the right amount of guidance and support to work toward the intended outcome of the scenario.

- **Review Questions:** All activities include review questions to help reinforce and connect the activity to the information you learned.

- **Activity Time:** All activities include an estimate of total activity time, to help you plan your learning.

- **Graphics:** Graphics are used in activities to provide visual support for you to identify the location in the computer interface where you need to complete a particular step, or to check the result of the step against your work.

Supplements

Element K provides supplemental materials for instructors using this text in a classroom. The material is designed to reduce instructor preparation time, and to provide additional resources that will be helpful in the classroom when using this text.

Instructor Resource Kit CD-ROM

The Instructor Resource Kit is a CD-ROM that accompanies the Instructor version of this text includes the following materials:

Exam*View* Software: Exam*View* is an innovative assessment/test generation software that enables instructors to create tests with questions that map to the text. Tests can be distributed on paper, a LAN, or on the Internet. Instructors can also customize the tests, as well as add additional questions. A printed copy of a Get Started User Guide accompanies the CD-ROM. The Guide will walk the instructor through setting up the Exam*View* software.

Course Outline: This outline provides a summary of the course content by chapter title and sub-topic. Many instructors find this useful to provide to students so they know what to expect from the course.

Course Syllabus: This syllabus is a template that instructors can provide to students that will specify hardware and software requirements, course objectives, and other useful information about the course.

Data Files: The data files map to student exercises so students can practice their skills outside the classroom.

PowerPoint Slides and Viewer: A complete set of slides that complements the course material is included, as well as a PowerPoint Viewer that will allow you to view the slides, even if you do not have PowerPoint software.

Instructor Resource Web site: Instructors have access to an Instructor Resource Web site that provides the tools available on the Instructor Resource Kit CD-ROM as well as other resources. Additional information on the Web site includes: links to CompTIA information, additional technical information and resources to use in the classroom, and information about Element K textbooks, including how to order materials and how to obtain evaluation copies. This Web site is updated regularly to provide the most current information instructors need to be effective in the classroom.

Course Description

Target Student

This course is designed for persons with basic end-user skills with Windows-based personal computers, who wish to begin a career in information technology by becoming personal computer service technicians, or who wish to prepare to take the CompTIA A+ Core Hardware and Operating Systems examinations.

Course Prerequisites

End-user skills with Windows-based personal computers, including the ability to:

- Start up and shut down the computer.
- Log on to a computer or computer network.
- Run programs.
- Move, copy, delete, and rename files in Windows Explorer.
- Browse and search for information on the Internet.

Basic knowledge of computing concepts including:

- The difference between hardware and software.
- The functions of software components such as the operating system, applications, and file system.
- The function of a computer network.

You can obtain this level of skills and knowledge by taking any of the following Element K courses:

- *Introduction to Personal Computers Using Windows 95*
- *Introduction to Personal Computers Using Windows 98*
- *Introduction to Personal Computers Using Windows 2000*
- *Introduction to Personal Computers Using Windows XP*
- *Introduction to Networks and the Internet*

And also:

- *Hard Disk Management for DOS 6.22*

Course Objectives

In this course, you will install, remove, upgrade, maintain, and troubleshoot computer hardware, and support Windows 9x, Windows NT 4.0, Windows 2000, and Windows XP computers.

You will:

- explore foundational information about computers.
- install or remove devices on standard ports.
- install and remove internal hardware.
- upgrade system components.
- install, configure, and work with various portable computing devices.
- perform preventative maintenance procedures.
- troubleshoot and correct device problems.
- troubleshoot system problems.
- list Windows and command-line tools.
- manage applications.
- install network components.
- implement local security in Windows 2000/NT/XP.
- manage file and print resources in Windows 2000/NT/XP.
- manage file and print resources in Windows 9x.
- manage disk resources in Windows 2000/NT/XP.
- manage disk resources in Windows 9x.
- connect to Internet and intranet resources.
- implement virus protection.
- prepare for disaster recovery.
- recover from disaster.
- install client operating systems.
- automate client operating system installations.

Course Requirements

Hardware

For Chapters 1 through 7:

For each lab station, you will need the following hardware. It is recommended that the documentation and driver disks for each device be included for use by students as needed. For some of the more expensive items, or less common devices, you might perform an instructor demonstration, have one lab station install the item and others watch, or pass the device from one lab station to the next with each station installing then removing the device.

- An ATX-based system with PCI and ISA slots. Whenever possible, have enough components for each lab station to install each device. If the systems you are using have only PCI slots, have at least one other system that contains both ISA and PCI slots. The computer also needs at least one of each of the following ports: parallel, VGA, keyboard and mouse PS/2 ports, serial, USB, FireWire, and sound including Line In, Line Out, Mic, and Game ports. If Windows XP cannot be installed on this additional system, you can install Windows 98 or Windows 2000 on it.

- PCI Cards.

- ISA Cards.

- Printer with a Parallel port.

- Printer with a Serial port.

- Printer with an Infrared port.

- Printer with a USB port.

- Internal and external modems.

- USB hub.

- USB devices.

- Network cards (and any required networking equipment for students to reach the Internet).

- PDA with serial, USB, and/or Infrared ports.

- Extra RAM to install.

- Additional IDE Hard Drive, CD-ROM, CD-RW, DVD, or DVD-R Drive to install.

- Additional SCSI Hard Drive or CD/DVD drive to install.

- External SCSI device.

- Additional parallel port devices.

- FireWire port.

- FireWire devices.

- FireWire hub.

- Speakers.

- Microphone.

- Joystick or other game controller that connects to the 15-pin game port.

- MIDI device.
- Other quarter-inch mini-jack device (cassette player, musical keyboard, and so on).
- Digital camera.
- Laptop with docking station and/or port replicator.
- External SCSI devices.
- PC Cards (Type I, II, and III if possible).
- UPS.
- ESD protection devices such as workbench mats with wrist strap and grounding cord, or floor mat with grounding cord and shoe straps.
- PC cleaning supplies such as compressed air canisters, mini-vacuum suitable for laser printers, swabs, alcohol, monitor wipes, and other PC cleaning solutions.
- Audio CD.
- AGP video card.
- RAID controller and drives.
- Wireless devices including mouse and/or keyboard and networking devices.
- Cartridge drive and cables (Iomega Zip or Jaz, SuperDisk, or similar drives).
- At least one system with dual processors.
- Cables for all devices. In addition, you also need the following cables: Null modem, RJ-45, RJ-11, RG 6, RG 8, RG 58, RG 59, STP, Fiber Optic.

Optional Hardware for Chapters 1 through 7:

Some topics describe hardware that you are less likely to have. However, if you do have access to the hardware, it will enhance the learning experience for the students. Any of the following items will be of benefit to students in installing, configuring, working with, and troubleshooting.

- Digital flat panel monitor with DVI connection.
- DVI port.
- CPU cooling systems including temperature sensors, liquid cooling systems, thermal compounds, heat sinks, and fans.
- Riser cards for audio and communications (also known as daughter boards).
- Mini PCI adapters for notebook computers.
- Different kinds of memory packages.
- Different kinds of CPU packages.
- Touchscreen monitor or panel to attach to a monitor.
- External tape drive.
- CAD/CAM devices.
- Cable modem.
- DSL modem.

- Special function video card such as those with TV tuner or TV connection capabilities.
- Various types of RAM.
- Solid Ink printer.
- Thermal printer.
- Dye sublimation printer.
- Printers with features such as the ability to add memory, hard drives, NICs, operational trays and feeders, finishers such as staplers, and/or functions such as scanning, fax, and copier built into the printer.
- Battery operated printer.

Non-working Devices for Chapters 1 through 7:

For the troubleshooting chapters, if you have access to any non-working devices, the devices can be installed for students to troubleshoot.

- Any of the devices students have worked with (from the hardware list for the course) that are not working are suitable for this purpose.
- Some suggestions for simulating problems are included as Instructor Notes in the activities, but actual non-working devices can often be beneficial in helping students identify when something is broken as opposed to not correctly configured.
- Damaged CD-ROM.
- Broken or damaged cables.
- Any non-working items which can be broken open to show students the internal workings of devices.

For Chapters 8 through 21:

Except where noted, the requirements listed are for the student and instructor computers.

- 300 MHz Pentium processor or higher.
- 10 GB hard disk or larger for the student and instructor computers.
- 12 GB hard disk or larger for the classroom domain controller. (You will need an even larger hard disk if you want each student to use Ghost to create a computer image.) You will need approximately 2 GB of disk space per computer image stored on the server.
- 128 MB of RAM or more. For the classroom domain controller, 256 MB of RAM or more.
- 800 x 600-capable display adapter and monitor.
- Floppy disk drive and bootable CD-ROM drive.
- One computer installed as a Windows 2000-based classroom domain controller. This computer's hardware must be on the Windows 2000 Hardware Compatibility List (HCL).
- Network adapter and cabling connecting each classroom computer.
- A projector system to display the instructor's screen output.
- 17 3.5" floppy disks for each student and the instructor.

- Bootable Windows XP Professional CD-ROMs for the ASR recovery topic.
- Internet access.

Software

For Chapters 1 through 7:

- Windows XP.
- Device drivers for any cards and devices students will install.
- A MIDI sequencer. You can download one of the many MIDI sequencers listed at **www.hitsquad.com/smm/win95/MIDI_SEQUENCERS/**. Several are Freeware, some are Shareware, and some are demos.

For Chapters 8 through 21:

- For the classroom domain controller, you can use either Windows 2000 Server or Windows 2000 Advanced Server. Make sure you have enough per-server licenses for the classroom.
- Windows XP Professional for each student and instructor computer. Be sure you have met the licensing or activation requirements for your situation.
- Windows 2000 Professional for each student and instructor computer. Be sure you have met the licensing or activation requirements for your situation.
- Service Pack 2 or later for Windows 2000.
- Bootable Windows 98 Second Edition CD-ROM for each student and instructor computer. Be sure you have met the licensing or activation requirements for your situation.
- Norton AntiVirus 2002 Professional Edition or McAfee VirusScan Professional Edition. If you choose to use McAfee VirusScan, students will not be able to manually update their virus definitions unless they register their software.
- Norton Ghost.
- PowerQuest Partition Magic or Norton Disk Commander.
- If you want to teach students how to install and configure Netscape Navigator instead of Internet Explorer, you will need Netscape Navigator 7.01 or later. You can download Netscape Navigator at **http://channels.netscape.com/ns/borwsers/download.asp**.
- There are additional requirements for some of the chapter-level lab activities. Please see the setup procedures for each lab activity for these requirements.
- You will need an email account for each student. Obtain these accounts either by installing Microsoft Exchange Server on the classroom domain controller and creating the necessary accounts, or by creating the accounts with one of the free email services that support Outlook Express, such as Hotmail. You can create one account for each student or create a single account and have students share this account.

Class Setup

For Chapters 1 through 7:

1. A working PC for each lab station is configured for the class. The computer has the following ports configured at the start of class:

    *   Parallel
    *   Serial
    *   USB
    *   VGA
    *   Sound card with line in, line out, mic, and game port
    *   FireWire
    *   PS/2 Keyboard and Mouse

    It is recommended that each lab station have no more than two students. Having two students per lab station boosts confidence for those who have never worked with hardware previously. The computers have Internet access; default DHCP configuration for network access is assumed for the course. If your network requires different settings, configure accordingly.

    *   Install Windows XP Professional using the entire hard disk as an NTFS partition.
    *   When prompted, use Typical Settings.
    *   When prompted to add the system to be a member of the domain, select No, and then continue with the installation.
    *   All other settings should be as appropriate to your system and location.

2. Additional hardware is located in bins in a central location.

3. Any equipment that is to be shared (such as laptops, dual processor systems, printers, or other more expensive items that you don't have enough of for each lab station) should be accessible by all lab stations.

4. One or more systems are connected to the Internet to be used as reference stations if students need to access documentation for a particular card or device, for troubleshooting help, or for other system information.

5. To test the network components installation, students will need to connect to a network. Internet access via DHCP is assumed. If your location uses static IP addresses, or needs additional TCP/IP settings, assign accordingly.

6. For any devices that you do not have the original drivers disk for, download the drivers to student systems in a folder named C:\Drivers.

7. The class should start with the computers turned off and the monitor unplugged.

8. Monitors that students will be installing should have the image slightly messed up. Change the brightness so it is very dim, and lower the contrast. Also, adjust the settings so that the image is not centered on the screen. If the monitor buttons or menu allow it, adjust the monitor so that the lines displayed on screen appear to not be straight. This could be pincushion, trapezoid/parallel, hourglass/hooking, tilt, or a combination. However, be sure that students will be able to see the screen well enough to log on.

For the Classroom Domain Controller (for Chapters 8 through 21):

1. Perform a clean installation of Windows 2000 Server or Advanced Server on the C drive in the default installation location. To start the Windows 2000 Server Setup program, you can either boot the computer from the Windows 2000 Server installation CD-ROM, create Setup boot disks by using the appropriate command (Makeboot.exe or Makebt32.exe) and then boot from the Setup boot disks, or create a network boot disk and install from a network share. Use the following installation parameters:

   - Create a single C partition using the entire disk.
   - Format the C partition to use NTFS.
   - Set the appropriate regional settings for your country.
   - Enter the appropriate user name and organization for your environment.
   - Enter the product key.
   - Configure enough per-server licenses so that all classroom computers can connect.
   - Use a computer name of 2000SRV.
   - Set the administrator's password to password.
   - Install the Domain Name System (DNS), Dynamic Host Configuration Protocol (DHCP), and Windows Internet Name Service (WINS) networking services.
   - Configure the date and time settings that are appropriate for your locale.
   - Select Custom networking settings. Assign a static IP address of 192.168.200.200 and a subnet mask of 255.255.255.0. Enter this IP address as the Preferred DNS Server address and also the WINS server address.
   - Accept the default workgroup membership.
   - When installation is complete, log on as Administrator.
   - Uncheck Show This Screen At Startup and close the Windows 2000 Configure Your Server window.

2. Configure the DNS domain name properties for this computer to be class.com.

   - Open the Properties for My Computer.
   - Select the Network Identification tab.
   - Click Properties, and then click More.
   - In the Primary DNS Suffix Of This Computer text box, type class.com and click OK.
   - Click OK to close all open windows.

- Restart the computer when prompted and log on as Administrator.

3. Using the DNS console, create a standard primary forward lookup zone and a reverse lookup zone for the class.com domain.

- From the Start menu, choose Programs→Administrative Tools→DNS.

- In the console tree, expand and select your 2000SRV computer.

- Choose Action→Configure the Server.

- Click Next.

- Make sure that Yes, Create A Forward Lookup Zone is selected and click Next.

- In the Zone Type portion of the wizard, verify that Standard Primary is selected and click Next.

- In the Zone Name portion of the wizard, in the Name text box, type class.com and click Next.

- In the Zone File portion of the wizard, verify that Create A New File With This File Name is selected along with a file name of class.com.dns, and then click Next.

- Verify that Yes, Create A Reverse Lookup Zone is selected and click Next.

- In the Zone Type portion of the wizard, verify that Standard Primary is selected and click Next.

- In the Network ID text box, type 192.168.200 and click Next.

- On the Zone File Page, click Next to accept the default file name of 200.168.192.in-addr.arpa.dns.

- Click Finish.

4. Configure the class.com forward lookup zone and the 200.168.192 reverse lookup zone to accept dynamic updates.

- Select and right-click each zone and choose Properties.

- On the General page, from the Allow Dynamic Updates drop-down list, choose Yes.

- Click OK to configure the zone to accept dynamic updates.

- Close the DNS console.

5. Promote this computer to Active Directory domain controller status for the class.com domain.

- From the Start menu, choose Run. Enter dcpromo and click OK.

- Click Next to advance through the Welcome To The Active Directory Installation Wizard page.

- Create a domain controller for a new domain.

- Create a new domain tree.

- Create a new forest of domain trees.

- In the Full DNS Name For New Domain text box, type class.com.

- Accept the default NetBIOS name, database, and log locations.

- Accept the default location for the Shared System Volume.

A+ Certification Troubleshooting and Repair Lab Guide, Third Edition

- Set the permissions to be compatible with only Windows 2000 servers.
- Enter password for the Directory Services Restore Mode password.
- When prompted, restart the computer and log on as Administrator.
- If necessary, close the Windows 2000 Configure Your Server window.
- If desired, configure the W32Time Service.

6. Configure DHCP so that this server can assign IP addresses to the instructor and student computers.
    - From the Start menu, choose Programs→Administrative Tools→DHCP.
    - Select and right-click 2000srv.class.com and choose New Scope.
    - On the Welcome page, click Next.
    - In the Name text box, type Class Scope and click Next.
    - In the Start IP Address text box, type 192.168.200.1.
    - In the End IP Address text box, type 192.168.200.199.
    - Verify that the Length is 24 and the Subnet Mask is 255.255.255.0, and then click Next.
    - Do not create any exclusions (unless required by your network).
    - Accept the default lease duration of eight days.
    - When prompted as to whether you want to define options, verify that Yes, I Want To Configure These Options Now is selected, and then click Next.
    - If you're using a router to access the Internet from the classroom, on the Router page, enter the IP address of the router and click Add. Click Next to continue.
    - On the Domain Name And DNS Servers page, in the Parent Domain text box, type class.com. In the IP Address text box, type 192.168.200.200 and click Add. Click Next.
    - On the WINS Servers page, in the IP Address text box, type 192.168.200.200 and click Add. Click Next to continue.
    - Verify that Yes, I Want To Activate This Scope Now is selected and click Next.
    - Click Finish.
    - Right-click 2000srv.class.com and choose Authorize to authorize the DHCP server in the Active Directory.
    - Close DHCP.

7. In Active Directory Users And Computers, create two users for each student. Name the first user Admin#, where # is a unique number for each student. Assign each user the password of password. Add these users to the Domain Admins group. Grant the Dial-In Permission to each of these users. Name the second user User#, where # is a unique number for each student. Assign each user the password of password.

8. Install an HP Laser Jet 5si MX printer on this server. Share the printer as NetPrint.

9. Install the server as a VPN server.

- Configuring the server as a VPN server requires the server to have two network cards. You can install the Microsoft Loopback Adapter to simulate a second network card if your server doesn't have two network cards. (You're going to use this network card to simulate a connection to the Internet.)
    - In Control Panel, double-click Add/Remove Hardware.
    - Click Next.
    - Verify that Add/Troubleshoot A Device is selected and click Next.
    - Select Add A New Device and click Next.
    - Select No, I Want To Select The Hardware From A List and click Next.
    - Select Network Adapters and click Next.
    - Below Manufacturers, select Microsoft.
    - Below Network Adapter, verify that Microsoft Loopback Adapter is selected and click Next.
    - Click Next.
    - Click Finish.
    - On the desktop, right-click My Network Places and choose Properties.
    - Right-click Local Area Connection 2 and choose Properties.
    - Select Internet Protocol (TCP/IP) and click Properties.
    - Choose Use The Following IP Address. In the IP Address text box, type 10.0.0.1. Verify that the Subnet Mask is 255.0.0.0. Click OK.
    - Click OK to close the Local Area Connection 2 Properties dialog box.
    - Close Network And Dial-Up Connections and Control Panel.
- From the Start menu, choose Programs→Administrative Tools→Routing And Remote Access.
- In the console tree, right-click 2000SRV and choose Configure And Enable Routing And Remote Access.
- Click Next.
- On the Common Configurations page, select Virtual Private Network (VPN) Server and click Next.
- On the Remote Client Protocols page, verify that TCP/IP is selected and click Next.
- Below Internet Connections, select Local Area Connection 2 (the one with Microsoft Loopback Adapter in the Description column) and click Next.
- On the IP Address Assignment page, verify that Automatically is selected and click Next.
- Do not specify that you have a RADIUS server. Click Next.
- Click Finish.
- Click OK to close the message box about the DHCP Relay Agent.
- In Routing And Remote Access, configure the DHCP Relay Agent.
    - In the console tree, expand the 2000SRV (local) object.

- Right-click DHCP Relay Agent and choose Properties.
- In the Server Address text box, type 192.168.200.200.
- Click Add.
- Click OK.
- Close Routing And Remote Access.

10. Install the latest Service Pack for Windows 2000.

11. Create a directory named C:\Support and share it as Support. Copy the contents of the \Support\ Tools folder from the Windows 2000 Professional CD-ROM to the C:\Support folder.

12. Create a directory named C:\AntiVirus and share it as AntiVirus. Copy the installation files for Norton AntiVirus to this share.

13. Create a directory named C:\VirusScan and share it as VirusScan. Copy the installation files for Norton AntiVirus to this share.

14. Create a directory named C:\Ghost and share it as Ghost. Copy the installation files for Norton Ghost to this share.

15. Create a directory named C:\Images and share it as Images. Copy C:\Ghost\Ghost.exe and C:\Ghost\Ghost.env to C:\Images.

16. Create at least one email account for students to use in Exercise 8-4. Create these accounts on your own mail server (such as Microsoft Exchange Server) or by using a free email service such as Hotmail.

17. Create a directory named C:\Win2000 and share it as Win2000. Copy the contents of the \i386 folder from the Windows 2000 installation CD-ROM to this folder.

18. Create a directory named C:\WinXP and share it as WinXP. Copy the contents of the \i386 folder from the Windows XP installation CD-ROM to this folder.

For the Student and Instructor Computers (for Chapters 8 through 21):

1. Delete all partitions on the computers' hard disks.

 Do not use all of the available disk space when you install Windows 98.

2. Perform a clean installation of Windows 98 using the following parameters:
- Create a C partition of 2 GB in size. Do not enable large disk support on this partition or Setup will use all available disk space.
- Install Windows 98 Second Edition to the default C:\Windows folder.
- Perform a Typical installation.
- Select the Install The Most Common Components (Recommended) option.
- Name the computer WIN98-#, where # is a unique number for each student (such as 1, 2, 3, and so on). Install the computer into the default workgroup (named Workgroup).
- Select the appropriate country or region for your location.
- When prompted, restart the computer.

- On the User Information page, enter the appropriate Name and Company information.

- Accept the Windows 98 license agreement.

- If necessary, type your Windows 98 product key. After copying some additional files, Setup will restart your computer again.

- Select your time zone.

- After configuring the startup environment, Setup will restart your computer again.

- Log on to the computer as Admin# (where # is the same number you assigned to the computer) with a password of password. When prompted, re-enter the password.

- In the Welcome To Windows 98 dialog box, uncheck Show This Screen Each Time Windows 98 Starts. Close the dialog box.

- Close the Channels bar. Click No to configure Windows 98 to no longer display the Channels bar when Windows 98 starts.

- Rename the My Computer icon to WIN98-#, where # is the number you assigned to the computer.

- In the Network dialog box, enable File and Printer Sharing for Microsoft Networks.

3. In Windows 98, create a folder named C:\WIN98. Copy the contents of the \WIN98 folder from the Windows 98 CD-ROM to the C:\WIN98 folder.

4. Configure Windows 98 so that the computer can connect to the Internet. Open Internet Explorer and configure it to use this connection.

> ⚠️ You must use Partition Magic or Norton Disk Commander to create these partitions. If you create the partitions during the installation of Windows 2000 and Windows XP, setup will create a single extended partition using all of the remaining free space on the disk. A single extended partition will prevent students from creating partitions later on in the course.

5. Use Partition Magic or Norton Disk Commander to create two additional 2 GB primary partitions on the hard disk.

> ⚠️ Do not upgrade Windows 98 to Windows 2000 Professional. Perform a clean install instead.

6. After you've successfully installed Windows 98 and created the two additional primary partitions, insert the Windows 2000 Professional CD-ROM. When you're prompted to upgrade to Windows 2000, click No. Click Install Windows 2000 to install Windows 2000 Professional with the following parameters:

- Choose Install A New Copy Of Windows 2000 (Clean Install).

- Enter the appropriate product key.

- If you need to install additional languages for your location, click Language Options and make the appropriate selections.

- On the Windows Setup page, click Advanced Options. Check I Want To Choose The Installation Partition During Setup so that you can create a new partition on which you can install Windows 2000.

- If you need to install Accessibility Options, click Accessibility Options and make the appropriate selections.

- Install Windows 2000 into the D primary partition. Format this partition to use the NTFS file system.

- Configure the regional settings that are appropriate for your country.

- Enter the appropriate user name and organization for your environment.

- Name the computer WIN2000-#, where # is the same number you chose for this computer when installing Windows 98.

- Set the Administrator's password to password.

- If the computer on which you're installing Windows 2000 has a modem, you'll be prompted to configure the modem dialing options. Enter the appropriate area code and number for accessing an outside line for your environment.

- Configure the date and time settings that are appropriate for your locale.

- Select Typical Settings for the network configuration.

- Install the computer into the default workgroup.

- When the installation is complete, restart the computer. In the Network Identification Wizard, on the Users Of This Computer page, select Users Must Enter A User Name And Password To Use This Computer.

- Rename the My Computer icon to WIN2000-#, where # is the number you assigned to this computer.

- In Computer Management, create a user account named Admin#, where # is the computer's assigned number. Assign a password of password to this user. Configure the password so that it never expires. Add the Admin# account to the Administrators group.

> If you find that you need to load hardware drivers from the manufacturers' disks instead of the Windows 2000 Professional installation CD-ROM, students will need these drivers when they install Windows 2000.

7. Configure Windows 2000 so that the computer can connect to the Internet. Open Internet Explorer and configure it to use this connection.

8. After you've completed the installation of Windows 2000, install Windows XP Professional with the following parameters:

- Select New Installation (Advanced) as the installation type.

- Enter the appropriate product key.

- On the Setup Options page, click Advanced Options. Check I Want To Choose The Install Drive Letter And Partition During Setup so that you can create a new partition on which you can install Windows XP.

- Configure the Accessibility Options and Language as appropriate for your environment.

- Do not upgrade the Windows 98 FAT partition to NTFS.

- Do not download updated Setup files.

- Install Windows XP into the E primary partition. Format this partition to use the NTFS file system.

- Configure the regional and language options that are appropriate for your locale.

- Enter the appropriate user and organization names.

- Name the computer WINXP-#, where # is the same number you assigned to this computer for the other operating system installations.

- Set the Administrator's password to password.

- If necessary, enter the appropriate area code and number for accessing an outside line for your environment.

- Configure the date and time settings that are appropriate for your locale.

- Select Typical Settings for the network configuration.

- Install the computer into the default workgroup.

- After the computer restarts, use the Setup program to create a user account named Admin#, where # matches the computer number. Set the password to password. (This account should become a member of the local Administrators group by default.) Use the following steps to set the password:

  - Open Control Panel.

  - Click User Accounts.

  - Click the Admin# user account.

  - Click Create A Password.

> If you find that you need to load hardware drivers from the manufacturers' disks instead of the Windows XP Professional installation CD-ROM, students will need these drivers when they install Windows XP.

9. Configure Windows 2000 Professional as the default operating system.

- In Windows XP, from the Start menu, choose Control Panel.

- Click Performance And Maintenance.

- Below Or Pick A Control Panel Icon, click System.

- In the System Properties dialog box, select the Advanced tab.

- Below Startup And Recovery, click Settings.

- From the Default Operating System drop-down list, select Windows 2000 Professional.

10. Configure the C, D, and E drives with the following drive labels:

- In Windows 2000, open Computer Management. In the console tree, select the Disk Management tool.

- In the right pane, right-click C: and choose Properties. In the Label text box, type Win98. Click OK to save your changes.

- In the right pane, right-click D: and choose Properties. In the Label text box, type Win2000. Click OK to save your changes.

- In the right pane, right-click E: and choose Properties. In the Label text box, type WinXP. Click OK to save your changes.

11. Configure Windows XP so that the computer can connect to the Internet. Open Internet Explorer and configure it to use this connection.

12. Extract the data files to both the C and D drives on each student and instructor computer prior to class. Remove the Read-only attribute from the data files after extracting them.

For the Instructor's Computer Only (for Chapters 8 through 21):

1. If you've chosen to use McAfee VirusScan and you want to be able to demonstrate manually updating virus definitions during the class, install McAfee VirusScan on the instructor's computer.

2. Register the McAfee VirusScan software.

To Provide Data File and Overhead Access Throughout the Course:

1. Keep the courseware CD-ROM available at the instructor computer to display PowerPoint slides. The CD-ROM includes the PowerPoint viewer.

CHAPTER 1

Introduction to Computers

Activities included in this chapter:

- Exercise 1-1 Tracing the Computer's Evolution
- Exercise 1-2 Identifying System Components
- Exercise 1-3 Identifying Software and Firmware
- Exercise 1-4 Understanding the Decimal Number System
- Exercise 1-5 Understanding the Binary Number System
- Exercise 1-6 Understanding the Hexadecimal Number System
- Exercise 1-7 Applying Number Skills
- Lab 1-1 Examining Computer Basics

EXERCISE 1-1

Tracing the Computer's Evolution

Scenario:

During a conversation one day, you are asked to provide information about the evolution of the personal computer.

1. **Match the inventor on the left with his contribution on the right.**

    ___ John Napier

    ___ Blaise Pascal

    ___ Gottfried von Leibniz

    ___ Herman Hollerith

    ___ Charles Baggage

    a. Processed census data using punched cards.

    b. Designed a mechanical calculator that could add, subtract, multiply, and divide.

    c. Designed the Difference Engine and the Analytical Engine.

    d. Developed a series of rods that let users do multiplication by adding numbers.

    e. Developed the first digital calculating machine that could add and subtract.

2. **Arrange the following devices in the order in which they were invented.**

    Pascaline Machine

    Stepped Reckoner

    Babbage's Difference Engine

    Abacus

    Napier's Bones

    Punch cards

3. **Match each technology with its description.**

___ Vacuum tubes

    a. Replaced vacuum tubes to make electronic computers faster, smaller, and more efficient.

___ Transistors

    b. Allowed multiple transistors to exist on the same base material and connected transistors without using wires.

___ Integrated circuits

    c. Eliminated the need to manually wire a machine and set switches for each different program that was to be executed.

___ Microprocessors

    d. Allowed an entire computing device to reside on a single chip whose function could be controlled by programmed instructions.

4. **Arrange the following technologies in the order they were invented.**

UNIVAC

Apple Macintosh

EDSAC

IBM PC

Altair 8800

Integrated circuits

Review Questions

1. What's the name of the special pen used to write on tablet computers?

2. Who founded Apple Computer?

3. What was the name of the first popular personal computer?

4. Which electronic component acts like a one-way valve, often used to change AC to DC?

5. Which early electronic computer did Dr. John W. Mauchly invent?

Exercise 1-2

Identifying System Components

Scenario:

One day you open a computer to swap out a failed processor. Somebody standing next to you has asked you to identify various system components in a computer.

1. **Match the system component to its description.**

    ___ System board   a.   Main circuit board of the computer

    ___ Processor   b.   The actual chips that keep track of
                                     computer data

    ___ Memory   c.   Means of connecting devices to the
                                     system board so that they can com-
                                     municate with the microprocessor.

    ___ Interfaces   d.   The collection of wires that connect
                                     an interface card and the micropro-
                                     cessor, and the rules that describe
                                     how data should be transferred
                                     through the connection.

    ___ Bus   e.   The real brains of the computer
                                     where most of the calculations take
                                     place

Review Questions

1. Which interface transmits data across multiple channels at once: parallel or serial?

2. Which bus architecture was the first standard bus architecture?

3. How many bits at a time do SIMMs transfer?

4. Which type of RAM needs to be refreshed?

5. The original IBM PCs where based on which Intel CPU?

_____

Exercise 1-3

Identifying Software and Firmware

Scenario:

You have been asked to identify the different types of software and firmware.

1. _____ software enables users to complete specific kinds of task; for example, writing a memo, developing a budget, or maintaining a mailing list.

2. _____ software performs basic tasks, such as recognizing input from the keyboard, sending output to the display screen, keeping track of files and directories on the disk, and controlling peripheral devices, such as disk drives and printers.

3. _____ software enables the operating system and applications software to communicate with the hardware; for example, a printer driver enables you to print your word-processing document.

4. **Match the term with its definition.**

____	ROM	a.	A memory chip that can be programmed only once.
____	PROM	b.	A memory chip that can be programmed, erased, and programmed again. Erases and writes can affect the entire contents of the chip or portions of the chip.
____	EPROM	c.	A special type of EEPROM that can be erased and written to in blocks.
____	EEPROM	d.	A memory chip whose contents can only be read, not written.
____	Flash memory	e.	A memory chip that can be programmed, erased entirely, and then programmed again.

Review Questions

1. What type of software enables the operating system and a peripheral device to communicate with each other?

_____

2. What type of interface does the Windows operating system have?

_____

3. Macintosh, OS/2, and DOS are examples of what type of software?

_____

4. What do you use to erase EPROM memory chips?

_____

5. Which have a longer life span—EEPROMs or EPROMs?

_____

EXERCISE 1-4

Understanding the Decimal Number System

Scenario:

A user has asked you to convert exponential notation into decimal values.

1. The decimal value for the exponential notation $7*10^0$ is ___.

2. The decimal value for the exponential notation $4*10^1 + 3*10^0$ is ___.

3. The decimal value for the exponential notation $4*10^2 + 6*10^1 + 5*10^0$ is ___.

4. The decimal value for the exponential notation $8*10^3 + 6*10^2 + 7*10^1 + 2*10^0$ is ___.

Review Questions

1. The decimal number system is based on how many discrete units?

2. What is the value of $3*105$?

3. Which character can you use to indicate multiplication besides and "x"?

4. What's another term to denote the decimal number system?

5. Any number raised to the power of 0 is what value?

EXERCISE 1-5

Understanding the Binary Number System

Scenario:

You've encountered some numbers that need to be converted from binary to decimal and from decimal to binary. Convert the numbers and provide the appropriate answers.

1. The decimal value of the binary number 1 is __ .

2. The decimal value of the binary number 10 is __ .

3. The decimal value of the binary number 101 is __ .

4. The decimal value of the binary number 1101 is __ .

5. The binary value of the decimal number 72 is _____ .

6. The binary value of the decimal number 283 is _____ .

7. The binary value of the decimal number 4,096 is _____ .

Review Questions

1. What's another term to denote the binary number system?

2. The binary number system is based on how many discrete units?

3. What are the two electrical states that computer recognize?

4. Which number represents the On electric state and which number represents Off?

5. What's the decimal equivalent of the binary value 1011011011?

EXERCISE 1-6

Understanding the Hexadecimal Number System

Scenario:

You've come across more numbers that you need to convert, this time from decimal to hexadecimal. Convert the numbers and provide the appropriate answers.

1. The hexadecimal equivalent of the decimal number 8 is __.

2. The hexadecimal equivalent of the decimal number 57 is ___.

3. The hexadecimal equivalent of the decimal number 166 is ___.

4. The hexadecimal equivalent of the decimal number 3,416 is ____.

Review Questions

1. What's another term to denote the hexadecimal number system?

2. How many discrete states in the hexadecimal number system?

3. Hexadecimal numbers are often preceded by what symbol?

4. What's the decimal equivalent of the hexadecimal value 2A14?

5. What's the hexadecimal value of the decimal value 1,750?

EXERCISE 1-7

Applying Number Skills

Scenario:

You've been asked to apply your number skills to answer the following questions.

1. You try to save a 1.4 MB file on a disk with 1,400 KB of free space, but the computer states you don't have enough room. What is going on?

2. The value of 4,095 (Base 10) in binary is _____ .

3. The value of 4,095 (Base 10) in hexadecimal is ___ .

4. How many different values can you store in a binary number that is 16 bits long? What is the maximum value you can store?

Review Questions

1. What is a single binary digit called?

2. Eight (8) bits is called what?

3. A kilobyte is how many bytes?

4. A gigabyte is how many bytes?

5. What's a group of 4 bits called?

_____

LAB 1-1

Examining Computer Basics

Scenario:

As part of your application for a job supporting Windows 2000 and Windows XP computers, you've been asked to answer some questions. Provide appropriate answers to all the questions below.

1. Arrange the following mechanical computers in the order they were invented.

> Difference Engine
>
> Arithmometer
>
> Abacus
>
> Pascaline Machine
>
> Stepped Reckoner

2. **Arrange the following technologies in the order they were invented.**

> UNIVAC
>
> Mark I
>
> Integrated circuits
>
> 8008 microprocessor
>
> ENIAC
>
> Transistors

3. **Match the technology with its description.**

____ Chipset

a. The collection of wires that connect an interface card and the micropro-cessor, and the rules that describe how data should be transferred through the connection.

____ CMOS RAM

b. Special memory that stores informa-tion about the computer setup that the computer refers to each time it starts.

____ Hard disk

c. A fixed unit inside a computer that magnetically stores data on rigid cir-cular platters.

____ CD-R

d. A CD on which you can write information.

____ Bus

e. The set of chips on the system board that support the CPU and other basic functions.

4. **Match the decimal number with its binary or hexadecimal equivalent.**

____	5	a.	7A120
____	500	b.	1100001101010000
____	5000	c.	1388
____	50,000	d.	101
____	500,000	e.	1F4

CHAPTER 2

Setting Up a Personal Computer

Activities included in this chapter:

- Exercise 2-1 Discussing Display Characteristics
- Exercise 2-2 Installing a CRT Monitor
- Exercise 2-3 Installing an LCD Monitor
- Exercise 2-4 Adjusting Video Settings
- Exercise 2-5 Changing Video Settings
- Exercise 2-6 Installing PS/2 Devices
- Exercise 2-7 Installing a Parallel Printer
- Exercise 2-8 Connecting Additional Parallel Devices
- Exercise 2-9 Installing a Serial Device
- Exercise 2-10 Connecting Sound Devices
- Exercise 2-11 Installing a USB Device
- Exercise 2-12 Installing a FireWire Device
- Exercise 2-13 Connecting Digital Radio Devices
- Exercise 2-14 Connecting Infrared Devices
- Lab 2-1 Setting Up PCs for a New Home Office

EXERCISE 2-1

Discussing Display Characteristics

Activity Time:

10 minutes

Objective:

To identify some of the key technical characteristics of common display devices.

Scenario:

You have been asked several questions by users lately about the specifications regarding their displays. Your manager wants to verify that you understand the questions and the answers.

---

1. **An average TV has a dot pitch of 0.70 mm. How does this compare to a computer monitor with a dot pitch of 0.25 mm?**

---

2. **Which resolution produces the smallest image that will enable you to fit more on the screen at a time?**

    a) 640 x 480

    b) 1024 x 768

    c) 1600 x 1200

3. **What refresh rate is the lowest at which most people don't notice flickering?**

Review Questions

1. Which display characteristic determines the maximum number of pixels on a monitor?

---

2. Which display characteristic determines the distance between the same color dots on a monitor?

---

3. Which display characteristic determines the number of times per second that the entire monitor is scanned and pixels are illuminated?

_____

4. Which screen setting can cause an "aura" effect if you set it too high?

_____

5. How much memory is required when you configure the display to use 24-bit color at 1600 x 1200 resolution?

_____

Exercise 2-2

Installing a CRT Monitor

Activity Time:

10 minutes

Objective:

To install and test a CRT monitor.

Setup:

You have a working computer with a 15-pin VGA-style monitor port. The computer is turned off and the monitor is unplugged.

Scenario:

It is your first day on the job as a hardware support technician. You have been assigned the task of setting up the computers for the marketing department as employees move into their new offices. The standard VGA CRT monitors have been delivered to each office. Employees want to begin using their computers as soon as possible.

What You Do	How You Do It
1. **Plug in the monitor.**	a. **Verify that the power is off at the computer.**
The pins can be easily bent, so alignment is critical to successfully adding a monitor to your system. Bent pins can result in poor video display or no video display.	b. **Identify the VGA adapter port.**
	c. **Locate the monitor cable and examine the connector.**
	d. **Insert the monitor cable into the VGA adapter, being sure to align the pins carefully.**
	e. **Tighten the screws.**

2. Verify that the monitor is functional.

    a. Turn on the monitor power.

    b. Turn on the computer power.

    c. After the system has started to boot, **verify that the power light on the monitor is green and is not flashing.**

Review Questions

1. How many pins does a VGA monitor cable contain?

   _____

2. What three components must you have for Plug and Play to succeed in automatically installing a hardware device?

   _____

   _____

3. What utility should you use if Windows fails to detect and install a Plug and Play device?

   _____

EXERCISE 2-3

Installing an LCD Monitor

Activity Time:

10 minutes

Objective:

To install and test an LCD monitor.

Setup:

You have a computer equipped with a digital video interface, and you have a digital flat-panel LCD monitor that uses the 29-pin DVI connector.

Scenario:

One of the marketing managers is replacing their CRT with a digital flat-panel LCD monitor as they move in to their new office. Their system already has a DVI interface installed.

What You Do	How You Do It
1. Plug in the LCD monitor.	a. Verify that the power is off at the computer.
	b. Locate the DVI port on the computer.
	c. Locate the LCD monitor cable and examine the connector.
	d. Insert the LCD monitor connector into the DVI port, being sure to align the pins with the holes.
2. Verify that the monitor is functional.	a. Turn on the monitor power.
	b. Turn on the computer power.
	c. Watch the monitor and verify that the display is clear.

A+ Certification Troubleshooting and Repair Lab Guide, Third Edition

Review Questions

1. How many pins does a DVI monitor cable contain?

   _____

2. After installing a new monitor, what steps should you take to verify that it works?

   _____

   _____

   _____

   _____

EXERCISE 2-4

Adjusting Video Settings

Activity Time:

10 minutes

Objective:

To adjust a variety of display settings to conform to user requirements.

Setup:

The computer is turned on and the Windows Login dialog box is displayed on the screen.

Scenario:

A monitor was recently moved from the old location to the new location. The employee reports that the display does not appear in the center of the monitor. The images are too dark, making it difficult to see, and they can't see as much on the screen as they would like to see. He would also like to use bigger fonts. The employee needs you to resolve these issues so that he can get back to work.

What You Do	How You Do It
1. Adjust the monitor display.	a. **Log in as Administrator.**
	b. **Referring to documentation as necessary, locate the control to adjust the brightness of the display image.**
	c. **Adjust the brightness** so that the monitor is comfortable to view.
	d. **Adjust the contrast** so that you can view all screen elements easily.

A+ Certification Troubleshooting and Repair Lab Guide, Third Edition

2. **Adjust the horizontal and vertical position of the image.**

    a. Referring to documentation as necessary, **locate the controls to adjust the size and centering of the display image.**

    b. **Adjust the vertical display position** so that the display is centered top-to-bottom on the screen.

    c. **Adjust the horizontal display position** so that the display is centered side-to-side on the screen.

    d. **Adjust the height and width of the image** so that there is either no border or the smallest border allowed.

3. **Change the resolution.**

    a. **Right-click the Desktop, and then choose Properties.** The Display Properties dialog box is displayed.

    b. **Click the Settings tab** to display this page of the dialog box.

    c. In the Screen Resolution box, **drag the slider to the right or click** to select the highest supported setting.

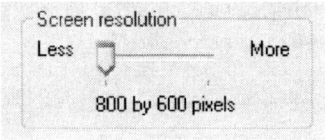

    d. **Click Apply.**

    e. If prompted, **click OK** to acknowledge the informational message.

    f. In the Monitor Settings dialog box, **click Yes** to confirm the changes.

4. Change the font size.

    a. **Right-click the Desktop and choose Properties.**

    b. **Click the Appearance tab.**

    c. **Display the Font Size drop-down list.**

    d. **Choose Large Fonts.**

    e. **Click OK.**

Review Questions

1. How do you adjust the horizontal and vertical position of the image on a monitor?

   _____

2. How do you adjust the font size displayed on a monitor?

   _____

3. Which display characteristics do you typically configure by using the monitor and not the Windows operating system?

   _____

4. Which display characteristics do you typically configure by using Windows and not the control buttons on the monitor?

   _____

EXERCISE 2-5

Changing Video Settings

Activity Time:

10 minutes

Objective:

To adjust a monitor's font setting.

Scenario:

The manager decided that the font you installed for him was too large. He would like to try something a little smaller.

---

1. How do you configure fonts by using the DPI method?

   By clicking Advanced on the Settings tab of the Display Properties dialog box.

---

2. **Change the font to Normal Size.**

    If the resolution of the monitor is too high for you, you can change it to something more comfortable for you at this time.

---

3. **Reboot the system and verify that the fonts are an acceptable size.**

Review Questions

1. How do you adjust the horizontal and vertical position of the image on a monitor?

2. How do you adjust the font size displayed on a monitor?

3. Which display characteristics do you typically configure by using the monitor and not the Windows operating system?

4. Which display characteristics do you typically configure by using Windows and not the control buttons on the monitor?

_____

Exercise 2-6

Installing PS/2 Devices

Activity Time:

15 minutes

Objective:

To install and test a PS/2 keyboard and mouse.

Setup:

Your computer is shut down. You have a keyboard and mouse that have been unplugged from your working computer.

Scenario:

The next pieces of equipment to be delivered are the company standard input devices. As you continue moving the marketing employees in to their new offices, you need to connect these devices to the systems before employees can begin using their systems.

What You Do	How You Do It
1. **Plug in the keyboard.**	a. **Verify that the power is off at the computer.**
⚠ You should have the power turned off when adding or removing keyboard and mouse peripherals.	b. **Identify the keyboard port.**
	c. **Locate the keyboard and examine the connector.**
	d. **Insert the keyboard connector in to the keyboard PS/2 port on the computer, being sure to align the pins with the holes.**
2. **Plug in the mouse.**	a. **Identify the PS/2 mouse port.**
	b. **Locate the mouse and examine the connector.**
	c. **Insert the PS/2 mouse connector in to the PS/2 mouse port on the computer, being sure to align the pins with the holes.**

3. Verify that the keyboard and mouse are fully functional.

    a. Turn on the computer power switch.

    b. Watch the monitor for error messages.

    c. If an error message indicating "no keyboard found" is displayed, **turn off the computer, and then switch the connections and reboot again.**

    d. **Log in as Administrator.**

    e. **Click the Start button, and then choose All Programs→Accessories→Notepad** to start an application and verify that the mouse works.

    f. In Notepad, **type *Does this keyboard work?*** to verify that the keyboard works.

    g. **Choose File→Exit** to close Notepad.

    h. When prompted to save changes, **click Yes.**

    i. In the File Name text box, **type *test.txt* and click Save.**

Review Questions

1. What components make up the PS/2 interface?

2. If the PS/2 ports on a computer are color-coded, what color is the mouse port?

3. If the PS/2 ports on a computer are color-coded, what color is the keyboard port?

4. What is the first step you should take before attempting to install a PS/2 device?

_____

_____

5.   You're attempting to install a new mouse. Windows XP doesn't have the necessary drivers for the mouse. Where should you obtain the drivers?

2

_____

_____

Exercise 2-7

Installing a Parallel Printer

Activity Time:

20 minutes

Objective:

To set up and test a parallel printer, and plan cable needs if the printer is relocated in the future.

Setup:

The drivers for the parallel printer that you install will be provided to you by your instructor. They will be in one of the following locations: in a directory on your local drive, on a network drive, on floppy disks, or on CD-ROM.

Scenario:

As you continue to unpack equipment for the marketing department manager, you next take out a printer and a parallel port cable. You will install it so the manager can use it.

What You Do	How You Do It
1. Connect the cable between the parallel printer and the system.	a. Turn off the power at the computer.
	b. Locate an available parallel port.
	c. Connect the Centronix end of the cable to the printer, securing the clips on either side of the connector.
	d. Connect the 25-pin male end of the cable to the parallel port on the system.
	e. Plug in the printer's power cord.

2.   **Install the driver.**

    a. **Turn on the power to the device and the computer.**

    b. If prompted, **follow the New Hardware Wizard prompts.**

    c. If you are not prompted with the New Hardware Wizard, **note the System Notification bubble pop-up in the System Tray stating that the device was installed.**

---

3.   **Verify that the correct printer driver was installed.**

    a. From the Start menu, **choose Printers And Faxes.**

    b. **Verify that the correct printer make and model is listed.**

    c. If it is not listed, **click Add Printer, and then follow the prompts in the Add Printer Wizard.**

---

4.   **Test the connection by printing a test page.**

    a. **Right-click the printer and choose Properties.**

    b. **Click Print Test Page.**

    c. **Click OK twice.**

    d. **Close all open windows.**

---

5.   **The manager would like the printer on the far side of the office so that it is out of his way. You measure the distance the cable would need to reach (down the desk leg, across the floor next to the file cabinet, and then around the edge of the room to the far corner) and find that the cable would need to be 25 feet long. Explain to the manager whether moving the printer to this location is possible. Also, explain any issues or problems that might arise from the longer cable.**

Review Questions

1. How many parallel ports does a PC support? What are the names of these ports?

   _____

2. What type of connector is used on a parallel cable to connect it to a printer?

   _____

3. How can you test a parallel printer?

   _____

   _____

4. What types of parallel ports are defined by the IEEE standard? What is the advantage of these ports?

   _____

   _____

   _____

5. What is the maximum cable length supported by the IEEE 1284 specification?

   _____

EXERCISE 2-8

Connecting Additional Parallel Devices

Activity Time:

20 minutes

Objective:

To install and test two piggy-backed parallel devices.

Setup:

You have been given a parallel port device such as a portable drive, scanner, or other device, a parallel cable, documentation, and any drivers needed for the device. The device has a "piggy-back" port through which you can connect another parallel port device including a printer.

Scenario:

Some of the employees you provide hardware support for have devices that connect through the parallel port in addition to having parallel port printers. They need your help in connecting both the second parallel port device and the printer so that both can be used without the need to disconnect one and then use the other.

What You Do	How You Do It
1. Connect the parallel device (the non-printer parallel device).	a. Turn off the printer and the computer.
	b. Disconnect the printer from LPT1.
	c. Connect the parallel cable between the non-printer parallel device and the computer.
	d. Plug in the power cord for the device you just connected.

2.	Install the device driver.	a.	Turn on the device and the computer.
		b.	If prompted, **install the device driver software.**
		c.	If you are not prompted to install the device drivers, **verify that the System Notification message indicates that the drivers were installed.**
		d.	If no System Notification message is displayed, **manually install the drivers for the device following the installation instructions in the documentation for the device.**
3.	**Connect the printer to the other parallel port through the parallel port connection on the device.**	a.	**Turn off the device and the computer.**
		b.	**Connect the printer cable to the parallel port on the parallel device.**
		c.	**Turn on the parallel port device, the printer, and the computer.**
4.	**Test that both devices function properly.**	a.	**Read from, write to, or use other functions of the device connected directly to LPT1.**
		b.	**Print a test page from the printer's Properties dialog box.**

Review Questions

1. You would like to install both a parallel printer and a CD-ROM drive with a parallel interface on a computer. The computer has a single parallel port (LPT1). What do you need in order to install both devices on the computer?

2. You have installed a portable drive on a computer's parallel port. How can you verify that this device is working correctly?

3. What step should you take first before connecting a parallel device to a computer?

_____

4. You have connected a parallel port CD-ROM drive to a computer, and plugged a printer into the piggy-back parallel port on the CD-ROM drive. How can you verify that the printer is working correctly?

_____

5. If a computer uses color-coding to identify its ports, what color is assigned to a parallel port?

_____

Exercise 2-9

Installing a Serial Device

Activity Time:

15 minutes to 30 minutes

Objective:
To install and test a serial device.

Setup:
You have been given a serial device. If a separate serial cable is required, it has been provided to you. Any drivers needed have also been provided.

Scenario:
A user bought a piece of equipment and doesn't know how to connect it to her system. After you install the serial device on the computer, you need to confirm that the configuration of the serial port meets the company standard. You have been given a document with the settings the company uses for serial devices such as modems and serial printers.

Device	Settings
Modem	8 Data Bits, 1 Stop Bit, No Parity, Bits Per Second to match the modem.
Mouse	Defaults.
Printer	9600 Bits Per Second, 8 data bits, No parity, 1 Stop Bit, X-on/X-off protocol.
Other serial devices	Defaults.

What You Do	How You Do It
1. Connect the serial device to the serial port on the computer.	a. Turn off the power at the computer.
	b. Identify an available serial port and determine if it is a 9-pin or 25-pin port.
	c. Locate the connector on the device and determine if it requires a 9-pin or 25-pin cable, and whether the cable needs to have a male or female connection on the device end.
	d. Locate a serial cable that meets the requirements as determined.
	e. If necessary, **plug the serial cable into the device.**
	f. **Plug the other end of the serial cable into the serial port on the computer.**
	g. **Secure the cable at both ends by turning the screws on each side of the cable's connector.**
	h. **Boot the computer.**
	i. If prompted, **install drivers.**
2. **Display the Port Settings list in Device Manager.**	a. From the Start menu, **choose Control Panel.**
	b. In the Control Panel window, **click Performance And Maintenance, and then click the System link** to display the System Properties window.
	c. **Click the Hardware tab, and then click Device Manager.**
	d. **Expand Ports (COM & LPT).**

3.	Configure the settings for the serial device you installed.	a.	**Right-click the COM port to which the serial device is connected and choose Properties.**
		b.	**Display the Port Settings page** of the Communications Port (COM#) Properties dialog box.
		c.	Through the Communications Port (COM#) Properties dialog box, **match the settings to those required for the device to function properly as given in the scenario for this activity.**
		d.	**Click OK** to save the changes.
		e.	**Close Device Manager.**
		f.	**Close Control Panel.**
		g.	**Click OK** to close the System Properties dialog box.
4.	**Test the device.**	a.	If you installed a modem, on the Diagnostics page of the modem's Properties sheet, **click Query Modem.**
		b.	If you installed a serial printer, on the Properties page for the printer, **click Print Test Page.**
		c.	If you installed a serial mouse or other pointing device, **move the mouse or pointing device around on the screen, and then click an icon to select it.**

Review Questions

1. What two types of connectors do you find on serial cables?

   _____

2. Which Windows utility should you use to configure the settings for a serial port?

   _____

3. Which ITU modem standards define a data receiving rate of greater than 56 Kbps and a data sending rate of 33.6 Kbps?

_____

4. How many serial ports can you have in a computer?

_____

5. How many serial ports can be used at the same time on a computer?

_____

EXERCISE 2-10

Connecting Sound Devices

Activity Time:

20 minutes

Objective:

To install and test several sound devices.

Scenario:

A group in the marketing department is responsible for creating and presenting audio visual presentations. These users have sound cards installed in their systems. They all have speakers and microphones connected to their sound cards. Some of them also have MIDI instruments and instruments that connect through an eighth-inch stereo jack. The users have just received these sound devices and want to begin using them.

What You Do		How You Do It	
1.	Connect the speakers to the sound card.	a.	Determine if you need to connect the speakers to each other, and if so, connect them to each other.
		b.	Locate the speaker jack on the sound card.
		c.	Plug the speaker into the jack.
2.	Connect an external device to the Line In jack.	a.	Locate the Line In jack.
		b.	Connect a eighth-inch stereo jack from the device to the computer.
3.	Connect a microphone to the MIC jack.	a.	Locate the MIC jack on the sound card.
		b.	Connect the microphone to the MIC jack.

4.	If you have a MIDI device, **connect the MIDI device through the game port.**	a.	**Locate the game port.**
		b.	**Connect the MIDI adapter to the game port.**
		c.	If necessary, **connect MIDI cables to the MIDI adapter.**
		d.	**Connect the MIDI cable to the MIDI instrument.**
		e.	If necessary, **install drivers for the MIDI instrument.**
5.	**Test the sound components.**	a.	**Choose Start→All Programs→Accessories→ Entertainment→Sound Recorder** to test the microphone.
		b.	With the Sound Recorder window open, **click the Record button** .
		c.	**Speak into the microphone and say a few words.**
		d.	**Click the Stop button** .
		e.	**Click the Play button** to test the speakers. The words you just recorded should be played back.
		f.	If you installed a MIDI device, **play a few notes** to verify that it works correctly.
		g.	**Close the Sound Recorder without saving changes.**

Review Questions

1. You've been called in to install a non-MIDI device for a user. To what port on a sound card do you connect the device? What color is this port if it's color-coded?

2. You've been asked to install a MIDI device. To what port on a sound card do you connect the device? What color is this port if it's color-coded?

_____

3. To what port on a sound card do you connect speakers? What color is this port if it's color-coded?

_____

4. To what standard are sound cards typically designed?

_____

5. What type of connector is used by MIDI devices?

_____

Exercise 2-11

Installing a USB Device

Activity Time:

10 minutes

Objective:

To install and test a USB device.

Setup:

You have a USB device, any cables needed, and any drivers required for the device.

Scenario:

You are a technician who has been assigned to install and support new peripherals for users when they purchase them at your store. A customer has purchased a device which contains a USB interface. The customer's computer has two USB ports. The device was packaged with the appropriate USB cable, drivers, and manuals.

What You Do	How You Do It

 Your instructor will provide you with one of a variety of USB devices and the supporting cables and documentation to be able to install it.

1.	Connect the USB device to your computer.	a.	Turn off your computer.
		b.	Locate the USB port on your system.
		c.	Locate the USB cable.
		d.	Locate the USB connection port on the USB device.
		e.	Connect the Type B end of the cable to the USB device.
		f.	Connect the Type A end of the cable from the USB device to the USB port on your computer.
		g.	Restart your computer.
2.	Install the USB device driver.	a.	When prompted that new hardware was detected, **insert the disk containing the driver.**
		b.	Follow the wizard's steps to install the device driver.
3.	Verify that the device works.	a.	Turn on the USB device.
		b.	Access the device through the software available on your computer.

Review Questions

1. Which end of a USB cable do you connect to a device?

2. Which end of a USB cable do you connect to a computer?

3. What is the maximum speed of a USB 2.0 device?

4. What is the maximum length of a USB cable for high-speed devices?

_____

5. What is the maximum speed of a USB 1.1 device?

_____

Exercise 2-12

Installing a FireWire Device

Activity Time:

10 minutes

Objective:

To install and test a FireWire device.

Scenario:

You are a technician who has been assigned to install and support new peripherals for users when they purchase them at your store. A customer has purchased a device which contains a FireWire interface. The customer's computer has a FireWire port. The device was packaged with the appropriate FireWire cable, drivers, and manuals.

What You Do	How You Do It
1. Connect the FireWire device to your computer.	a. Turn off your computer.
	b. Locate the FireWire port on your computer.
	c. Locate the FireWire cable.
	d. Locate the FireWire connection port on your FireWire device.
	e. Connect the cable to the FireWire device.
	f. Connect the cable from the FireWire device to the FireWire port on the computer.
	g. Restart your computer.

2. Verify that the FireWire device works properly.

    a. Access the FireWire device.

    b. Transfer the data from the FireWire device to your system.

Review Questions

1. What is the maximum data transfer rate of a FireWire device?

    _____

2. What versions of Windows do not support FireWire?

    _____

3. What is the maximum length of a FireWire cable?

    _____

4. You have two FireWire devices: a digital video camera and an external hard drive. You currently have the digital video camera connected to your computer. You would like to use the external hard drive instead. What should you do?

    _____

    _____

5. What is the name of the standard proposed by Compaq, Intel, and Microsoft that combines the FireWire and USB interfaces?

    _____

EXERCISE 2-13

Connecting Digital Radio Devices

Activity Time:

15 minutes

Objective:

To install and test the software, receiver, and transmitter for a wireless input device.

Scenario:

Several of the employees in your company have purchased wireless keyboards and mice. You have been assigned to install them so users can begin using them.

What You Do	How You Do It
1. If device documentation requires software installation prior to installing wireless devices, **install the wireless device software.**	a. If necessary, **insert the CD-ROM containing the wireless device software into the CD-ROM drive.**
	b. If the CD-ROM doesn't auto-run, **choose Start→Run, and then browse for the file on the CD-ROM to start the installation. Click Open, and then click OK.**
	c. **Install the software by following the on-screen prompts.**

2. Connect the receiver device.

    a. If necessary, **plug the receiver into an electrical outlet.**

    b. If necessary, **power the receiver on.**

        This is usually connected to the USB, PS/2, or serial port.

    c. **Connect the receiver to the port matching the cable.**

    d. If the New Hardware Wizard runs, **follow the prompts to install the device.**

---

3. Connect the transmitter device(s).

    a. **Insert batteries in the device.**

    b. **Click the Connect button on the receiver and/or transmitter** (depending on the manufacturer—check documentation).

    c. If the New Hardware Wizard runs, **follow the prompts to install the device.**

    d. **Test the device.**

---

4. Disconnect any hardwired connection devices you are replacing with the newly installed wireless devices.

    a. **Turn off the system.**

    b. **Disconnect the devices to be removed.**

    c. **Reboot the system.**

    d. If necessary, **uninstall any software for the devices you removed.**

Review Questions

1. What two methods are used to establish wireless connections?

_____

2. Which wireless connection method requires line-of-sight communications?

_____

3. Which wireless connection method does a BlueTooth device use?

_____

4. What step should you perform first to install a digital radio device?

_____

Exercise 2-14

Connecting Infrared Devices

Activity Time:

5 minutes

Objective:

To connect and configure an infrared device.

Setup:

You can only complete this activity if you have a computer with an infrared port or can add an infrared port to your system and a device that uses infrared.

Scenario:

The head of the marketing department uses wireless devices in order to keep her desk clear from cables. She has a wireless mouse, keyboard, PDA, and printer devices. She has asked you to set up her equipment.

What You Do	How You Do It
1. Position the device and computer so that you can make the connection between the wireless device and the computer.	a. Power on the computer and the device. b. Position the devices so there is a direct line of sight between the two infrared ports.

2.	Configure the device as appropriate to the system.	a. If you are connecting an infrared device to a serial or USB port, **open Control Panel, and then click Add Hardware.**
		b. **Click Next.**
		c. **Click Add A New Hardware Device, and then click Next.**
		d. **Select Install The Hardware That I Manually Select From A List, and then click Next.**
		e. **Select Infrared Devices, and then click Next.**
		f. If you have a driver for the device, **click Have Disk, and then click Next.**
		If you don't have a driver for the device, **select the manufacturer and device that match your device, and then click Next.**
		g. **Click Next.**
		h. **Select the port your infrared device is attached to, and then click Next.**
3.	Transfer data between the devices.	a. **Position the devices with a direct line of sight between the infrared port on the computer and the wireless device.**
		b. Following the directions in the device documentation, **transfer data between the devices.**

Review Questions

1. What is the recommended maximum distance between two infrared devices for communications to succeed?

2.   What is the range of data transfer rates for infrared devices?

3.   What step should you perform first to install an infrared device?

LAB 2-1

Setting Up PCs for a New Home Office

Activity Time:

2 hour(s)

Objective:

To assemble a typical set of components and peripherals to create a new, working desktop personal computer system.   .

Data Files:

- Setting Up PCs for a New Home Office Lab Results.txt

Setup:

To perform this lab, you will need:

- 1 Pentium 4 desktop computer with a Windows operating system pre-installed, containing:
  — 1 parallel port
  — 1 serial port
  — 2 USB ports
  — 1 SCSI port
  — 1 FireWire port
  — Sound card with game port
  — DVI-style monitor port
- 1 LCD flat-panel monitor with a DVI cable
- 1 wireless keyboard and mouse set
- 1 PS/2-style keyboard and mouse set
- 1 SVGA CRT-style monitor
- 2 PDAs with serial, infrared, and USB connection options and a cradle
- 1 laser printer with parallel port and infrared connection options
- 1 color inkjet printer with parallel port and USB connection options
- 1 scanner with a USB connection
- 1 digital camera with a USB connection
- 1 USB hub
- 1 digital video camera with an iLink/FireWire interface cable
- 2 sets of speakers

- 2 microphones
- 1 joystick
- 1 MIDI keyboard
- 4 USB cables
- 1 parallel printer cable
- Any other cables included with the various devices
- Any equipment manufacturer's manuals included with the various devices
- Access to the Windows installation media and to any other device drivers needed for the various devices

Scenario:

You work for the R. A. Kash Computer Sales and Support company. A customer is setting up a new home business with her husband. They purchased equipment for a new desktop computer that you will be setting up at their home office.

R. A. Kash has the opportunity to become this customer's single source vendor for all hardware purchases and support requirements. You have been assigned to this account and need to set up all of the equipment so that the customer can begin using it tomorrow morning.

 When you have finished the lab, you can refer to the Setting Up PCs for a New Home Office Lab Results.txt file to check your work.

1. **Remove the system from the box, and then connect the included PS/2-style keyboard and mouse to the system.**

2. **Remove the LCD digital flat-panel monitor from the box and connect it to the DVI port.**

3. **Connect the laser printer to the system using the parallel printer cable.**

4. **Connect the PDA cradle to the serial port.**

5. **Connect the speakers, a microphone, the MIDI keyboard, and the joystick to the sound card.**

6. **Connect the USB hub to the system.**

7. **Connect the color inkjet printer, the scanner, and the digital camera to the USB hub using USB cables.**

8. Connect the digital video camera using the FireWire/iLink port.

---

9. Connect the second PDA through an infrared connection.

---

10. Power on the system and install any drivers you are prompted for.

---

11. Test each device to verify that it works.

---

12. Power down and remove the PS/2-style keyboard and mouse from the system in preparation for replacing them with the wireless units.

---

13. Connect the wireless keyboard and mouse to the desktop system, and then verify that they work correctly.

---

14. Print to the laser printer through the infrared connection.

CHAPTER 3

Installing or Removing Internal Hardware

Activities included in this chapter:

- Exercise 3-1 Establishing an ESD-free Work Area
- Exercise 3-2 Identifying Card Types
- Exercise 3-3 Installing ISA Cards
- Exercise 3-4 Installing PCI Cards
- Exercise 3-5 Installing AGP Cards
- Exercise 3-6 Installing a Network Card
- Exercise 3-7 Installing an IDE Drive
- Exercise 3-8 Partitioning and Formatting the New Drive
- Exercise 3-9 Installing an Internal SCSI Drive
- Exercise 3-10 Formatting an Internal SCSI Hard Drive
- Exercise 3-11 Connecting External SCSI Devices
- Exercise 3-12 Choosing an Appropriate RAID Level
- Lab 3-1 Installing Internal System Components

EXERCISE 3-1

Establishing an ESD-free Work Area

Activity Time:

20 minutes

Objective:

To create an action plan for establishing an ESD-free work area, and to establish and test the work area.

Scenario:

Your company has established ESD-free workstations with grounding wrist straps, anti-static workbench mats, and anti-static floor mats. The hardware technicians carry vinyl notebooks containing pages encased in plastic sheet protectors, because they need to refer to the documents frequently throughout the day. The technicians recently received nylon jackets and plastic styrofoam-covered coffee mugs to celebrate a major project they completed.

There has been a recent increase in ESD damage to systems and components they have been working on. You have been called in to resolve the problem. A new branch office has been set up and you need to establish an ESD-free work area for repairs to be completed at the branch office.

What You Do	How You Do It

1. **What recommendations would you make to reduce the ESD damage that has been occurring?**

2. **List the objects that need to be purchased to establish an ESD-free work area at the new branch office.**

3. Using the list you created, **create an ESD-free work area at your lab station.**

    a. **Install a grounded anti-static work surface mat on your lab table.**

    b. **Place a grounded anti-static floor mat at your lab area.**

    c. **Connect a grounded wrist or foot strap to your work area.**

    d. If necessary, **use a can of anti-static spray in case you notice any static electricity in your clothes.**

4. **Test the resistance on the work surfaces to verify that the ESD-damage potential has been neutralized.**

    a. **Clip the black clip from the multimeter to a ground.**

    b. **Clip the other clip to the snap on the mat.**

    c. Using your multimeter, **verify that the maximum resistance of your anti-static mat is less than 1 ohm.**

Review Questions

1. What steps should you take to establish an ESD-free work area?

    - _____

    - _____

    - _____

    - _____

2. How can you verify that the ESD-damage potential has been neutralized in your work area?

_____

_____

3. At what range of humidity levels do computers function best?

_____

4. What should you do if you suspect that the humidity level in your work area is too high?

_____

EXERCISE 3-2

Identifying Card Types

Activity Time:

10 minutes

Objective:

To identify the connector types for several sample adapter cards.

Scenario:

A customer discovered boxes full of cards when they cleaned out the storage room. The cards are in containers marked as to their purpose (for example, network cards, sound cards, modems, and so forth). They are unsure which of the cards can be connected to their systems since the cards have various types of edge connectors. They would like you to identify the card types and to help them identify the slots in which they can be used.

1. The card shown in the following graphic uses a(n) ____ connector type.

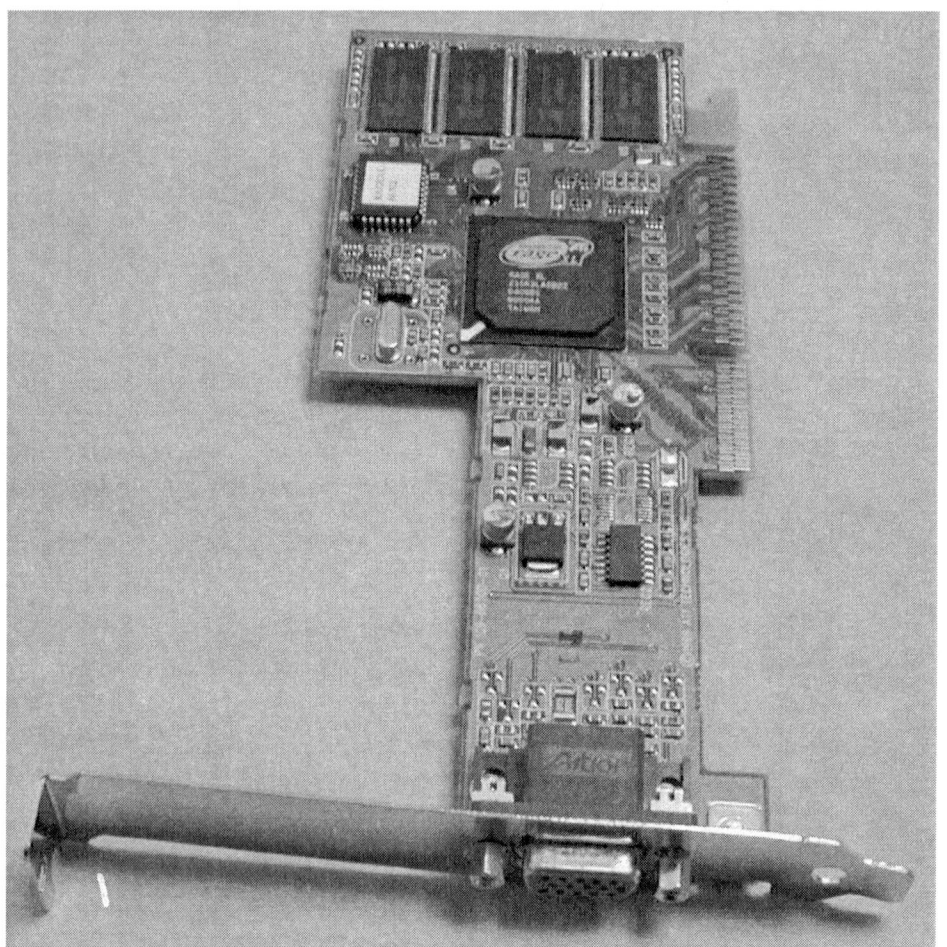

2. The card shown in the following graphic uses a(n) ___ connector type.

3. The card shown in the following graphic uses a(n) ___ connector type.

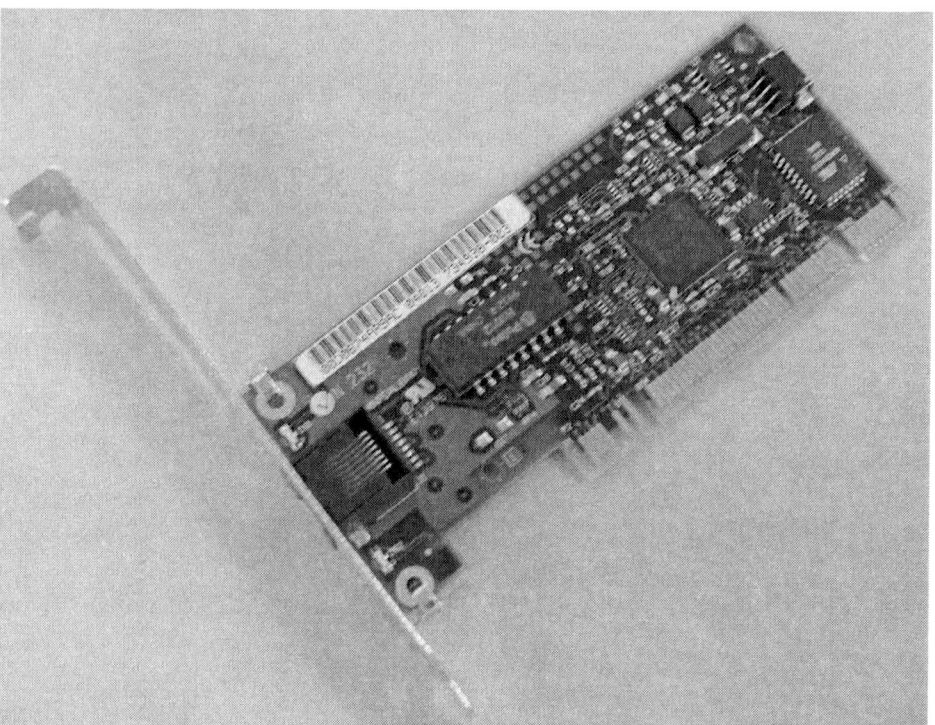

4. The card shown in the following graphic uses a(n) _____ connector type.

5. Identify the cards that can be installed in each slot on this system board.

_____   _____ System 1, Slot 2

6. **Identify the cards that can be installed in each slot on this system board.**

_____   _____ System 2, Slot 2

Review Questions

1. Which type of adapter card is typically found in older server class computers?

   _____

2. Which type of adapter card do you connect to the white slot on the motherboard?

   _____

3. Which type of adapter card is optimized for speed and ideal for video adapters?

   _____

4. Which type of adapter card has an 8-bit or 16-bit bus and cannot be configured through Plug and Play?

   _____

Exercise 3-3

Installing ISA Cards

Activity Time:

30 minutes

Objective:

To install, configure, and test an ISA adapter card.

Setup:

You have at least one open ISA slot on the system board. You have an ISA card and any drivers needed for the ISA card you install are available to you.

Scenario:

You have been asked to install several expansion cards in a user's system. You determine that the first card is an ISA card. The appropriate drivers for the card are also available to you should you need them.

1. Determine the IRQ, DMA, and I/O Addresses in use on your system.	a. Choose Start→Control Panel. Click Performance And Maintenance, and then click System.
	b. Display the Hardware page of the System Properties.
	c. Click Device Manager.
	d. Choose View→Resources By Type.
	e. Select the computer.

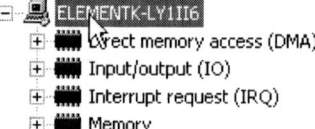

	f. Choose Action→Print to print a Resource Summary report.
	g. With your printer and System Summary selected, **click Print.**

2. **Open the system cover and access the slots.**

    a. **Turn off the system power.**

    b. **Unplug peripherals from the system.**

    c. **Unplug the computer from the electrical outlet.**

    d. **Undo the screws, latches, or sliders** to prepare to remove the cover.

    e. Referring to documentation for how your cover comes off, **pivot, slide, or lift the cover off the chassis.**

    f. **Determine if any components need to be moved or removed in order to access the slots.**

3. **Insert the ISA card in an available slot.**

    ⚠ Do not rock the card side-to-side when installing or removing it.

    a. **Locate an open ISA slot.**

    b. **Remove the slot cover.**

    c. **Firmly press the card into the slot.**

    d. **Secure the card to the chassis with the screw from the slot cover.** Normally, you would now secure the cover back on to the system, but since we will be working inside the system for the rest of the chapter, we will leave it off.

4. **Configure the card for the system.**

    a. **Reconnect the peripherals you disconnected in the previous step.**

    b. **Power on the system.**

    c. **Install any required drivers.**

    d. **Configure DMA, I/O Addresses, and/or interrupts as required for the device.**

5. Verify that the card is functioning properly.

    a. Connect any devices to the card that are required for testing the card functionality.

    b. Access or use the device connected to the card.

Review Questions

1. How does a hardware device signal the computer's processor when it needs to perform work?

_____

2. Which hardware resource enables a hardware device to bypass the computer's processor and communicate directly with the computer's RAM?

_____

3. How do you configure the hardware resources for an ISA adapter card that is not PnP-compatible?

_____

_____

4. What Windows utility should you use to verify that the hardware resources you set on an ISA adapter card don't conflict with the existing resources already in use on the computer?

_____

5. What memory address is reserved for LPT1?

_____

EXERCISE 3-4

Installing PCI Cards

Activity Time:

10 minutes

Objective:

To install, configure, and test a PCI adapter card.

Setup:

The cover has been removed from the system. You have a PCI card and any drivers needed for the PCI card you install are available to you. There is an open PCI slot on the system board.

Scenario:

Now that you have installed an ISA card in the system from the stash of cards the customer discovered, the next card you decide to install is a PCI card. The appropriate drivers for this card are also available if you are prompted for them.

What You Do	How You Do It
1. Insert a PCI card in an open PCI slot.	a. Turn off the system power.
	b. Unplug peripherals from the system, but leave the system plugged into the electrical outlet.
	c. Locate an open PCI slot.
	d. Remove the slot cover.
	e. Firmly press the card into the slot.
	f. Secure the card to the chassis with the screw from the slot cover.

2.	Configure the card for the system.	a.	Reconnect the peripherals you disconnected in the previous step.
		b.	Power on the system.
		c.	Install any required drivers.
		d.	If a SCSI card was installed, reboot when prompted.
		e.	In Device Manager, verify that the device's properties show that the device is working properly and that there are no IRQ, I/O Address, or DMA conflicts, and then click Cancel.
3.	Verify that the card is functioning properly.	a.	Connect any devices to the card that are required for testing the card functionality.
		b.	Access or use the device connected to the card.

Review Questions

1. What step should you take first before attempting to install a PCI adapter card into a computer?

2. What Windows utility enables you to verify that a PCI adapter card is functioning correctly?

3. What steps can you use to test a PCI adapter card?

Exercise 3-5

Installing AGP Cards

Activity Time:

10 minutes

Objective:

To install and test an AGB video adapter card.

Setup:

You can complete this activity if you have an AGP video card to install in your system.

Scenario:

One of your customers wants to run a game that requires a 3D video card. He is currently using the built-in video on the system board. He has purchased an AGP 3D card that was listed on the game box as being supported by the game.

What You Do	How You Do It
1. Install the AGP video card.	a. Shut down and turn off the computer.
	b. Locate the AGP slot.
	c. Insert the video card in the AGP slot.
2. Test the video card.	a. Restart the system.
	b. If prompted, install drivers for the video card.
	c. Verify that the image on the screen is satisfactory.

Review Questions

1. What color is the AGP slot on the motherboard?

_____

2. What is the maximum throughput on an AGP Pro adapter?

    _____

3. What does it mean when an AGP card is described as having a dual head?

    _____

    _____

Exercise 3-6

Installing a Network Card

Activity Time:

15 minutes

Objective:

To install and test a network adapter card.

Setup:

There is a server set up with DHCP to automatically issue IP addresses to each student. Drivers for the network card are provided.

Scenario:

The computers that were deployed for the marketing department need to be connected to the network. Some systems might already have a network card installed and need a second network card to connect to a separate test network.

What You Do	How You Do It
1. Install the network card.	a. Determine the edge connector type of the network card.
	b. Turn off the computer.
	c. Insert the network card in the slot that matches the edge connector of the network card.
	d. Connect the network cable from the network access point to the network card.

2. **Test the network card.**

    a. **Turn on the computer.**

    b. If prompted, **install network card drivers.**

    c. **Choose Start→Run, and then type** *cmd* **and press Enter** to open a Command Prompt window.

    d. **Type** *ipconfig* to display the current settings for your network connection.

        If no network number has been assigned or if the network number is 169.254.0.1, **type** *ipconfig /release* **and press Enter.**

        Type *ipconfig /renew* **and press Enter** to obtain a new IP address.

    e. **Type** *ping www.yahoo.com* **and press Enter** to verify that you can communicate with another system.

    f. **Type** *exit* to close the command window.

Review Questions

1. What type of cable is used to link all portions of a network together?

   _____

2. Which configuration properties are required when you install the TCP/IP protocol?

   _____

3. What are the two methods you can use to automatically configure the TCP/IP protocol?

   _____

4. List five methods you can use to establish an Internet connection.

   _____

   _____

5. What are the four steps for installing a network adapter?

   _____

   _____

   _____

   _____

Exercise 3-7

Installing an IDE Drive

Activity Time:

30 minutes

Objective:

To prepare, install, and test an IDE hard-disk drive.

Setup:

There is an available power cable in your system. The IDE data cable has an available connection. There is an empty drive bay. You have been provided with either an IDE hard drive or IDE CD-ROM drive and documentation. All cables and documentation have been provided with the drive.

Scenario:

One of your customers needs an IDE drive added to his system.

What You Do	How You Do It
1. Locate available bay, power, and data connection resources for the drive.	a. Power off the system.
	b. Locate an available drive bay and determine if the bay is the same form factor as the drive. If you are using a 5.25-inch drive bay and a 3.5-inch drive, you will need to install the drive using rails to adapt the drive to the larger bay.
	c. If you are installing an IDE CD-ROM, CD-RW, or DVD drive, remove the face plate from the drive bay into which you are installing the drive.
	d. Locate an available IDE data connection on an IDE data cable. If necessary, connect an IDE data cable to the IDE controller connection on the system board.
	e. Locate an available power connector. If necessary, connect a power splitter to an existing power connection.
2. Prepare the drive for installation.	a. Set the jumpers or switches to Cable Select or Slave.
	b. If necessary, attach rails to the drive to fit in the bay.
3. Install the IDE drive into the system.	a. Slide the drive into the bay.
	b. Connect the data cable to the drive.
	c. Connect the power cable to the drive.
	d. Secure the drive to the bay chassis with screws.

4. **Verify that the drive is accessible.**

a. **Plug all peripherals back into the system.**

b. **Restart the system.**

c. **If prompted, access CMOS and set the disk type according to the drive documentation.**

d. **If you accessed CMOS, exit CMOS and save your settings.**

Review Questions

1. What is the maximum number of IDE drives you can install into a single channel?

   _____

2. True or False: You install the IDE controller separately from an IDE hard disk.

   _____

3. You are planning to install a single IDE hard disk into a computer. You've jumpered the drive to use a cable select cable. Which connector on the cable should you use to plug in the hard disk?

   _____

   _____

4. You are installing two IDE hard disks into a computer. Both hard disks support cable select cables (and have been jumpered appropriately), and you are using such a cable. One of the hard disks already has an operating system and should be used as the master drive. To which connectors on the cable should you connect the two disks?

   _____

   _____

5. You have installed a second IDE hard disk into a computer. When you turn on the computer, the computer's power-on self test (POST) identifies only the first IDE disk. What step should you take next so that the computer can access the second hard disk?

   _____

   _____

EXERCISE 3-8

Partitioning and Formatting the New Drive

Activity Time:

15 minutes

Objective:

To partition and format a newly-installed IDE hard-disk drive to use the NTFS file system.

Scenario:

You just installed the new hard drive. Before the user can use the drive, you need to prepare it for use. The company standard is NTFS.

What You Do	How You Do It
1. Open the Disk Management utility.	a. From the Start menu, **right-click My Computer.**
	b. **Choose Manage.**
	c. **Click Disk Management.**

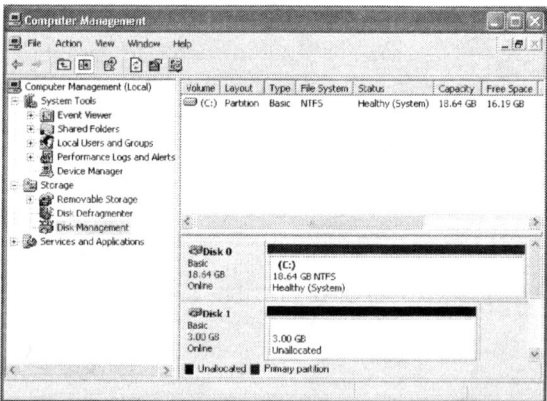

A+ Certification Troubleshooting and Repair Lab Guide, Third Edition

2. **Partition and Format the new drive.**

a. **Right-click the unallocated space for Disk 1.** The new disk is all unallocated.

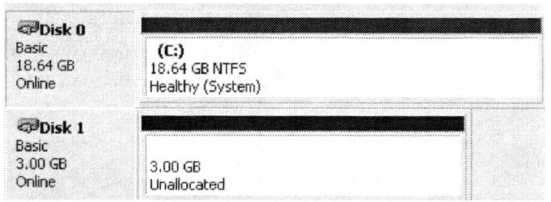

b. **Choose New Partition.** The New Partition Wizard starts.

c. **Click Next.**

d. With Primary Partition selected, **click Next.**

e. **Accept defaults for partition size and click Next.**

f. **Accept the default drive letter and click Next.**

g. **Format the partition as NTFS using Default as the Allocation Unit Size and New Volume as the Volume Label. Click Next.**

h. **Click Finish.**

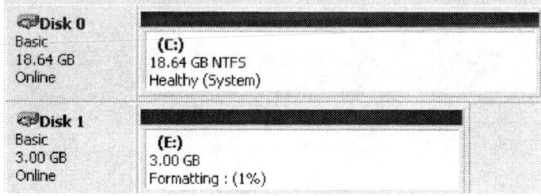

Review Questions

1. You have just installed a second IDE hard disk into a computer that's running Windows XP. When you turn on the computer, the computer's power-on self test (POST) identifies both hard disks as being installed. When you open Windows Explorer in Windows XP, however, you are unable to access the second hard disk. What should you do?

   _____

2. What operating system function prepares a hard disk for storing data?

   _____

3. What step must you perform first before attempting to format a newly installed hard disk?

   _____

EXERCISE 3-9

Installing an Internal SCSI Drive

Activity Time:

30 minutes

Objective:

To install a SCSI host bus adapter, and to prepare, install, and test an internal SCSI hard-disk drive.

Scenario:

You have been given an internal SCSI drive to install in a customer's system. There is no SCSI HBA in the system.

What You Do	How You Do It
1. Install a SCSI HBA in the system.	a. Power down the system.
	b. Locate an available slot that matches the bus type of the SCSI HBA card.
	c. Install the SCSI HBA card in the slot.
	d. Restart the system, and if prompted, configure the HBA.

2.	Locate available bay, power, and data connection resources for the drive.	a.	Power off the system.
		b.	Locate an available drive bay and determine if the bay is the same form factor as the drive.
		c.	If you are installing a SCSI CD-ROM, CD-RW, or DVD drive, **remove the face plate from the drive bay into which you are installing the drive.**
		d.	Connect the internal SCSI data cable to the SCSI host bus adapter.
		e.	Locate an available power connector. If necessary, **connect a power splitter to an existing power connection.**
3.	Prepare the drive for installation.	a.	Set the SCSI ID to an unused ID number.
		b.	If necessary, **attach rails to the drive** to fit in the bay.
		c.	If the drive is at the end of the SCSI chain, **terminate the device and,** if necessary, **remove termination from the previously terminated device.**
4.	Install the SCSI drive into the system.	a.	Slide the drive into the bay.
		b.	Connect the data cable to the drive.
		c.	Connect the power cable to the drive.
		d.	Secure the drive to the bay chassis with screws.

5. **Verify that the drive is accessible.**

    a. **Plug all peripherals back into the system.**

    b. **Restart the system.**

    c. If prompted, **access SCSI BIOS and set the disk type according to the drive documentation.**

    d. If you accessed CMOS, **exit CMOS and save your settings.**

Review Questions

1. You are planning to install a new SCSI hard drive into a computer. What step should you perform before attempting to install the hard drive?

    _____

    _____

2. What is the data transfer rate of Ultra 320 SCSI on an 8-bit bus?

    _____

3. To what type of adapter card must you connect a SCSI drive?

    _____

4. You are installing a SCSI hard drive into a computer. This hard drive will be at the end of the chain of SCSI devices. What must you do when you install the hard drive?

    _____

    _____

5. You have installed a SCSI hard disk into a computer that does not yet have an operating system installed. How can you verify that the hard disk is working properly?

    _____

EXERCISE 3-10

Formatting an Internal SCSI Hard Drive

Activity Time:

15 minutes

Objective:

To partition and format a newly-installed internal SCSI hard-disk drive.

Scenario:

You just installed an internal SCSI hard drive. Now you need to prepare it for use by the customer.

 Only perform this activity if the internal SCSI drive you installed is a hard drive.

1.

   1.   You have successfully installed a SCSI hard disk and verified that the computer can access it. What do you need to do next in order for the drive to be accessible within Windows XP?

       You must partition and format the hard disk.

   2.   What Windows XP utility should you use to prepare a hard disk?

       The Computer Management utility.

---

2.   In the Computer Management utility, **open Disk Management.**

---

3.   **Partition and format the new drive.**

Review Questions

   1.   You are planning to install a new SCSI hard drive into a computer. What step should you perform before attempting to install the hard drive?

_____

_____

2. What is the data transfer rate of Ultra 320 SCSI on an 8-bit bus?

_____

3. To what type of adapter card must you connect a SCSI drive?

_____

4. You are installing a SCSI hard drive into a computer. This hard drive will be at the end of the chain of SCSI devices. What must you do when you install the hard drive?

_____

_____

5. You have installed a SCSI hard disk into a computer that does not yet have an operating system installed. How can you verify that the hard disk is working properly?

_____

EXERCISE 3-11

Connecting External SCSI Devices

Activity Time:

20 minutes

Objective:

To install and test multiple external SCSI devices.

Setup:

A self-terminated SCSI adapter or built-in SCSI port is available on the system.

Scenario:

The artist in the Marketing department often needs to access clip art from CD-ROMs while needing to have the application CD-ROM in the drive to use the graphics application. She would like to have the ability to access both CD-ROMs at the same time. She also has a SCSI scanner to connect to the system.

What You Do	How You Do It
1. **Install the first SCSI device.** ⚠ Be sure that you do not install it into the parallel port, which looks identical to the SCSI ports on some systems.	a. With the computer powered off, **connect the SCSI cable from the CD-ROM drive to the SCSI port on the computer.** b. If necessary, **remove termination from the device** in preparation for adding the second SCSI device.
2. **Install the second SCSI device.**	a. **Connect the SCSI cable from the CD-ROM drive to the scanner.** b. **Terminate the second device.**

3. **Verify that both SCSI devices work.**

    a. **Boot the computer.**

    b. **Install any required device drivers.**

    c. **Insert a CD-ROM in the external SCSI CD-ROM drive, and then change to that drive letter and list the files.** You can list the files through Explorer or from the command line.

    d. **Place your manual on the scanner bed, and then scan the page into the system.**

Review Questions

1. You are preparing to install a SCSI scanner on a computer that already has an external SCSI CD-ROM connected to it. You plan to connect the scanner to the CD-ROM. What must you do before installing the CD-ROM?

2. You have just installed an external SCSI CD-ROM and a Jaz drive. How do you verify that the new SCSI devices are working properly?

Exercise 3-12

Choosing an Appropriate RAID Level

Activity Time:

10 minutes

Objective:

To determine the appropriate RAID level to implement in various scenarios.

Scenario:

Evaluate the needs of each customer to determine which level of RAID should be implemented.

1. If the customer can only afford to add a second disk to the system, they should implement _____ .

2. If the customer needs to improve fault tolerance and performance, and they also need to hot swap failed drives, they should implement _____ .

3. If the customer would like to write everything to two separate disks, and they have duplicate controller cards as well, they should implement _____
   .

Review Questions

1. What is the minimum number of hard drives you need to implement RAID level 0?

2. What is the difference between disk mirroring and disk duplexing?

3. True or False: You can implement RAID with either IDE or SCSI hard disks.

4.   What is the minimum number of hard drives you need to implement RAID level 5?

_____

3

LAB 3-1

Installing Internal System Components

Activity Time:

1 hour(s), 30 minutes

Objective:

To install new internal system components into a desktop computer system.

Setup:

To perform this lab, you will need:

- 1 Pentium 4 desktop computer with:
  - A Windows operating system installed
  - 2 expansion slots available to install the additional adapter cards
  - 2 empty drive bays to install the additional drives
- 1 PCI SCSI host bus adapter card
- 1 PCI network adapter
- 1 IDE DVD drive
- 1 SCSI hard drive

Scenario:

You work for the R. A. Kash Computer Sales and Support company. The customer for whom you set up a new home business has purchased several new internal system devices for the destkop computer at their home office. The customer has contracted with your company to have you install the new devices.

 When you've finished the lab, you can refer to the Installing Internal System Components Lab Results.txt file to check your work.

1. **Establish an ESD-free work area in which to work on the systems.**

2. **Install the SCSI host bus adapter in the system.**

3. **Install the network adapter in the system.**

---

4.   **Install the IDE drive in the system.**

5.   **Install the SCSI internal drive in the system.**

3

CHAPTER 4

Upgrading System Components

Activities included in this chapter:

- Exercise 4-1 Determining the Appropriate Type of RAM
- Exercise 4-2 Adding RAM to a System
- Exercise 4-3 Upgrading the CPU
- Exercise 4-4 Adding and Removing a Second Processor
- Exercise 4-5 Upgrading the System BIOS
- Exercise 4-6 Upgrading the Power Supply
- Exercise 4-7 Upgrading the System Board
- Exercise 4-8 Determining Whether to Upgrade
- Lab 4-1 Upgrading System Components

EXERCISE 4-1

Determining the Appropriate Type of RAM

Activity Time:

15 minutes

Objective:

To identify important technical characteristics for RAM.

Scenario:

You've been asked to help another A+ technician determine the type and quantity of RAM to be ordered. He has several questions he needs you to answer before he is able to place the order with the vendor.

1. **Match the type of RAM with its description.**

   ___ VRAM
   ___ DDR SDRAM

       a. A replacement for SDRAM.
       b. A special type of DRAM used on video cards that can be written to and read from at the same time. It also requires less refreshing than normal DRAM.

   ___ SRAM

       c. A special type of video memory which can be simultaneously read from and written to in blocks.

   ___ DRAM

       d. Used for cache memory. It does not need to be refreshed to retain information. It can use synchronous, asynchronous, burst, or pipeline burst technologies.

   ___ WRAM

       e. Used on SIMMs and DIMMs. It needs to be refreshed every few milliseconds. Uses assigned memory addresses.

2. **True or False? RAM will not run any faster than the motherboard's bus speed.**

   ___ True

   ___ False

3. **True or False? A nanosecond is one-trillionth of a second.**

    ___ True

    ___ False

4. **On a typical system with RAM that runs at a speed of 10 ns, you could add RAM that runs at which speed?**

    a) 6 ns

    b) 10 ns

    c) 12 ns

    d) All of the above

5. **Match the cache with its description.**

    ___ L1   a. Memory on the motherboard between the processor and RAM when there's a built-in L2 cache on the processor.

    ___ L2   b. A type of high-speed RAM that is placed between the processor and conventional RAM to improve computing speed.

    ___ L3   c. A type of high-speed RAM that is added directly to a processor to improve computing speed.

6. **The number of SIMMs or DIMMs needed to create a bank is the width of the CPUs data bus divided by the width of the _____ .**

7. **On a system with a CPU with a 64-bit data bus, how many SIMMs would you need to create a bank?**

    a) 2

    b) 4

    c) 8

    d) 16

8. On a system with a CPU with a 32-bit data bus, how many SIMMs would you need to create a bank?

    a) 2

    b) 4

    c) 8

    d) 16

Review Questions

1. Which type of memory is used to store the system configuration information?

   _____

2. Which type of memory is used on an adapter card?

   _____

3. What units of measure are used to describe the speed of RAM?

   _____

4. You have installed 100 MHz and 133 MHz RAM into a computer. At which speed will the RAM run?

   _____

5. What type of memory is included on the same microchip as the CPU?

   _____

   _____

Exercise 4-2

Adding RAM to a System

Activity Time:

15 minutes

4

Objective:

To install and test additional RAM in a computer system.

Scenario:

The systems your customer purchased have been performing sluggishly. Additional RAM has been purchased for these systems.

What You Do	How You Do It

1. **Determine how much RAM is currently installed.**

    a. From the Start menu, **choose My Computer.**

    b. **Click View System Information.**

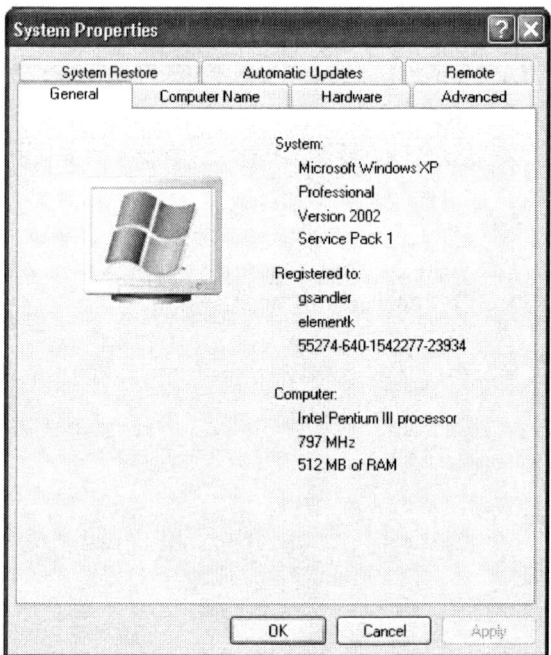

2. **How much memory is currently installed?**

3. **Install more memory in the system.**

    a. **Shut down your computer.**

    b. **Disconnect the power cord.**

    c. **Discharge any static electricity from yourself and your clothes.**

    d. **Locate the memory expansion sockets in your system.**

    e. If there is at least one empty memory expansion socket, **proceed to the next step.** If there are no empty memory expansion sockets, **push the ejector tabs on each end of the memory module out** to release the memory module, **and then remove the memory module.**

    f. **Align the notched edge of the memory module with the memory expansion slot, and then firmly press the module down into the socket.**

    g. If the ejector tabs did not automatically lock into each end of the memory module, **push both ejector tabs up until they lock into the notches on each end of the memory module.**

4. **Verify that the additional memory is recognized by the system.**

    a. **Plug in the power cord and restart the system.**

    b. If prompted at startup, **follow any on-screen prompts** to make the system recognize the memory.

    c. **Display the System Properties dialog box and record the amount of memory shown.** If the additional memory isn't recognized, you can check documentation to see if any steps need to be performed. Also, verify that the memory was correctly seated in the slots and was the correct type of memory for the system.

Review Questions

1. How can you determine how much RAM is currently installed in Windows XP?

2. What type of memory package is used in Pentium IV systems?

3. What type of memory package is used in Apple iMac systems?

4. You just installed additional RAM into a computer. You know that the RAM previously worked because it was in use in a different computer. You are unable to get the RAM to work in the new computer. What might be the problem?

5. You have installed additional RAM into a computer that does not yet have an operating system. How can you verify that the computer can access this RAM?

EXERCISE 4-3

Upgrading the CPU

Activity Time:

20 minutes

Objective:

To upgrade a system's CPU.

Scenario:

One of your clients has an older system that they need to try to upgrade. The CPU in the system doesn't meet the requirements for the application they need to run on it. They have purchased a CPU upgrade and would like you to install it for them.

What You Do	How You Do It
1. Remove the existing CPU.	a. Shut down the system and unplug the power cord.
	b. Ground yourself and dissipate any static electricity you might be carrying.
	c. If necessary, **undo the clip to remove the heat sink and fan from the top of the CPU.**
	d. If necessary, **unplug the power cable from the CPU fan.**
	e. **Pull up the lever on the side of the ZIF-socket CPU.** If you have a different style CPU, refer to the system documentation for how to remove it.
	f. Now that the CPU has been released, **pick the CPU straight up** so as not to bend any pins.
	g. **Place the old CPU in a safe location in an appropriate container** to prevent damage to the CPU should you need or want to reinstall it later.

2. Install the replacement CPU.

    a. Align the pins on the CPU with the holes in the ZIF socket on the system board.

    b. Press the CPU lever back down to lock the CPU in place.

    c. Lock the heat sink and fan clip.

    d. Plug the CPU fan power plug in to the motherboard.

    e. Connect any power connections to the appropriate power connectors.

3. Verify that the CPU is recognized.

    a. Restart the system.

    b. Display the System Properties dialog box.

    c. Verify that the CPU listed on the General page matches what you just installed.

Review Questions

1. You are attempting to upgrade the CPU in a computer. How can you remove the old CPU?

2. You have just replaced the CPU in a computer. How do you know if it's functioning properly?

3. What utility can you use in Windows XP to verify that a newly upgraded CPU is reporting the correct information?

4. What is the maximum amount of RAM a Pentium 4 processor can address?

5. What is the core speed of a Pentium 4 processor?

_____

4

Exercise 4-4

Adding and Removing a Second Processor

Activity Time:

30 minutes

Objective:

To create a plan for installing a second processor, and to remove and reinstall a second processor in a dual-processor system.

Setup:

The hands-on steps in this activity can only be completed if you have a dual-processor system board, two matching processors, and a termination board.

Scenario:

One of your users is a software developer. She has a system with dual processor capability. She needs to test the application she is writing to see how much the second processor affects the processing speed.

What You Do	How You Do It
1. If you are running a dual-processor system with only one processor, which socket does the processor go in?	
2. If you are running a dual-processor system with only one processor, what do you need to do to the empty socket?	
3. What needs to be similar about both processors? How is it best to make sure of this?	

4. **Remove the second processor.**

    a. **Shut down the system and unplug the power cord.**

    b. Following the directions shown in the system board or processor documentation, **locate the second processor, and remove it from the socket.**

    c. Following the directions shown in the system board or processor documentation, **insert the terminator or other device in the second processor socket.**

5. **Verify that the single processor is functioning properly.**

    a. **Reboot the system and verify that it can boot successfully with a single processor.**

    b. **Open Device Manager and record the processor information.**

      Processors
           Intel(r) Pentium(r)III processor

6. **Install the second processor.**

    a. **Shut down the system and unplug the power cord.**

    b. Following the directions shown in the system board or processor documentation, **locate the second processor socket and remove any devices from the socket.**

    c. Following the directions shown in the system board or processor documentation, **insert the processor in the second processor socket.**

7. **Verify that both processors are functioning properly.**

    a. **Reboot the system and verify that it can boot successfully with dual processors.**

    b. **Open Device Manager and record the processor information.**

Review Questions

1. You just installed a second processor in a computer. What Windows XP utility can you use to verify that the processor is functioning correctly?

2. You are planning to install a second processor into a computer. What changes must you make on the motherboard before attempting to insert the second processor?

3. You currently have a computer with a Pentium IV 2 GHz processor. This computer supports dual processors. You would like to install a second processor. What requirements must the second processor meet?

4. You just removed the second processor from a computer. What must you do next in order for the computer to boot properly?

5. What steps should you take first before attempting to add or remove a second processor?

EXERCISE 4-5

Upgrading the System BIOS

Activity Time:

30 minutes

Objective:

To perform and verify a system BIOS upgrade.

Scenario:

A new version of the system BIOS for the computers in one of your customer's locations has been released. It should help with one of the problems they have been experiencing.

What You Do	How You Do It
1. **Determine the BIOS manufacturer for your system.**	a. **Choose Start→All Programs→Accessories→ System Tools→System Information.**

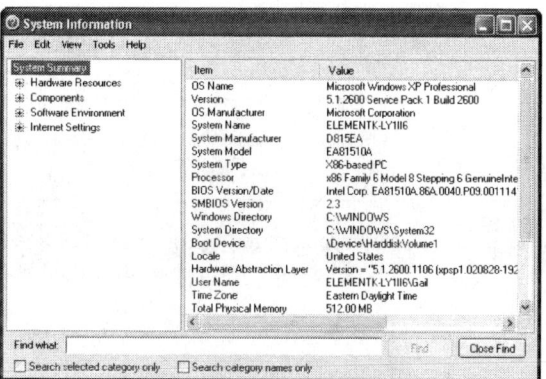

b. **Record the BIOS Version/Date:**

   _____.

c. **Record the SMBIOS Version:**

   _____.

d. **Close the System Information window.**

2.	Upgrade the BIOS.	a.	Access the Web site for your system.
		b.	Locate the upgrade for your particular BIOS.
		c.	Perform the steps indicated on the Web site to upgrade your BIOS.
3.	Verify that the BIOS upgrade was successful.	a.	Reboot the system.
		b.	Open the System Information window and check that the BIOS version/date and SMBIOS version have been updated.

Review Questions

1. Which Windows XP utility enables you to determine the BIOS manufacturer for your computer?

   _____

2. How do you obtain a BIOS upgrade for a computer?

   _____

3. Where are the BIOS settings stored on a computer?

   _____

4. You are attempting to access the system settings on a computer that uses AMD BIOS. What key(s) should you press after cold booting the computer?

   _____

5. You are attempting to access the system settings on a computer that uses Compaq BIOS. What key(s) should you press after cold booting the computer?

   _____

EXERCISE 4-6

Upgrading the Power Supply

Activity Time:

20 minutes

Objective:
To replace a system's power supply and test the replacement.

Setup:
You have a power supply to install into the system. If you don't have another power supply, you can just reinstall the one you take out.

Scenario:
After calculating the power needed for all of the components added to a user's system, you have determined that it exceeds the capacity of the installed power supply.

What You Do	How You Do It
1. Remove the existing power supply.	a. Shut down and turn off the system.
	b. Unplug the power cord from the electrical outlet.
	c. Remove any components necessary in order to access the power supply and its connection to the system board.
	d. Unplug all power connections from devices, marking where each connection went to as you go.
	e. Unplug the power supply from the system board.
	f. Unscrew the power supply from the case.
	g. Remove the power supply from the case.

2.	Install the replacement power supply.	a.	Insert the power supply into the case.
		b.	Secure the power supply to the case.
		c.	Plug all power connections into the devices.
		d.	Plug the power supply into the system board.
		e.	Reinstall any components you removed to access the power supply.
		f.	Plug the power cord from the power supply to the electrical outlet.
3.	Test the power supply.	a.	Turn on the system.
		b.	Log in as Administrator.
		c.	Test all components.

Review Questions

1. You just replaced the power supply in a computer. How can you verify that it is working correctly?

   _____

   _____

2. What type of power connector is used to supply power to floppy drives? How many of these power connectors are typically available on the power supply?

   _____

3. What type of power connector is used to supply power to hard disk drives? How many of these power connectors are typically available on the power supply?

   _____

4. You are building a computer from scratch. How do you determine the minimum wattage you need for the power supply?

5. What effect does using Suspend mode have on a computer?

Exercise 4-7

Upgrading the System Board

Activity Time:

1 hour(s)

Objective:

To remove and replace a system board, and test the replacement.

Scenario:

A lightning storm fried the system board in one of your customers' systems. You have been assigned the task of replacing the system board. While doing so, the customer would like you to put in an upgraded system board to improve system performance.

What You Do	How You Do It
1. Remove cards and cables.	a. Shut down the system and unplug the power cord.
	b. Disconnect all external devices.
	c. Remove all cards from the expansion slots and store them in appropriate anti-static containers.
	d. As you disconnect each cable in the system, attach a piece of masking tape to each cable and record where each connection goes as you remove it.
	e. Unplug the power and data cable connectors for all drives in the system. Mark which cable is connected to the primary and which to the secondary IDE connector.
	f. Unplug connectors attached to any front-panel switches or LEDs.
	g. Unplug the power supply from the system board.
	h. If necessary, remove the drive bay assembly and any other components needed to access all the screws on the system board.
2. Remove the existing system board.	a. Unscrew the system board from the case. Be sure to set the screws aside to use in mounting the new system board.
	b. Lift the system board, and then if necessary, slide it forward, and then lift it up and out of the case.

4

| 3. | Install the new system board. | a. | Slide the new motherboard into the case, aligning the mounting holes. |
| | ⚠ Be sure not to screw the system board in too tightly, because this can damage the motherboard. | b. | Secure the motherboard to the case using the screws you removed from the old system board. |

| 4. | Install RAM and a processor on the new system board. | a. | Install memory DIMMs beginning with Bank 0. |
| | | b. | Install the CPU according to the manufacturer's directions. |

5.	Reinstall the cards and cables.	a.	Reconnect all internal cables and cards, including any LED or front-panel switch connections.
		b.	Reinstall adapter cards.
		c.	If you needed to remove any drive bay assemblies or other components to access the system board, **replace any of those components.**
		d.	Reconnect the power supply to the system board.
		e.	Reconnect all external devices.

| 6. | Test the system. | a. | Plug in the power cord. |
| | | b. | **Start the system.** If all went well, it should boot. Windows might attempt to reboot several times as it discovers new components. |

Review Questions

1. Which motherboard form factor is the standard for new computers?

2. A user has asked you to transfer her computer from a desktop case to a micro tower. What should you do before attempting the upgrade?

_____

_____

_____

3. You have just replaced the motherboard in a computer. How do you know the upgrade succeeded?

_____

4

EXERCISE 4-8

Determining Whether to Upgrade

Activity Time:

15 minutes

Objective:

To make recommendations as to whether to upgrade hardware components in various scenarios.

Scenario:

You're an A+ technician who supports users and systems in a publishing company. You've been given a list of computers and their configuration, and you've been asked to determine if you need to upgrade any of their hardware components.

---

1. Computer A is a Pentium II computer running Windows NT 4.0. The system has a video card that does not support 3D graphics or the new 21-inch monitor its user has acquired. The user needs the monitor to create and modify the graphics for one of your company's top publications. A new video card will cost $200. Should you upgrade the video card?

    a) Yes

    b) No

    c) Maybe

---

2. Computer B has a Pentium II processor, 64 MB of RAM, and it's running Windows 98. The user needs to install several new programs to create and manage large files used in the layout of several publications. You will also need to upgrade this computer to Windows XP within the next six months as part of the upgrade within that user's department. Should you upgrade or add more memory?

    a) Yes

    b) No

    c) Maybe

---

3. **Computer B also has a 20 GB hard disk that has 8 GB of free space. Should you upgrade the hard disk too?**

    a) Yes

    b) No

    c) Maybe

4. **Computer C is a Pentium III computer with 256 MB of RAM and a 30 GB hard disk with 10 GB of free space. The user is an administrative assistant who uses the computer for email and word processing. She complains that the computer isn't as fast as the computer she has at home. Upon further investigation you find that at most she has only three programs open at one time. A new processor will cost $450 and more memory will cost $175. Should you upgrade the processor and the memory?**

    a) Yes

    b) No

    c) Maybe

5. **If you're planning to upgrade from Windows 98 to Windows 2000, which component(s) might you need to consider upgrading?**

    a) Hard disk

    b) Processor

    c) Sound card

    d) System BIOS

    e) Network card

Review Questions

1. What are two symptoms that indicate you should upgrade a computer's processor?

    _____

    _____

2. What are two symptoms that indicate you should upgrade a computer's RAM?

    _____

    _____

3. In what scenario might you decide that buying a new computer is more cost effective than upgrading your existing computer?

    _____

Lab 4-1

Upgrading System Components

Activity Time:

2 hour(s)

Objective:

To upgrade system components in a desktop computer system.

Setup:

To perform this lab, you will need:

- 1 Pentium 4 desktop computer with Windows 2000 Professional or Windows XP Professional installed
- A new dual-processor capable system board
- Two identical CPUs
- Additional RAM

Scenario:

You work for the R. A. Kash Computer Sales and Support company. The customer for whom you set up a home business has purchased some new system components, and has contracted with your company to have you upgrade the equipment at their home office. They currently have a single-processor system, and one of the applications they share would benefit from a dual-processor system. They have also purchased additional RAM to improve system performance.

You have been assigned to this project and need to complete it as soon as possible because the original system will be unavailable to them while you are performing the upgrade. You have brought your toolkit, including boot disks, with you.

 When you have finished the lab, you can refer to the Upgrading System Components Lab Results.txt file to check your work.

1. **Establish an ESD-free work area in which to work on the systems.**

2. **Disconnect and remove all components from the system.**

3. **Remove the original system board.**

4. **Install the new system board into the case.**

5. **Install the CPUs on the new system board.**

6. **Install the RAM from the old system board and the new RAM onto the new system board.**

7. **Connect all components.**

4

8. **Boot the system and verify that all components are recognized and functioning properly.**

9. If necessary, **upgrade the system BIOS.**

CHAPTER 5

Supporting Portable Computing Devices

Activities included in this chapter:

- Exercise 5-1 Docking Portable Systems
- Exercise 5-2 Exchanging Portable Computer Drives
- Exercise 5-3 Installing PC Cards
- Exercise 5-4 Managing PC Cards
- Exercise 5-5 Installing a Mini-PCI Card
- Exercise 5-6 Adding Memory to Portable Computing Devices
- Exercise 5-7 Connecting a PDA to the Computer
- Lab 5-1 Supporting Portable Computing Devices

EXERCISE 5-1

Docking Portable Systems

Activity Time:

20 minutes

Objective:

To configure and test a docking solution for a portable computer.

Scenario:

Many members of the Marketing department have portable systems. They have all requested a docking solution for their system so that they don't have to plug and unplug the external peripherals when they switch between working at work and working on the road or at home. The systems are from a variety of vendors. Some of the users have received port replicators and some have received docking stations. They need your assistance in connecting the external peripherals to the docking solution and in how to insert and remove their portable system from the docking solution.

What You Do	How You Do It
1. Connect peripherals to the docking solution.	a. Connect the monitor to the monitor port on the docking solution.
	b. Connect the keyboard to the keyboard port on the docking solution.
	c. Connect the mouse to the mouse port on the docking solution.
	d. Connect the printer to the appropriate port for your printer on the docking solution.
	e. Connect the power source from the docking solution to the electrical outlet.

2.	Verify that the portable can use the peripherals while docked.	a.	Insert the computer into the docking solution.
		b.	**Turn on the power.** This might be the power switch on the portable system or it might be a power switch on the docking solution.
		c.	**Turn on the power to the monitor and to any other external peripherals that require powering on.**
		d.	**Test that the external keyboard, mouse, monitor, and printer work properly.**
3.	Verify that the portable can use its integrated peripherals while undocked.	a.	**Turn off the power to all peripherals and to the portable system.**
		b.	**Undock the system.**
		c.	**Power on the portable and verify that the integrated keyboard, mouse, and monitor work correctly.**

Review Questions

1. What step should you take first before attempting to connect a portable computer to a docking station or port replicator?

2. How should you test to make sure that the portable computer is communicating with its docking station or port replicator?

3. What types of batteries are used by portable computers?

4. True or False: You can usually interchange the power cords between brands of notebook computers.

5. How many times can you recharge a Nickel Cadmium battery?

_____

Exercise 5-2

Exchanging Portable Computer Drives

Activity Time:

15 minutes

Objective:

To replace the floppy drive in a portable computer with a CD or DVD drive.

Scenario:

Sally Mendez recently received a new portable computer. Her system only has one drive bay to use for the floppy drive and CD/DVD drive. The floppy drive is currently in the drive bay and she needs to use the CD/DVD drive. She is not sure how to remove the drive from her system.

What You Do	How You Do It

 If the system you are using does not have drive bays for the floppy drive and CD or DVD drives, they are either in a docking solution or are attached using a cable. You will need to adapt this activity to match your system if this is the case.

1.	Remove the floppy drive from the drive bay or cable connector.	a.	In the System Tray, **double-click the Removable Device icon** to display a list of the devices that can be stopped.
		b.	**Select the drive you want to remove.**
		c.	**Click Stop** *drive description* (where *drive description* identifies the floppy drive you want to remove).
		d.	In the Stop A Hardware Device information box, **click OK.**
		e.	**Close the Safely Remove Hardware dialog box.**
		f.	Referring to the documentation and any symbols on the system case, **locate the floppy drive and its release mechanism.**
		g.	If the documentation specifies to, **shut down the system before continuing.**
		h.	**Press the release mechanism for the floppy drive** to release it from the system.
		i.	**Slide the floppy drive out of the drive bay or disconnect it from the cable.**
2.	Insert the CD/DVD drive in the bay or connect it to the cable.	a.	**Slide the CD/DVD drive into the drive bay or connect it to the cable.**
		b.	**Verify that the Removable Drive icon appears in the System Tray.**
		c.	**Access the CD/DVD drive** to verify that it was correctly installed.

Review Questions

1. You are currently using a portable computer that has only one extra drive bay. You had been using the floppy drive, but now need to use the DVD drive. What should you do in Windows XP before attempting to remove the floppy drive?

   _____

   _____

   _____

2. How can you verify in Windows XP that the new drive you inserted into the extra drive bay in a notebook is working properly?

   5

   _____

EXERCISE 5-3

Installing PC Cards

Activity Time:

10 minutes

Objective:

To install and test a PC card in a portable computer.

Setup:

There is an empty PC Card slot and an available PC Card to insert.

Scenario:

Several users received new portable systems. These came with various expansion cards. You need to install the PC Cards so that the users can use them.

What You Do	How You Do It
1. Install the PC Card.	a. Locate the PC Card slot on your portable system.
	b. Slide the PC Card into the slot until it is fully inserted.
	c. If prompted, install any required drivers for the PC Card.

<table>
<tr><td>2.</td><td>Verify that the PC Card was recognized by the system.</td><td>a.</td><td>**Determine if an icon for the PC Card appeared in the System Tray.** Most cards will add an icon Unplug Or Eject Hardware.
</td></tr>
<tr><td></td><td></td><td>b.</td><td>**Open Device Manager.**</td></tr>
<tr><td></td><td></td><td>c.</td><td>**Select the hardware you just installed.** You will need to expand the category under which the device is located to select it.</td></tr>
<tr><td></td><td></td><td>d.</td><td>**Right-click the device and choose Properties.**</td></tr>
<tr><td></td><td></td><td>e.</td><td>**Verify that Device Status indicates that This Device Is Working Properly.**</td></tr>
<tr><td></td><td></td><td>f.</td><td>**Click OK.**</td></tr>
</table>

Review Questions

1. You just inserted a new SCSI adapter PC card into a computer. Which Windows XP utility can you use to verify that it works correctly?

2. Which type of PC card is used for miniature hard disks?

3. What is the thickness of a Type II PC card?

4. What type of connector is used to connect a PC card to the PC card slot in a computer?

5. What advantage does bus mastering offer?

EXERCISE 5-4

Managing PC Cards

Activity Time:

15 minutes

Objective:

To test and verfiy the replacement procedures for several PC cards on a system with only one PC card slot.

Scenario:

Toby Macintosh has recently received a laptop system. He needs to connect it to the network while he is at work and to the phone line when he is at home. The system has only one PC Card slot. It came with both a network card and a modem card. He would like your help in learning how to insert and remove the cards and to test them to verify that they work properly.

What You Do	How You Do It
1. **Install the network card in the portable computer system.**	a. **Locate an empty PC Card slot.**
	b. Holding the card with the connectors facing the slot and the label with the Insert indicator on top, **slide the card into the slot.**
	c. **Verify that the Removable Device icon appears in the System Tray** to indicate that the card was fully inserted and recognized.
	d. If prompted, **install network card drivers.**
2. **Test the network card** to verify that it was properly installed and that the computer can connect to the network.	a. If necessary, **connect the dongle to the network card.**
	b. **Connect a network cable to the network card.**
	c. **Access a network or Internet location.**

3.	Remove the network card from the portable computer system.	a.	In the System Tray, **click the Removable Device icon.**
		b.	**Choose the option to stop the network card device.**
		c.	**Disconnect the network cable from the card.**
		d.	**Push the PC Card slot release lever once** to pop it out.
		e.	**Push the PC Card slot release lever again** to release the card from the slot.
		f.	**Slide the card out of the slot.**
4.	**Install the modem card in the portable computer system.**	a.	**Insert the modem card in the PC Card slot.**
		b.	If prompted, **install drivers for the modem card.**
5.	**Test the modem** to verify that the modem can connect over the phone line to the network.	a.	**Connect the phone line to the modem.**
		b.	**Open Device Manager.**
		c.	On the Modem Properties Diagnostics page, **click the Query Modem button.**

Review Questions

1. What Windows XP utility should you use if you want to remove a PC card from a computer and replace it with a different card?

2. You have inserted a PC card modem into a notebook computer for the first time. What must you do next before you can use the modem?

3. Which Windows XP utility can you use to verify that a PC card device is working properly?

Exercise 5-5

Installing a Mini-PCI Card

Activity Time:

15 minutes

Objective:

To install and test a Mini-PCI card in a notebook computer.

Scenario:

You've been asked to install a new Mini-PCI card in a user's notebook computer to replace one that just failed. You know from your previous experience with this type of notebook that it has a dedicated Mini-PCI bay.

What You Do	How You Do It
1. **Install the wireless Mini-PCI card.**	a. Shut down the system, close the cover, and unplug the power cord.
	b. If necessary, **remove the computer from the docking station or disconnect any peripheral devices.**
	c. **Ground yourself and dissipate any static electricity you might be carrying.**
	d. **Turn over the laptop and follow the manufacturer's instructions to locate the Mini-PCI bay cover.**
	e. **Remove the screw that secures the Mini-PCI bay cover.**
	f. **Remove the Mini-PCI bay cover.**
	g. **Secure the card inside the bay using supplied screws or clamps.**
	h. **Replace the cover on the bay and fasten it with the screw.**
2. **Verify that the card is installed properly.**	a. **Plug in the computer or replace it in the docking station.**
	b. **Turn the power on.**
	c. **Verify that the new Mini-PCI card has been recognized. If necessary, install any updated drivers.**

Review Questions

1. Where do you install a Mini-PCI card in a notebook computer?

_____

2.	Which type of Mini-PCI card must be located against the computer's chassis? Why?

_____

_____

3.	Which type of Mini-PCI card uses a SODIMM connector?

_____

EXERCISE 5-6

Adding Memory to Portable Computing Devices

Activity Time:

20 minutes

Objective:

To install additional system memory in a portable computer, and to install memory in a peripheral device for a portable computer.

Scenario:

You have just received the memory modules that were ordered for several portable computing devices. You need to deploy them to the devices for users.

What You Do	How You Do It
1. Install memory in a portable computer.	a. Shut down and unplug the portable computer.
	b. Locate and remove the memory cover on the case.
	c. Verify that the memory module you are about to install matches the specifications for the memory slot.
	d. Following the directions in the documentation, install the memory module.
	e. Replace and secure the cover to the memory.
	f. Restart the computer.
	g. Verify that the additional memory was recognized.

2. **Install a memory module in an MP3 player, a PDA, or a digital camera.**

    a. **Turn off the device.**

    b. **Locate the expansion slot for the memory card.**

    c. If necessary, **remove the existing memory card.**

    d. **Verify that the memory card matches the specifications for adding memory to the device.**

    e. **Insert the memory card into the slot.**

    f. **Turn on the device.**

    g. **Verify that the memory was recognized.**

Review Questions

1. What types of memory modules are used in notebook computers?

    _____

    _____

2. How can you differentiate between a 5 V and a 3.3 V SmartMedia card?

    _____

    _____

3. What is the maximum storage capacity of a SmartMedia card?

    _____

4. What is the maximum storage capacity of a CompactFlash card?

    _____

5. What step should you perform first before attempting to insert Flash memory into a digital camera?

    _____

EXERCISE 5-7

Connecting a PDA to the Computer

Activity Time:

10 minutes

Objective:

To set up and test the hardware and software to support a PDA device on a portable computer.

 This activity was developed using Palm PDAs. If you have another brand of PDA, check the documentation if the steps are not appropriate for your device.

Scenario:

Users recently received Palm PDAs. Some users have notebook computers and others have desktop computers. They all need to be able to connect their PDAs to their computers, in order to synchronize the calendar and update their To Do lists.

What You Do	How You Do It
1. Set up the cradle or docking station for the PDA.	a. If necessary, **connect the AC cable to the cradle or docking station connector.**
	b. **Connect the cradle or docking station to the computer port that matches the connector on the cable.**
	c. **Connect the PDA to the cradle or docking station.**
2. Install the PDA software on the computer.	a. **Insert the PDA software CD-ROM in the CD-ROM drive.**
	b. **Follow the on-screen instructions to install the software.**

Review Questions

1. To what types of ports can you connect a PDA to a computer?

_____

2. What types of input methods do PDAs support?

_____

3. What type of device is typically used to connect a PDA to a computer?

_____

4. You have connected a PDA to your computer but are still unable to access it in Windows XP. What should you do next?

_____

Lab 5-1

Supporting Portable Computing Devices

Activity Time:

30 minutes

Objective:

To configure a typical portable computer system, including docking station and peripheral devices.

Setup:

To perform this lab, you will need:

- A portable computer with a Windows operating system installed
- A compatible docking station
- Standard desktop peripheral components, including monitor, keyboard, and mouse
- A PDA device and software
- A digital camera
- An MP3 player

Scenario:

You work for R. A. Kash Computer Sales and Support company. One of the customers you support is expanding their business. Everyone in the company spends a lot of time traveling, so they have purchased PDAs for all employees. The new employees will be traveling several days each month, so they will be set up with notebook computers and a matching docking solution so that they can use a full size monitor, keyboard, and mouse when they are at the home office. One of the users has a digital camera and needs to upload the pictures to the home office each day while traveling. She also has an MP3 player she would like to use while flying.

 When you have finished the lab, you can refer to the Supporting Portable Computing Devices Lab Results.txt file to check your work.

1. **Set up the notebook computer.**

---

2. **Set up the docking solution connecting all of the desktop components the user will use through it while the notebook is docked.**

---

3. Set up the PDA.

---

4. Install the PDA software on the computer.

---

5. Connect the digital camera to the notebook or insert the flash media in the PDA.

---

6. Connect the MP3 player to the computer.

CHAPTER 6

Performing Preventative Maintenance

Activities included in this chapter:

- Exercise 6-1 Defragmenting a Hard Disk
- Exercise 6-2 Maintaining Printers
- Exercise 6-3 Using a UPS
- Exercise 6-4 Cleaning Peripherals
- Exercise 6-5 Cleaning Internal System Components
- Exercise 6-6 Disposing of Computer Equipment
- Lab 6-1 Performing Preventative Maintenance

Exercise 6-1

Defragmenting a Hard Disk

Activity Time:

15 minutes to 1 hour(s)

Objective:

To scan, analyze, and defragment a hard disk to improve disk performance.

Scenario:

One of your clients is complaining that his hard disk in his Windows XP computer is very slow. He says that he can hear the hard disk "crunching away" whenever he attempts to save a file to the hard disk. He's asked you to do what you can to resolve the problem.

What You Do	How You Do It
1. Run Chkdsk on the hard disk to scan for file-system errors.	a. Choose Start→Run, and enter *CMD* to open a Command Prompt window.
	b. Enter `chkdsk c:`
	c. Type `exit` to close the command prompt window.
2. Did you find any errors on your drive?	

3. **Analyze the fragmentation on the hard disk.**

   a. From the Start menu, **choose All Programs→ Accessories→System Tools→Disk Defragmenter.**

   b. In the Volume list, **select the C drive.**

   c. **Click Analyze.**

   d. In the Disk Defragmenter message box, **click View Report.**

   e. In the Volume Information area, **scroll to the Volume Fragmentation statistics.** You can determine the overall fragmentation percentage here.

   f. In the Most Fragmented Files list, **click the Fragments column heading** to sort by this column. The larger files have the greatest amount of fragmentation.

   g. **Click Close.**

4. **Based on the analysis you see in the report, should you defragment this disk?**

5. **Defragment the disk.**

   a. **Click Defragment.** The information displayed in Disk Defragmenter and the status bar changes as the defragmentation progresses.

    If you don't want to take the time for defragmentation to complete, click Stop.

   b. **Close Disk Defragmenter.**

Review Questions

1. Which command-line utility enables you to search a hard disk for bad sectors or errors in the file system and repair those errors?

2. How can you counteract fragmentation on a computer's hard disk?

   _____

3. Which operating systems contain a graphical version of the Chkdsk utility?

   _____

4. Which switch should you use with the Chkdsk utility if you want to not only examine the hard disk for errors but also repair those errors?

   _____

5. How can you determine if a hard disk needs to be defragmented?

   _____

EXERCISE 6-2

Maintaining Printers

Activity Time:

45 minutes

Objective:

To perform standard printer-maintenance tasks on a dot-matrix printer, an inkjet printer, and a laser printer.

Setup:

You have compressed air canisters, a printer vacuum, tweezers, and lens cloths, as well as replacement parts, ribbons, ink cartridges, toner cartridges, and cleaning supplies that correspond to the manufacturer of each printer. You also have a mild household cleaning solution, a lint-free cloth, toothpicks, an artist paint brush, cotton swabs, and printer cleaning sheets to run through the paper path.

Scenario:

Your company developed a schedule for maintaining printers. The following table documents what procedures need to be completed for each type of printer and how often it needs to be performed. It is the end of the quarter.

Frequency	Tasks to be Performed
Daily	Check consumables such as ink, ribbons, and paper. Print a test page to verify that the print quality is acceptable.
Monthly	Surface dust and debris removal.
Quarterly	Cleaning of the entire printer.

1. **Perform preventative maintenance for a dot-matrix printer.**

   a. **Print a test page** to verify that the ribbon prints satisfactorily.

   b. Based on the results of the previous step, if necessary, **replace printer ribbon.**

   c. **Verify that there is enough paper for a day's printing.** If necessary, have extra paper available for users to install.

   d. **Use the compressed air canister and/or vacuum to remove dust and paper bits from the inside of the printer.**

   e. **Use tweezers to remove any paper caught in the paper feed mechanism.**

   f. **Use a mild household cleaner to wipe down the exterior of the printer case.**

2. **Perform preventative maintenance for an inkjet printer.**

a. **Print a test page** to verify that the printer prints satisfactorily.

b. Based on the results of the previous step, if necessary, **replace printer ink cartridges.**

c. **Verify that there is enough paper for a day's printing.** If necessary, have extra paper available for users to install.

d. **Use the compressed air canister and/or vacuum to remove dust and paper bits from the inside of the printer.**

e. **Use tweezers to remove any paper caught in the paper feed mechanism.**

f. **Use a mild household cleaner to wipe down the exterior of the printer case.**

g. **Place an inkjet cleaning sheet in the paper tray and use the form feed button(s) to send it through the paper path.**

6

3. **Perform preventative maintenance for a laser printer.**

a. **Print a test page** to verify that the printer prints satisfactorily.

b. Based on the results of the previous step, if necessary, **replace the toner cartridge.**

   Follow the directions to replace any other components that need to be replaced with replacing the toner cartridge, and reset any counters as needed.

c. **Verify that there is enough paper for a day's printing.** If necessary, have extra paper available for users to install.

d. **Use the compressed air canister and/or vacuum to remove dust and paper bits from the inside of the printer.**

e. **Use tweezers to remove any paper caught in the paper feed mechanism.**

f. **Use a mild household cleaner to wipe down the exterior of the printer case.**

g. **Place a laser printer cleaning sheet in the paper tray and use the form feed button(s) to send it through the paper path.**

Review Questions

1. What is the first task you should complete when performing preventative maintenance on any printer?

   _____

2. You suspect that dust and bits of paper are preventing a dot-matrix printer from printing satisfactorily. What should you do?

   _____

   _____

3. What tasks should you also perform each time you replace the toner cartridge in a laser printer?

_____

4. You printed a test page on an inkjet printer and the print is very faint. What should you do next?

_____

5. What should you use to clean the exterior of the printer case?

_____

6

EXERCISE 6-3

Using a UPS

Activity Time:

20 minutes

Objective:

To install, configure, and test a UPS.

Scenario:

There are periodic power outages at your customer's site due to old power lines and high winds. They have had several corrupted files due to power loss. They have purchased a UPS and have contracted with you to install and test it for them.

What You Do	How You Do It
1. Set up the UPS to power a computer system.	a. If necessary, **connect the battery in the UPS.**
	b. **Plug the UPS into the power outlet.**
	c. **Shut down each of the components that will be powered through the UPS.**
	d. **Unplug the components from the wall or surge protector, and then plug them into the UPS.**
	e. If your UPS is equipped with a cable to connect to a peripheral port on your computer, **connect the UPS to the USB or COM port.**

2.	**Configure what happens when the UPS encounters a power failure.**	a.	**Open Control Panel.**
		b.	**Click Performance And Maintenance.**
		c.	**Click Power Options.**
		d.	If available, **click the UPS tab.**
			If no UPS tab is displayed, **click the tab related to UPS configuration.**
		e.	If necessary, **configure the UPS port, manufacturer, and model.**
		f.	Following the directions that came with your UPS, or using the UPS tab in the Power Options Properties dialog box, **configure the computer to sound an alarm as soon as there is a power failure and to repeat it every minute.**
		g.	**Configure the settings to perform a shutdown when the critical alarm threshold is reached.**
3.	**Test the UPS.**	a.	**Turn on the components** to make sure they can be powered through the UPS.
		b.	When all of the components plugged into the UPS have come up to the functional state, **unplug the UPS from the power outlet** to simulate a power outage. All equipment should remain on with no blips in power.
		c.	**Plug the UPS back into the wall outlet.**
		d.	If your UPS is equipped with a test button, **press the Test button.**

6

Review Questions

1. How do you manually determine the appropriate capacity for an Uninterruptible Power Supply (UPS)?

   _____

   _____

   _____

2. What utility do you use in Windows XP to configure the actions you want the UPS to perform when the power fails?

   _____

   _____

3. What two methods can you use to verify that a UPS is functioning correctly?

   _____

4. What is an online UPS?

   _____

5. What is a standby UPS?

   _____

Exercise 6-4

Cleaning Peripherals

Activity Time:

50 minutes

Objective:

To clean the peripheral equipment on a computer system.

Scenario:

In an effort to cut down on the number of peripheral problems that have been occurring, your company has decided to perform preventative maintenance on peripherals each month. As one of the junior members of the support team, you have been assigned the task of cleaning the department's keyboards, mice, and monitors at the beginning of each month. If users have PDAs or scanners, you are also to clean those peripherals. You have compiled a peripheral cleaning kit containing the following items:

- Monitor cleaning wipes
- Keyboard cleaning wipes
- Lint-free cloths
- Rubbing alcohol
- A mild household cleaner
- Cotton swabs (tightly wound)
- Lens cloth
- Window cleaner
- Toothpicks
- Artist paint brush
- Compressed air canisters
- Computer vacuum

What You Do	How You Do It
1. Clean the keyboard.	a. **Turn the keyboard upside down and gently shake it** to remove debris from under the keys.
	b. **Spray compressed air under the keys** to dislodge particles of dust and dirt.
	c. **Drag a small paint brush or a business card between the keys to remove any particles left behind.**
	d. **Wipe each key with keyboard wipes or a soft cloth with rubbing alcohol applied to it.**
	e. **Verify that all of the keys work.**

2. **Clean the mouse.**

a. **Shut down the system and unplug the mouse.**

b. **Turn the mouse upside down and rotate the cover** to unlatch it. Rotate the cover in the direction indicated on your mouse.

c. **Place your hand over the cover and ball, and then turn the mouse right side up and the cover and ball should drop out into your hand.** If they don't drop out, gently shake the mouse. If they still don't drop out, make sure that the cover has been turned far enough to unlatch it.

d. Using a toothpick or your fingernail, **scrape off the line of dirt on each roller.** There should be three rollers and the dirt is usually in the center of each roller.

e. **Spray compressed air into the mouse** to remove any remaining debris, including the debris you scraped off the rollers.

f. **Wipe the ball, inside, outside, and the cord of the mouse with mouse cleaning wipes or a soft cloth dampened with rubbing alcohol.**

g. **Place the ball back inside the mouse.**

h. **Place the cover over the mouse and rotate it until it locks in place.**

i. **Plug the mouse in, and then start the system and verify that all of the mouse functions work.**

6

3. **Clean the monitor.**

 If you have an LCD monitor, do NOT use window cleaner on it. Instead, you should use a lint-free cloth to wipe the screen. If more cleaning power is needed, dampen the cloth with rubbing alcohol and wipe the screen.

a. **Shut down the system, turn off the monitor, and unplug the monitor cable and power cord.**

b. **Spray glass cleaner on a lint-free cloth.** Alternatively, you can use specially prepared wet monitor wipes and drying wipes.

c. **Wipe the monitor screen using the cloth.**

d. **Vacuum the exterior or wipe with a cloth dampened with a mild household cleaner** to remove dust and debris from the case.

e. **Plug the monitor in and connect it to the system, and then start the system and verify that it works.**

---

4. **Clean the PDA.**

a. **Turn off the PDA.**

b. **Dampen a lint-free cloth with rubbing alcohol and wipe the PDA screen.**

c. **Dampen a lint-free cloth with a mild household cleaner and wipe down the rest of the PDA.**

d. **Turn on the PDA and verify that it works properly.**

---

5.   Clean the scanner.

          a.   **Turn off the scanner and unplug it from the system and from the power outlet.**

          b.   **Dampen a lint-free cloth with rubbing alcohol and wipe the scanner glass.**

          c.   **Dampen a lint-free cloth with a mild household cleaner and wipe down the rest of the scanner.**

          d.   **Plug the scanner back in, and then verify that it works properly.**

6

Review Questions

1.   How do you clean a mouse?

_____

_____

2.   How do you clean a CRT monitor?

_____

_____

3.   How do you clean an LCD monitor?

_____

_____

4.   How do you clean a keyboard?

_____

_____

5.   How do you clean a scanner?

_____

_____

Exercise 6-5

Cleaning Internal System Components

Activity Time:

30 minutes

Objective:

To clean the case and internal components of a computer system.

Scenario:

To help prevent system problems, a yearly preventative maintenance plan has been put in place to clean the internal system components. This includes the system board, drives, and any adapter cards.

You have compiled a system cleaning kit containing the following items:

- Monitor cleaning wipes
- Keyboard cleaning wipes
- Lint-free cloths
- Rubbing alcohol
- A mild household cleaner
- Cotton swabs (tightly wound)
- Lens cloth
- Window cleaner
- Toothpicks
- Artist paint brush
- Compressed air canisters
- Computer vacuum
- CD-ROM cleaning kit
- Floppy drive cleaning kit
- Removable drive cleaning kit (SuperDisk, Zip, Jaz, and so forth, to match your removable drive)

What You Do	How You Do It
1. Clean the case.	a. Shut down the system, and then unplug the peripherals and the power cord.
	b. Remove the cover from the system.
	c. **Wipe the case with a water-dampened, lint-free cloth.** If the case requires additional cleaning power, use a mild household cleaner on the cloth instead of water.
2. Clean the system board.	a. **Position the system so that you can hold the compressed air canister upright.**
	b. **Spray the compressed air so that you blow the dust and debris off the system board and out of the case.**
	c. If you have a computer-safe vacuum, **vacuum any remaining particles from inside the system, being careful not to suck up any jumpers or other components.**
3. Clean the CD-ROM drive. ⚠ Refer to the instructions that come with your cleaning kit and use those steps if they are different from those listed here.	a. **Power on the system.**
	b. **Insert the CD-ROM cleaner disk in the drive.**
	c. **Access the CD-ROM drive.**
	d. **Remove the CD-ROM cleaner disk from the drive.**
	e. **Test the drive by reading a CD-ROM.**

6

4.	Clean the floppy disk drive.	a.	Insert the floppy disk cleaner disk in the drive.
		b.	Access the floppy disk drive.
		c.	Remove the floppy cleaner disk from the drive.
		d.	Test the floppy disk drive by writing to and reading from a floppy disk.
5.	Clean the removable media drive.	a.	Insert the compatible cleaning product in the drive.
		b.	Follow the manufacturer's directions to clean the drive.
		c.	Remove the product from the drive.
		d.	Test the drive by reading from and writing to compatible media in the drive.

Review Questions

1. What tools should you use to clean a computer's system board?

   _____

2. You are planning to use compressed air to clean a computer's system board. How should you complete the task?

   _____

   _____

3. What tools should you use to clean a CD-ROM drive?

   _____

4. Can you clean Iomega Zip and Jaz drives?

   _____

5. Can you clean Imation SuperDrives?

   _____

EXERCISE 6-6

Disposing of Computer Equipment

Activity Time:

10 minutes

Objective:

To determine the correct disposal methods for various types of computer equipment.

Scenario:

The warehouse department has several older pieces of equipment that have reached the end of their useful life. You have deployed new equipment to the department and now need to dispose of the old equipment. The company has also accumulated several broken pieces of equipment that need to be disposed. You are responsible for properly disposing of the equipment. Your manager asks you the following questions to find out how you will be disposing of the equipment.

---

1. **Why do CRTs need to be recycled rather than disposed of through normal waste management procedures?**

---

2. **Various types of batteries have been accumulated for disposal. These are from digital cameras, PDAs, laptops, and wireless devices among other sources. The following table shows the battery types you have accumulated. Indicate the proper disposal method for each battery type.**

   Alkaline

   Lithium

   Sealed lead batteries

   Nickel metal hydride

   Nickel cadmium

---

3. Which printer consumables need to be handled in a special manner and be recycled?

_____

4. What is an MSDS and where can you obtain them?

_____

Review Questions

1. How can you determine if computer equipment must be treated as hazardous material when you dispose of it?

   _____

2. While replacing a toner cartridge, the cartridge cracks and a large amount of toner spills on the floor. How should you clean up the spill?

   _____

3. Which types of batteries typically cannot be disposed of in the regular trash?

   _____

4. What materials are contained in a CRT monitor that prohibits you from disposing of them in a landfill?

   _____

5. How should you dispose of old CRT monitors and computers?

   _____

LAB 6-1

Performing Preventative Maintenance

Activity Time:

1 hour(s), 30 minutes

Objective:

To perform preventative maintenance on standard computer systems and peripherals, and to perform correct disposal procedures for obsolete computer equipment.

Setup:

To perform this lab, you will need:

- A desktop computer with a CRT monitor and a Windows operating system installed
- A laptop computer with an LCD screen and a Windows operating system installed
- Dot-matrix, inkjet, and laser printers
- Assorted peripheral equipment: for example, a scanner and a PDA
- A UPS
- Assorted obsolete equipment and batteries

Scenario:

The R. A. Kash Computer Sales and Support company has begun offering a preventative maintenance contract to its customers. Several customers have signed up to take advantage of this service. Today, you have been assigned the project of going to a customer's site and performing the preventative maintenance on all of his equipment. The customer also has some old equipment and batteries that need to be disposed of.

 When you have finished the lab, you can refer to the Performing Preventative Maintenance Lab Results.txt file to check your work.

1. **Perform printer maintenance on the dot-matrix, inkjet, and laser printers.**

2. **Check the UPS batteries.**

3. **Clean all peripherals.**

4. Clean the interior of the desktop system.

_____

5. Mark each of the pieces of obsolete equipment with the appropriate disposal method: computer recycler or regular garbage collection.

_____

Chapter 7

Troubleshooting Device Problems

Activities included in this chapter:

- Exercise 7-1 Troubleshooting Monitor Problems
- Exercise 7-2 Troubleshooting Keyboard and Pointing-device Problems
- Exercise 7-3 Troubleshooting PC Adapter Card Problems
- Exercise 7-4 Troubleshooting Why a Hard Drive Won't Boot
- Exercise 7-5 Troubleshooting Why a Newly Installed Hard Drive Isn't Recognized
- Exercise 7-6 Troubleshooting Hard Drive Data Access Problems
- Exercise 7-7 Troubleshooting Wrong Drive Size
- Exercise 7-8 Installing and Using IomegaWare Utilities
- Exercise 7-9 Troubleshooting Floppy Drive Problems
- Exercise 7-10 Troubleshooting Removable Cartridge Drive Problems
- Exercise 7-11 Troubleshooting CD or DVD Drive Problems
- Exercise 7-12 Identifying the Steps in the Laser Printing Process
- Exercise 7-13 Troubleshooting Printer Problems
- Exercise 7-14 Configuring the Parallel Port
- Lab 7-1 Creating Device Troubleshooting Plans

EXERCISE 7-1

Troubleshooting Monitor Problems

Activity Time:

1 hour(s)

Objective:

To diagnose and resolve various monitor problems.

Scenario:

Several users have opened trouble tickets with the support center about problems with their monitors. All of the users need their systems fixed before they can continue with their work. You need to resolve the problems and get the users back to work. The following is a list of the trouble tickets you are responding to:

- Ticket 296001:

  Location: Main building, 31H21

  User: Robert Allen

  The user's monitor is not coming on. The power light is not lighted up. The user has checked that the monitor is plugged in and the monitor is connected to the system.

- Ticket 296002:

  Location: Main building, 13B19

  User: Althea Gavin

  User's monitor is flickering and the display is distorted.

- Ticket 296003:

  Location: Elmwood Place, cube 32

  User: Chris Parker

The monitor power light is on, but there is no display.

- Ticket 296004:

  Location: Training center, room 4

  User: Tom Fisher

  The monitor comes on, and he works on the system for awhile. Then, he turns to do paperwork. When he turns back to work on the PC, the monitor is blank.

- Ticket 296005:

  Location: Main building, 62B35

  User: Joan Paris

  The monitor is making noises.

What You Do	How You Do It
1. **Resolve trouble ticket 296001.**	a. **Unplug the monitor from the electrical outlet and plug in a lamp or other device** to verify that the monitor is plugged into a working outlet. If the device works, **plug the monitor back into the outlet.** If the device does not work, **contact the electrician to fix the outlet and plug the monitor in to another outlet.** If the outlet is on a UPS, surge protector, or power strip, **verify that the unit is turned on.**
	b. **Verify that the connections of the power cord and monitor cable are secure on the monitor as well as on the PC and electrical outlet.**
	c. **Try to turn on the monitor again.** If the monitor still doesn't come on, **replace the monitor with a known good monitor.**

2. Resolve trouble ticket 296002.

    a. Verify that the monitor cable is firmly plugged in to the monitor and to the computer.

    b. If available, **press the degauss button.**

    c. Check the monitor cable for any bent pins and straighten if necessary.

    d. Move the monitor away from florescent light, speakers, other monitors, or other electronic devices with powerful motors.

---

3. Resolve trouble ticket 296003.

    a. Verify that the monitor cable is connected to the monitor and to the PC.

    b. Adjust the contrast using the buttons on the monitor.

    c. Adjust the brightness using the buttons on the monitor.

    d. If it still is not working, **swap the monitor with one that you know works** to determine if the problem is with the monitor or the video card.

---

4. Resolve trouble ticket 296004.

    a. Determine if the power light is glowing green or orange.

    b. If light is orange, **press a key** to arouse the system from doze or sleep mode.

    c. Change Power Management settings in CMOS to disable sleep or doze mode.

    d. Change all Settings For Always On Power Scheme to Never.

---

5. Resolve trouble ticket 296005.

a. **Determine whether noise is crackling or whining noise.**

b. If it is a crackling noise, **clean the monitor and try to vacuum or blow dust out of monitor vents. Do not open the monitor!** If necessary, send it out for more in-depth cleaning.

c. If it is a whining noise, try the following to fix it: **move the monitor or change the refresh rate.** If it won't stop whining, send it out for adjustment and **replace the monitor with a quieter one.**

7

Review Questions

1. You have been called in to troubleshoot a monitor. The monitor doesn't display an image. What should you check first?

   _____

2. You have been called in to troubleshoot a monitor that flickers. List two possible problems that could cause this symptom.

   _____

   _____

   _____

   _____

3. What symptom should you look for if you suspect that there is nothing wrong with a monitor other than it is in power-saving mode?

   _____

   _____

4. What steps should you take to troubleshoot a monitor that's making a whining noise?

   _____

5. A user has asked you to turn off the power-saving mode on his monitor. What Windows XP utility should you use to accomplish this task?

   _____

EXERCISE 7-2

Troubleshooting Keyboard and Pointing-device Problems

Activity Time:

45 minutes

Objective:

To diagnose and resolve various problems with keyboards and pointing devices.

Scenario:

Several users have opened trouble tickets with the support center about problems with their keyboards and pointing devices. All of the users need their systems fixed before they can continue with their work. You need to resolve the problems and get the users back to work. The following is a list of the trouble tickets you are responding to:

- Ticket 299001:

    Location: Elmwood Place, cube 24

    User: Al Mikels

    The user's keyboard is not working at all.

- Ticket 299002:

    Location: Training center, room 1

    User: Andy Potarnia

    User's keyboard is producing the wrong characters when he types.

- Ticket 299003:

    Location: Main building, 42B31

    User: Toma Wright

    User's mouse jumping around on the screen.

- Ticket 299004:

    Location: Main building, 31C93

    User: Jason Zeh

User has a cordless mouse, and the mouse pointer is not moving on the screen.

- Ticket 299005:

  Location: Main building, 26B15

  User: Daniel Bidlack

  Root beer has been spilled on user's keyboard.

- Ticket 299006:

  Location: Main building, 32B14

  User: Trudi Steele

  User's Palm touch screen is not responding when she touches it with her finger. Stylus input works sometimes.

7

What You Do	How You Do It
1. Resolve trouble ticket 299001.	a. Verify that the keyboard is plugged in to the keyboard port.
	b. Verify that the keyboard cable is securely connected.
	c. If the keyboard still does not work, **switch with a known good keyboard.**
	d. If the keyboard still does not work, **verify that the keyboard is recognized by the CMOS.**
	e. If the keyboard still does not work, **replace the system board.**
2. Resolve trouble ticket 299002.	a. Verify that no Function key, Scroll Lock, or other key is enabled or stuck down.
	b. If that is not the problem, **replace keyboard with a known good keyboard.**

3. Resolve trouble ticket 299003.

    a. Make sure the surface the mouse is being rolled on is clean and smooth.

    b. Clean the rollers inside the mouse.

    c. Clean the mouse ball by blowing on it or by using warm water and mild detergent.

    d. From the Start menu, choose Control Panel. Click Printers And Other Hardware. Click Mouse. Check the pointer speed, click speed, and other settings that might affect performance.

    e. If the problem is not resolved, replace the mouse.

4. Resolve trouble ticket 299004.

    a. Verify that there is no obstruction between the transmitter and receiver devices.

    b. Press the Reset or Connect buttons on each device to try to re-establish the connection.

    c. Replace the batteries in the mouse.

    d. Press the Reset or Connect buttons on each device.

    e. Verify that the receiver device is connected to the port.

    f. Try reinstalling the latest software or driver for the cordless mouse.

    g. If it still has not been resolved, try a corded mouse connected to the port.

    h. If the previous step worked, replace the cordless mouse with either a corded or another cordless mouse.

5. Resolve trouble ticket 299005.

    a. Remind users that all drinks must be covered when used near computer equipment.

    b. Unplug the keyboard and turn it upside down over the wastebasket.

    c. Move the keyboard around to remove as much liquid as possible.

    d. Rinse the keyboard in running water.

    e. Set on end to dry for several days.

    f. Replace the keyboard so user can get back to work until their keyboard is ready to use again.

6. Resolve trouble ticket 299006.

    a. Clean the PDA screen.

    b. Check the PDA for battery power, for cracks in the screen, or other physical problems.

    c. Access the home page of the Palm device and tap the Prefs icon. Choose Digitizer and follow the on screen prompts for calibrating the device.

    d. Test that the Palm device works correctly.

Review Questions

1. A user reports that the wrong characters are displayed on his screen when he presses keys on his keyboard. What should you check first?

_____

_____

2. You have been asked to troubleshoot a problem with a mouse where the pointer jumps around on the screen. List two possible problems that could cause this symptom.

_____

_____

_____

3. You are preparing to troubleshoot a touch screen device. Users report that the insertion point does not appear where they touch the screen. (It appears either well above the location they touch or not on the screen at all.) What should you do?

_____

4. You have been asked to troubleshoot a user's cordless mouse. You have tried pressing the Reset or Connect buttons on both the mouse and its receiver, but the mouse still is not working. What should you try next?

_____

5. You are cleaning a keyboard on which a user spilled his soda. You have already turned the keyboard upside down and shook it to empty it of whatever soda you can. What should you do next?

_____

Exercise 7-3

Troubleshooting PC Adapter Card Problems

Activity Time:

1 hour(s)

Objective:

To diagnose and resolve various problems with PC adapter cards.

Scenario:

The call center has received several trouble calls that have been assigned to you. All of the tickets on your list are related to internal PC adapter card problems. You need to resolve the problems and get the users back to work. The following is a list of the trouble tickets you are responding to:

- Ticket 399001:

  Location: Main building, 33J27

  User: Aminah Sinclair

  The user is still having problems with his video system. All monitor problems were reviewed and none of these resolved the problem. Therefore, it points toward a problem with the video card.

- Ticket 399002:

  Location: Main building, 31L19

  User: Randi Keene

  A second parallel-port adapter ISA card was added to the system by the user. Now, she cannot connect to the network and the new card is not working.

- Ticket 399003:

  Location: Elmwood Place, cube 14

  User: Conroy Ives

  Last night a lightning storm struck. Most equipment was fine, but this user is having problems with getting on the network. All other users in the area are connecting without problems.

- Ticket 399004:

  Location: Training center, room 8

  User: Kai Beyer

The user reports that the speakers connected to his sound card produce a hum all the time.

- Ticket 399005:

Location: Main building, 11A12

User: Ardon Blandon

The user reports no sound coming from the speakers connected to his sound card.

What You Do	How You Do It
1. **Respond to trouble ticket 399001.**	a. **Locate the video card and make sure it is fully seated into the slot, then see if this fixed the problem.**
	b. **Determine if the video card is in a PCI, ISA, or AGP slot.**
	c. If it is not in an AGP slot, **try moving the card to another slot.**
	d. If you are still having problems, **remove the card and press down on all four corners of socketed chips to verify they are fully seated, then reinstall the card.**
	e. If a hardware device has been recently added to the system, **check Device Manager and verify that there is not a resource conflict between the device and the video card.**
	f. If you are still having problems, **try a known good working video card.**

2. **Respond to trouble ticket 399002.**

            a.   **Open Device Manager and display the Resources By Connection view.**

            b.   **Determine if there is a conflict between the second parallel port and the network card.**

            c.   **Change the IRQ on one of the devices to an unused setting.**

            d.   **Verify that both devices now work properly.**

---

3. **Respond to trouble ticket 399003.**

            a.   **Check whether the network card is listed in Device Manager.**

            b.   **Display properties for the network card and verify whether the Device Status indicates it is working properly.**

            c.   If the device is not working properly, **click Troubleshoot and follow the Troubleshoot Wizard steps.**

            d.   If the problem is not resolved, **replace the network card.**

            e.   **Verify that the system can now connect to the network.**

---

4. **Respond to trouble ticket 399004.**

            a.   **Verify that it is a humming noise rather than a crackling noise.**

            b.   **Move the speakers apart and away from the system a bit.**

            c.   If the hum has not stopped, **verify that the speaker wires are not tangled with power cords.**

            d.   If the problem still exists, **replace the speakers with higher quality speakers.**

---

5. Respond to trouble ticket 399005.

a. Verify speakers are connected to the correct port on the sound card.

b. Verify speakers are turned on and power cord is plugged in.

c. Verify speaker sound is turned up.

d. Verify Windows volume control is turned up.

e. If none of these steps fixed the problem, verify that the audio cable from the CD-ROM is connected to the sound card.

f. Use Device Manager to verify that the sound card is working properly.

g. If the problem still persists, replace the sound card and/or speakers.

Review Questions

1. You have just installed a network adapter into a computer. When you tested the adapter with the computer's case open, it worked fine. Now, when you close the computer's case, the network adapter no longer works. What problem might cause this symptom?

   _____ _____

2. You have been asked to troubleshoot a network adapter that was installed by another technician. The user reports that the network adapter works only intermittently. List two problems that might cause this symptom.

   _____

   _____

   _____

3. What Windows utility can you use to troubleshoot a suspected hardware resource conflict?

   _____

4. List two problems that can cause speakers to hum constantly.

   _____

   _____

5. What steps should you take to troubleshoot a card that you suspect was damaged due to electrostatic discharge?

_____

_____

_____

_____

7

EXERCISE 7-4

Troubleshooting Why a Hard Drive Won't Boot

Activity Time:

30 minutes

Objective:

To diagnose and resolve a hard-drive related boot problem.

Scenario:

Georgetta Larsen cannot boot her system. She got an error message at POST, but did not write it down.

What You Do	How You Do It

1. List at least two POST messages that would indicate a problem with the hard drive. What does the message mean? How would you fix it?

2. **Determine what is causing the problem.**

   Go through the guided steps until your problem is resolved. You might not need to complete all steps shown.

   a. **Perform a cold boot.**

   b. **Verify that CMOS lists the correct drive settings.**

   c. **Listen to the drive or touch the drive to determine if it is spinning during POST.**

   d. **Using your multimeter, verify that power connection readings are +12v for Pin 1, and +5v for Pin 4.** Pins 2 and 3 should be ground.

   e. **Verify that data cable is correctly oriented.**

   f. **Check drive settings:**
      - IDE: Master, slave, or cable select
      - SCSI: Termination and device ID

   g. **Replace drive.**

3. **Test that the drive now works.**

   a. **Boot the system.**

   b. **Verify that you can read and write to the drive you repaired.**

Review Questions

1. A user reports that when she turns on her computer, she sees the message "Not Ready-System Halted." What are two problems could cause this symptom?

   _____

   _____

   _____

2. You have been asked to troubleshoot a hard disk on a computer that reports errors in the 17xx range during the power-on self test (POST). What troubleshooting steps should you take?

   _____

   _____

3. What two configuration errors cause 95 percent of the problems with SCSI hard disks?

_____

4. A user reports that his hard disk used to be very fast but now seems quite slow. What two problems might cause the hard disk to slow down?

_____

_____

5. What is the first step you should take when troubleshooting a hard disk that won't boot?

_____

_____

EXERCISE 7-5

Troubleshooting Why a Newly Installed Hard Drive Isn't Recognized

Activity Time:

15 minutes

Objective:

To determine the proper troubleshooting approach to take when a newly-installed hard drive is not recognized.

Scenario:

You just finished installing a new hard drive as the second drive in the system, but it is not being recognized by the system.

---

1. One of the things you need to check when a newly installed drive isn't recognized is the CMOS settings for the drive. What in particular do you need to check in CMOS for this problem?

---

2. Another thing you should check when you encounter this problem is that the drive was installed correctly. What exactly would you be checking?

---

3. In continuing to troubleshoot this problem and after checking that the drive was properly installed, you booted from a bootable floppy disk. You then entered the drive letter for the drive in question, and were unable to access the drive. What should your next step be?

Review Questions

1. You have just installed a new hard drive. When you power on the computer, it does not report that the new hard drive is available. You have verified that the hard drive is installed properly (checked the cable and jumper settings). What should you do next?

   _____

2. You have just installed a new hard drive. The computer reports that the new drive is installed during the boot process. When you attempt to access the hard drive in Windows XP, you are unable to do so. What should you do?

   _____

   _____

3. What utility can you use on a bootable floppy disk to troubleshoot a newly installed hard drive?

   _____

EXERCISE 7-6

Troubleshooting Hard Drive Data Access Problems

Activity Time:

15 minutes

Objective:

To determine the proper troubleshooting approach in various hard-drive data-access problem scenarios.

Scenario:

- Ticket: 112001

  Location: Main building, 25L17

  User: Reanna Kerwin

  System boots fine and everything works until the user tries to access data on the second hard drive, D. The message Can't Access This Drive is displayed when she tries to access the D drive. The user would also like an explanation about what the error message means.

- Ticket: 112002

  Location Elmwood Place, cube 58

  User: Leland Wolter

  When the user tries to access the hard drive containing his data, the system locks up and makes a clicking sound. From the DOS prompt, he can change to drive D, but when he tries to access a file or list the files on the drive, it locks up and begins clicking again.

- Ticket: 112003

  Location: Training center, main office

  User: Kamron Langley

  User reports that some of his folders have begun disappearing and some folder and file names are scrambled with strange characters in their names.

1. List some of the steps you might take to resolve trouble ticket 112001.

2. What steps might you take to attempt to resolve trouble ticket 112002? What is the most likely cause of the problem?

3. What steps might you take to attempt to resolve trouble ticket 112003? What is the most likely cause of the problem?

Review Questions

1. You have just installed a new hard drive in a computer. The computer boots successfully, but when you attempt to access data on the hard drive, you see a message stating that Windows is unable to access this drive. You know you are using the right drive letter. You're unable to copy a file to or from the hard drive. What should you do next?

2. A user reports that he is unable to access his second hard disk. When he tries to access this hard disk, he hears a clicking sound. What should you do first to troubleshoot this problem?

3. A user tells you that the names of files on the hard drive have strange characters. What are two problems that could lead to the filenames being scrambled?

7

EXERCISE 7-7

Troubleshooting Wrong Drive Size

Activity Time:

15 minutes

Objective:

To determine the proper troubleshooting approach when systems do not report the correct drive size.

Scenario:

Several older systems have been put back in service following a big hiring phase. These systems are being upgraded with larger hard drives and additional RAM. However, some systems are not reporting the correct drive size.

1. A 30 GB hard drive was installed, but the system reports that the drive is about 500 MB. What can be done to resolve this problem?

2. The system is running Windows 98 SE. After installing and partitioning a 70 GB drive with FDISK, FDISK reports that the drive is about 6 GB. Why is this happening? How can you resolve the problem?

3. A user is questioning the difference between the sizes in GB and bytes. Why is there such a big difference? 9.33 GB and 10,025,000,960 bytes. Why isn't it 10GB?

Review Questions

1. You have installed a new 10 GB hard disk in a computer. When you turn on the computer, however, its BIOS reports that the hard disk is only 500 MB in size. What should you try first to resolve this problem?

   _____

2. You have installed a new 10 GB hard disk in a computer. You have also updated the computer's BIOS. When you turn on the computer, its BIOS still reports that the hard disk is only 500 MB in size. What should you do?

   _____

   _____

Exercise 7-8

Installing and Using IomegaWare Utilities

Activity Time:

30 minutes

Objective:

To download and install IomegaWare utility software.

Setup:

An Iomega brand removable cartridge drive is installed on your system. This might be a Zip, Jaz, USB PocketZip (Clik!), HipZip, FotoShow, or Peerless device.

Scenario:

You installed an Iomega removable cartridge storage drive. You would like to install the IomegaWare utilities that shipped with the device, but the cartridge has been reformatted and used to store data files.

What You Do	How You Do It
1. What options are listed when you right-click the Iomega removable disk drive in My Computer?	
2. Download the IomegaWare software.	a. Access *www.iomega.com/software/ioware402pc.html*.
	b. Click the Download Now link.
	c. Fill out the Software Registration page, and then click Submit.
	d. Click Save.
	e. In the Save As dialog box, **verify that Save In is set to the Desktop.**
	f. Click Save.

3. **Install the IomegaWare software.**

    a. **Double-click ioware-w32x86402.exe that you saved to your Desktop.**

    b. **Click Next.**

    c. **Click Yes.**

    d. **Click Next.**

    e. **Click Close.**

    f. With Shut Down Now selected, **click OK.**

7

4. Verify that the installation was successful and that you can use the tools that were installed.

a. Open My Computer.

b. Right-click the removable cartridge drive.

c. Verify that some of the menu options have the Iomega symbol in front of them.

d. Choose Properties.

e. Click the Iomega tab.

f. In the Disk box, **click More Information.**

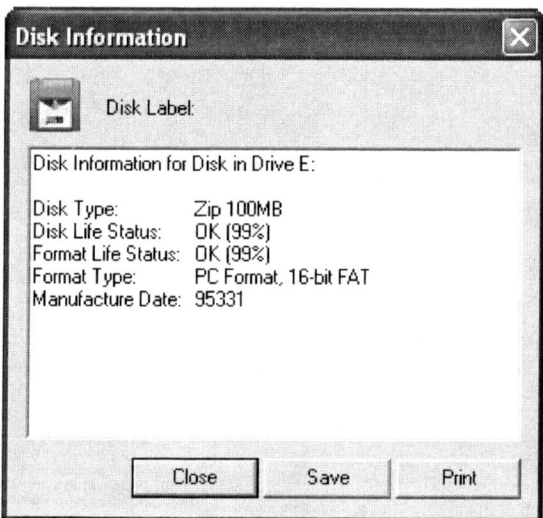

g. Click Close.

h. Click Cancel.

Review Questions

1. For what devices should you use the IomegaWare utilities?

_____

_____

2. How can you identify the IomegaWare utilities in Windows Explorer?

_____

_____

EXERCISE 7-9

Troubleshooting Floppy Drive Problems

Activity Time:

30 minutes

Objective:

To determine the proper troubleshooting approach in various floppy-drive problem scenarios, and to diagnose and resolve problems with floppy drives.

Scenario:

Users have opened trouble calls with the help center for the following problems which are related to the floppy drive on their systems.

- Ticket: 235001

    Location: Main building, 23D41

    User: Angharad Phatek

    When the user attempts to access the floppy drive, the message This Disk Is Not Formatted. Do You Want To Format It Now Or Insert Disk Now? is displayed.

- Ticket 235002

    Location: Main building, 32G37

    User: Gary Toomey

The user cannot write to a disk in the floppy drive.

- Ticket: 235003

  Location: Elmwood Place, cube 37

  User: Zoe Isaacs

  When trying to access the floppy drive from the command prompt, the user receives the message The System Cannot Find The Drive Specified.

- Ticket: 235004

  Location: Elmwood Place, cube 42

  User: Etta Romero

  User received a floppy disk containing important information from another user. When Etta tries to access the disk through Windows Explorer, she receives a message that the disk is not formatted.

- Ticket: 235005

  Location: Elmwood Place, cube 16A

  User: Wendy Jones

  It has been verified that the floppy disk is readable on other systems and that no floppy disks can be read on her drive and no floppy disks written on her drive can be read on any other systems.

---

1. **Identify some issues you should check in resolving trouble ticket 235001.**

---

2. List the issues to check in resolving trouble ticket 235002.

_____

3. What might cause the user to receive the error message shown in trouble ticket 235003?

_____

4. What would you recommend to the user to resolve trouble ticket 235004?

_____

5.   Resolve trouble ticket 235005.

a. Disconnect the power connector from the rear of the floppy disk drive.

b. Disconnect the controller cable from the rear of the floppy disk drive.

c. Remove the screws that mount the floppy disk drive in the chassis bay.

d. Slide the original floppy disk drive out of its bay.

e. Insert the new floppy disk drive into its bay.

f. Mount the disk drive to the chassis using the appropriate screws.

g. Connect the controller cable to the rear of the disk drive.

h. Connect the power connector to the rear of the disk drive.

i. Start the system and verify that the disk drive works properly.

Review Questions

1. What should you check first if a user is unable to write to a floppy disk?

2. A user reports that when she attempts to access a floppy disk, she receives the error message"The System Cannot Find The Drive Specified." What should you check first?

3. A user reports that he is unable to access a floppy disk he received from a graphics designer; the floppy disk contains your company's new logo. The user is receiving a message stating that the disk is not formatted. What might be the problem?

4. A user reports that he is able to read and write to floppy disks on his computer. When the user gives one of his floppy disks to another user, that user is unable to read or write to the floppy disk. What might be the problem?

_____

EXERCISE 7-10

Troubleshooting Removable Cartridge Drive Problems

Activity Time:

45 minutes

Objective:

To diagnose and resolve problems with removable cartridge drives.

Setup:

Prior to resolving each scenario in this activity, you will need to connect the drive if you don't have the specific drive indicated connected to your system. You can then have the instructor simulate the problem you are troubleshooting. The IomegaWare software has been installed.

Scenario:

Some of your users have high capacity removable cartridge drive systems including Zip, Jaz, LS120, and LS240 drives. The following are the trouble tickets that have been assigned to you related to those devices.

- Ticket: 234001

    Location: Main building, 42E51

    User: Daniel Price

User cannot access the Zip drive because no drive letter is being displayed for the device.

- Ticket: 234002

  Location: Main building, 24A61

  User: Naomi Lincoln

  User cannot write to Jaz drive. She can see the drive letter, but when she tries to write to the disk, she gets an error message.

- Ticket: 234003

  Location Elmwood Place, cube 18

  User: Yolande Vaughan

  The user is having problems accessing data on a Zip disk. She is not sure whether it was formatted for a Macintosh system or Windows system. She needs to access the information on a PC.

- Ticket: 234004

  Location: Training center, main office

  User: Sara Jenks

  User has a SuperDisk drive and the cartridge won't come out of the drive.

- Ticket: 234005

  Location: Main building, 41A41

  User: Kyria Shaver

  User has an older Zip drive attached through the Parallel port on a new system. The user is unable to access files on the Zip drive.

What You Do	How You Do It
1. Resolve trouble ticket 234001.	a. If necessary, **connect a Zip drive to your system.**
	b. **Open My Computer.**
	c. **Determine whether there is an icon for the Zip drive.**
	d. If not, **verify that the driver is loaded for the drive and load it if it has not been loaded.**
	e. **Verify that the drive is connected to the proper port with the proper cable.**
	f. **Restart the system.**
	g. If the problem is still not resolved, **access the troubleshooting guide at** *www.iomega.com/support/documents/11076.html*, **following links as needed until the problem is resolved.**
2. Resolve trouble ticket 234002.	a. If necessary, **connect a Jaz drive to your system.**
	b. **Right-click the Jaz drive icon and choose Protect.**
	c. **Select Not Protected, and then click OK.**
	d. If the disk still cannot be read, **try to use another disk in the drive.**
	e. If the disk still cannot be read, **verify that all cables are correctly connected.**
	f. If the disk still cannot be read, **move the drive as far from the monitor, speakers, power supplies, or other electronic devices as the cables will enable you to place the drive.**

7

3. **Resolve trouble ticket 234003.**

    a. If necessary, **connect a Zip drive to your system.**

    b. **Right-click the Zip drive letter and choose Properties.**

    c. **Display the Iomega panel, and then in the Disk Box, click More Information.**

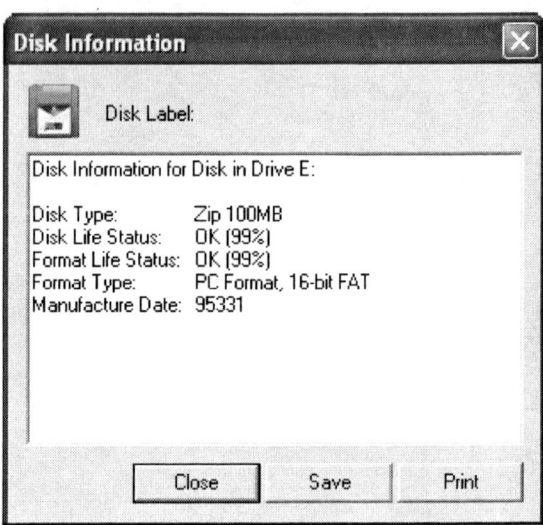

    d. **Verify that the disk is formatted for PC use.**

    e. **Click Cancel.**

4. **Resolve trouble ticket 234004.**

    a. If necessary, **connect a SuperDisk drive to your system.**

    b. **Right-click the drive letter and choose Eject.**

    c. If this does not work, **straighten a small paper clip.**

    d. **Insert the end of the paper clip in the hole to release the catch and eject the cartridge.**

5. Resolve trouble ticket 234005.

    a. **Open Device Manager.**

    b. **Verify that parallel port is not using unidirectional settings.**

    c. If necessary, **in the BIOS settings change parallel port mode settings to bidirectional.**

    d. **Restart the computer.**

    e. With ECP disabled, **attempt to access the drive.**

    f. In Device Manager, **display the LPT port properties Port Settings page.**

       Select Use Any Interrupt Assigned To The Port.

       Check Enable Legacy Plug And Play Detection.

       Click OK.

    g. **Restart the system and attempt to access the drive.**

7

Review Questions

1. You have been asked to troubleshoot a problem a user is experiencing with a removable cartridge drive. When the user attempts to access this drive in Windows Explorer, he does not see a drive letter for the drive. What should you check?

2. A user reports that she is unable to write to a removable cartridge drive. What should you check first?

3. You have been asked to remove a disk from a removable cartridge drive. How should you accomplish this task?

_____

_____

4. A user has asked you to move his original Zip drive from his old computer to his new computer. After attaching the Zip drive to the new computer, you are unable to access the drive. What might be the problem?

_____

_____

5. A user is unable to write to his removable cartridge drive. You have verified that the disk is not write-protected. What should you try next?

_____

EXERCISE 7-11

Troubleshooting CD or DVD Drive Problems

Activity Time:

45 minutes

Objective:

To determine the proper troubleshooting approach in various CD or DVD drive problem scenarios, and to diagnose and resolve problems with CD or DVD drives.

Scenario:

The following are the trouble tickets related to CD-ROM, CD-R/RW, DVD, and DVD-R drives that have been assigned to you for resolution.

- Ticket: 232001

    Location: Main building, 31A57

    User: Nichole Lombard

7

The door will not open on the CD-ROM drive. The user needs the CD that is in the drive.

- Ticket: 232002

  Location: Main building, 41A23

  User: Ruth Dalton

  User needs to be able to listen to audio CDs. System reads data and program CDs just fine.

- Ticket: 232003

  Location: Main building, 22C25

  User: Phillip Ward

  The user's system was recently upgraded to Windows XP. He can no longer access the CD-ROM drive on the system.

- Ticket: 232004

  Location: Main building, 11A10

  User: Richard Alston

  The user's CD-RW drive was listed as D. A new drive was added to the system and now, the D drive does not point to the CD-ROM drive. Some applications cannot find the CD-ROM when he attempts to run the application even though the CD is in the drive.

- Ticket: 232005

  Location: Main building, 12D52

  User: Mark Glick

  User needs to burn a CD and the drive keeps ejecting the CD media before he can write the disc.

- Ticket: 232006

  Location: Elmwood Place, cube 7

  User: Jennifer Kulp

  The user needs to be able to watch DVDs on her system. She can read CDs, play audio CDs, and read data DVDs in the drive.

What You Do	How You Do It
1. Resolve trouble ticket 232001.	a. Verify that there is power to the drive.
	b. Press the eject button on the drive.
	c. Verify that no applications are attempting to read from the CD-ROM.
	d. Open My Computer. Right-click the CD-ROM drive icon and choose Eject.
	e. Straighten out a small paper clip, and then insert the end into the hole on the front of the CD-ROM drive.

7

2. Resolve trouble ticket 232002.

a. Verify that you can read a data CD.

b. Verify that speakers are connected properly to the sound card.

c. Verify that speakers are properly powered and turned on.

d. Verify that volume is turned up on the physical speakers.

e. In the System Tray, **right-click the Volume icon and choose Open Volume Controls.**

    Verify that Volume Control is not all of the way down and that Mute is not checked.

f. **Play a system sound such as the Asterisk.**

g. Verify that the proper sound device drivers are installed.

h. In the Sounds, Speech, And Audio Devices window, under Troubleshooters, **click Sound. Follow the prompts in the Troubleshooting Wizard to attempt to resolve the problem.**

i. **Open the Windows Media Player and attempt to play the default song.**

j. Verify that the audio cable inside the case that connects the CD-ROM to the sound card is properly installed and that there are no broken wires.

k. Verify that the user can now play the audio CD.

3.   **Resolve trouble ticket 232003.**

a.   **Verify that the drive is on the Windows XP hardware compatibility list.**

b.   **Verify that the drive is properly installed.**

c.   **Verify that Windows Explorer lists a drive letter for the CD-ROM drive.**

d.   **Open My Computer, and then right-click the CD-ROM icon and choose Properties. Display the Hardware panel. Verify that the appropriate driver is listed.**

e.   **Click the Troubleshoot button and follow the prompts to troubleshoot the problem.**

7

4.   **Regarding trouble ticket 232004, explain to the user what the reason for their problem is and what needs to be done to correct it.**

5.   **What would you suggest that the user try in resolving trouble ticket 232005?**

6. **After checking over the hardware for the DVD drive on the system, you find no problems. What else might the problem be in trouble ticket 232006?**

Review Questions

1. A user reports that a CD is stuck in his CD-ROM drive. You have tried pressing the eject button and used the Eject option within My Computer to attempt to remove the CD. How can you manually remove the CD from the CD-ROM drive?

2. You have been asked to troubleshoot a problem where a user is able to read CD-ROM data and program disks but is unable to hear audio CDs. You have verified that you are able to read a data CD in the user's CD-ROM drive. You suspect the problem might be with the computer's speakers. What steps should you try next to troubleshoot the speakers?

3. A user reports that she upgraded her computer to Windows XP and is now unable to user her CD-ROM drive. What is the first step you should take to troubleshoot this problem?

4. What Windows utility should you use if you want to assign a specific drive letter to a CD-ROM drive?

5. A user is attempting to write to a blank CD in the CD-RW drive. When he inserts the CD, the drive ejects it before he can write to it. What are the two common causes of this problem?

EXERCISE 7-12

Identifying the Steps in the Laser Printing Process

Activity Time:

5 minutes

Objective:

To document the sequence of steps in the laser printing process.

Scenario:

In order to keep your laser printers working properly, you were told that it would help to know the steps used in the laser printing process. To make sure that you have the concept down, you wrote down the steps as you remembered them, and now you want to put them in the order that they occur.

1. Specify the order that each of the steps in the laser printing process occur.

   Developing

   Erasing

   Writing

   Cleaning

   Transferring

   Fusing

   Charging or conditioning

Review Questions

1. What step does a laser printer perform first when it prints a page?

2. What is the last step a laser printer performs when printing a page?

EXERCISE 7-13

Troubleshooting Printer Problems

Activity Time:

1 hour(s)

Objective:

To determine the proper troubleshooting approach in various printer problem scenarios, and to diagnose and resolve problems with printers.

Scenario:

The following is a list of the printer trouble tickets that have been assigned to you today.

- Ticket: 215001

  Location: Main building, 21L39

  User: Greg Berndt

  User prints a document from WordPad. Shortly after that he gets the message This Document Failed To Print. He is using an inkjet printer connected to the parallel port.

- Ticket: 215002

  Location: Main building, 32J45

  User: Estelle Royston

  Printer does not successfully print a test page using the buttons on the printer.

- Ticket: 215003

  Location: Main building, 13E41

  User: Mark Dawson

  Paper jam on laser printer.

- Ticket: 215004

  Location: Training center, main office

  User: Tomas Ridley

  Laser printer output has repeated streaks on the pages it produces. This is an HP LaserJet 5si printer.

- Ticket: 215005

  Location: Training center, room 1

  User: Toni Mancuso

Ink Jet printers in the room have various problems including:

- Poor print quality.
- No output.
- Fuzzy output.

- Ticket: 215006

  Location: Main building, 12B13

  User: Sheila Wright

  The dot matrix printer used for printing multi-part forms was printing poorly, and now, in addition, there is a paper jam.

- Ticket: 215007

  Location: Elmwood Place, cube 29

  User: Janice Wharton

  The user has a parallel port Zip drive and a printer plugged in to the piggy-back parallel port on the drive. The printer is not printing.

- Ticket: 215008

  Location: Main building, 13A36

  User: Terri Maximillion

  User has a USB ink-jet printer. The user is connecting it through the USB port on their keyboard. She received the message The Hub Does Not Have Enough Power Available To Operate The Device Driver Name. Would You Like Assistance In Solving This Problem? If You Click No, The Device May Not Function Properly.

What You Do	How You Do It
1. Resolve trouble ticket 215001.	a. Verify that the printer is turned on.
	b. Verify that the printer is online.
	c. Verify that the printer is connected with an IEEE 1284 cable to LPT1 on his system.
	d. Verify that LPT1 is configured for a bi-direction protocol.
	e. Perform a printer self test using the controls on the printer as specified in the printer documentation and verify that the printer passes this test.
	f. If the printer is piggy-backed on another device such as a Zip drive, scanner, or other daisy-chained device to the LPT port, **connect the printer directly to LPT1 and attempt to print again.**
	g. If you still cannot print, **replace the printer cable.**
	h. If the print process is still producing this error message, **move the printer and cable to another PC and attempt to print from Notepad or Wordpad.**

2. **Resolve trouble ticket 215002.**

    a. **From the Start menu choose Printers And Faxes.**

    b. **Right-click the printer and choose Properties.**

    c. **Click Print Test Page.**

    d. **If the page did not print, click Troubleshoot.**

    e. **Follow the Troubleshooting Wizard to help you resolve the problem.**

    f. **Check documentation for the printer and print a test page directly from the physical printer using printer controls.**

    g. **If the printer test does not print, refer to the printer's documentation for how to resolve this problem on your printer model.**

3. **Resolve trouble ticket 215003.**

    a. **Check the printer's documentation and follow the directions on how to remove paper from a paper jam for your printer.**

    b. **Check input and output trays for stuck paper.**

    c. **Check the rest of the paper path for jammed paper or stray bits of paper.**

    d. **Remove the tray and verify that the plates at the bottom of the tray move freely.**

        Reinsert the tray and try to print again.

    e. **Reset the printer and try printing again.**

4. Access the HP Web site and locate possible reasons for the repeated pattern on the output described in trouble ticket 215004. Identify which component is the potential reasons for the streaking to occur.

5. **List some of the things you should check and try to do when resolving trouble ticket 215005.**

6. **Resolve trouble ticket 215006.**

    a. **Open the tractor feeds and carefully remove the paper from the paper path.**

    b. **Remove any bits of paper that are loose in the printer from the paper path.**

    c. **With the printer off, align the paper and carefully guide it through the paper path, and align the holes with the tractor feed. Close the tractor feed over the edges of the paper feed holes.**

    d. **Determine if the poor print quality is due to needing a new ribbon, bent or damaged pins on the print head, the print head being too far from the platen, sheet fed is selected instead of pin feed, or another reason.**

        Make adjustments or replace the component as needed to resolve the problem.

7. Access the Iomega Web site and locate the document that describes how to resolve the problem described in trouble ticket 215007. After reviewing the steps, what are the two solutions they suggest?

8. How could you resolve the problem described in trouble ticket 215008?

Review Questions

1. A user reports that he is unable to print to his parallel printer. When you arrive at the user's desk, you notice that the printer is piggy-backed onto a scanner. What should you do?

2. You have attempted to print a test page on a printer, but the test page did not print. What Windows utility can you use to help you find the problem?

3. What step should you perform first when troubleshooting a paper jam?

4. A user reports that the print quality on her inkjet printer is very poor. What step should you take first?

5. A user is receiving this error message when she attempts to print to a USB printer:"The Hub Does Not Have Enough Power Available To Operate The Device Driver Name. Would You Like Assistance In Solving This Problem?" How can you resolve this problem?

EXERCISE 7-14

Configuring the Parallel Port

Activity Time:

15 minutes

Objective:

To enable ECP on a parallel port.

Scenario:

The company standard for parallel port configuration is ECP. It has been found that not all systems in the company adhere to this standard. You have been asked to check the systems you are setting up to make sure ECP is enabled. You have determined that you should check all of the systems to make sure that it is enabled.

What You Do	How You Do It
1. **Access the system BIOS.** Some older systems do not power off when you perform a shutdown.	a. **Shut down the computer and verify that the power is off.** If you missed the point in the boot process where you were to press the key(s) to access system bios (before the Windows splash screen is displayed), shutdown again and perform another cold boot and try again. b. **Turn the power on, and as the computer is booting, press the key (or key combination) indicated to access system setup.**

2.	Verify that ECP is enabled for the Parallel Port.	a.	**Find the Parallel Port settings.** This is usually under an Advanced menu or heading, then under Peripheral, and finally Parallel Port, but it might be accessed through a different set of choices depending on BIOS manufacturer.
		b.	**Verify that the Parallel Port settings are:**

- Parallel Port: Enabled
- Mode: ECP
- Base I/O Address: 378 (for LPT 1)
- Interrupt: IRQ 7 (for LPT1)
- DMA: 3 (for LPT1)

3.	Save BIOS Settings.	a.	**Press the key indicated in the BIOS to save changes and exit.**
		b.	**Verify that you want to save the changes.**

Review Questions

1. You suspect that a user's printing problem is caused by the configuration of the computer's parallel port. What should you examine to verify the parallel port's configuration?

_____

2. You have determined that you need to change a computer's parallel port from using SPP to ECP. What utility should you use?

_____

LAB 7-1

Creating Device Troubleshooting Plans

Activity Time:

45 minutes

Objective:

To research and document the appropriate steps to take in troubleshooting various hypothetical problems with computer devices.

Scenario:

You work for the R. A. Kash Computer Sales and Support company. The customer for whom you set up a home business has contracted with your company to provide full support including troubleshooting and repair of the equipment at their home office.

The client's company has grown greatly and they have purchased both new and used systems. Several of the devices have been giving the users problems. The customer has sent you an email with a general description of the problems. You plan to research and document your troubleshooting approach to each situation in advance, so that you can use your time efficiently when you go to the client's site later in the day to clear up the problems.

 When you have finished the lab, you can refer to the Creating Device Troubleshooting Plans Lab Results.txt file to check your work.

1. **A user with a wireless mouse is having problems with the mouse pointer jumping around on the screen or not moving at all. The mouse has worked well in the past, and there have been no changes to the computer's hardware configuration. What approach would you take to troubleshoot this problem?**

2. **There is a conflict between the settings on two of the internal adapter cards in one of the systems. What approach would you take to troubleshoot this problem?**

3. **A brand-new hard drive was added to one of the systems. The user can see the new second drive with its assigned drive letter in My Computer, but is unable to access it to read or write data. What approach would you take to troubleshoot this problem?**

4. **The CD-ROM drive on one of the systems is not working. It will not read any discs placed in the drive. What approach would you take to troubleshoot this problem?**

---

5. The floppy drive on a system will not read a specific disk, but can read other disks. What approach would you take to troubleshoot this problem?

_____

6. A printer is piggy-backed onto a daisy-chained device that is connected to the parallel port. The user cannot print to the printer. The printer works fine when it is directly attached to the parallel port. What approach would you take to troubleshoot this problem?

_____

CHAPTER 8

Troubleshooting System Problems

Activities included in this chapter:

- Exercise 8-1 Troubleshooting a Network Connection
- Exercise 8-2 Troubleshooting Modem Problems
- Exercise 8-3 Troubleshooting Power Problems
- Exercise 8-4 Troubleshooting Boot Problems
- Exercise 8-5 Troubleshooting Memory Problems
- Exercise 8-6 Troubleshooting System Board Problems
- Exercise 8-7 Correcting Portable System Problems
- Exercise 8-8 Diagnosing System Problems
- Lab 8-1 Creating System Troubleshooting Plans

EXERCISE 8-1

Troubleshooting a Network Connection

Activity Time:

20 minutes

Objective:

To diagnose and resolve a network connectivity problem on a computer system.

 It is possible that you will not need to perform all of the guided steps in this activity, or you might not be able to perform some steps. It will depend on the problem that the system is experiencing.

Scenario:

The network administrator has ruled out general network and server errors as the reason Alex Francis cannot connect to the network. He is located at the Elmwood Place facility in cube 21. He has been unable to connect to the Internet today. He needs to be able to access the Google.com Web site. All of the other users in the vicinity of his cube have been able to connect to the network.

What You Do	How You Do It

1. **Troubleshoot the network connection settings.**

   a. **On the system experiencing problems, enter** *ping www.google.com* **to verify that the system cannot connect to the Internet.**

   ```
   C:\>ping www.google.com
   Unknown host www.google.com.
   ```

   b. **On another system, log in to the network and at a command prompt, enter** *ping www. google.com* **to determine if the problem is just at the other system.**

   ```
   C:\>ping www.google.com

   Pinging www.google.com [216.239.33.99] with 32 bytes of data:

   Reply from 216.239.33.99: bytes=32 time=101ms TTL=42
   Reply from 216.239.33.99: bytes=32 time=90ms TTL=42
   Reply from 216.239.33.99: bytes=32 time=90ms TTL=42
   Reply from 216.239.33.99: bytes=32 time=90ms TTL=42

   Ping statistics for 216.239.33.99:
       Packets: Sent = 4, Received = 4, Lost = 0 (0% loss),
   Approximate round trip times in milli-seconds:
       Minimum = 90ms, Maximum = 101ms, Average = 92ms
   ```

   c. **On the system experiencing problems, open a command window and enter** *ipconfig*

   d. **Verify that the settings from the previous command are appropriate for your network. Change them if necessary.**

   e. **On another system, log in to the network. Then at a command prompt, ping the IP address of the system experiencing problems** to determine if you can reach the system over the network.

   f. **On the system you are troubleshooting, enter** *ping www.google.com* **to see if the problem has been resolved.**

2. Troubleshoot the local system's network connection hardware and cabling.

    a. Check that the network cable is firmly attached to the network card and to the network port.

    b. **Verify that the correct cable is being used to connect to the network.**

    c. If available, **run the diagnostics test for the network card from the software for that particular network card.**

    d. If necessary, **replace the network cable.**

    e. If necessary, **replace the network card.**

3. **Use the Help And Support Center to troubleshoot the network connection.**

    a. **From the Start menu choose Help And Support.**

    b. **Click Fixing A Problem.**

    c. **Click Networking Problems.**

    d. **Click Diagnose Network Configuration And Run Automated Networking Tests.**

    e. **Click Scan Your System.**

Modems and Network Adapters			
☐ Modems			˙ ˙
⊞ Network Adapters	[00000011] MAC Bridge Miniport	PASSED	
⊞ Network Clients			

    f. **Expand Network Adapters.**

4. **Did the Network Diagnostics point to any problems?**

5. Verify that the user can connect to the network and access the Google Web site.

    a. Log in to the network.

    b. Open a command prompt window and ping the Google Web site.

    c. Display the system's network settings.

    d. Close the command prompt window.

    e. In a Web browser, access *www.google.com*.

Review Questions

1. What three utilities can you use to troubleshoot network connection settings?

   _____

2. A user reports that he is unable to connect to the Internet. You have verified that his network settings are correctly configured. What should you try next?

   _____

3. A user cannot connect to the network. You have verified that the computer's network connection settings are correct. You have checked other users' computers, and those users are able to connect to the network. What should you check next?

   _____

   _____

4. What utility can you use to test a network card to verify that it's working properly?

   _____

5. What utility can you use in Windows XP to access the troubleshooting wizards?

   _____

8

EXERCISE 8-2

Troubleshooting Modem Problems

Activity Time:

45 minutes

Objective:

To diagnose and resolve several modem-related problems.

Setup:

You have access to an analog telephone and analog telephone line in order to test the modem connection. You have already installed and tested a modem in your system. You also have a dial-up account and phone number of a dial-up service to which you can connect.

Scenario:

The company has only recently started allowing employees to dial in to the network while on the road or working from home. The help center has been inundated with modem related trouble tickets. The following is the list of tickets you have been assigned to handle.

- Trouble ticket: 415001

    Location: Elmwood Place, cube 26

    User: Amy Schweib

User receives the message There Was No Dial Tone.

- Trouble ticket: 415002

  Location: Elmwood Place, cube 4

  User: Augusta Lindsay

  The error message Modem Not Responding There Was A Hardware Failure In The Modem is displayed when she attempts to dial in.

- Trouble ticket: 415003

  Location: Elmwood Place, cube 9

  User: Caitlyn Thorp

  After attempting to connect, the error message Dial-Up Networking Could Not Negotiate A Compatible Set Of Network Protocols is displayed, and the connection is dropped.

- Trouble ticket: 415004

  Location: Elmwood Place, cube 3

  User: Carm Traphagan

  After the modem dials, the user gets a message that the server is busy. She tried at various times of day and night and cannot believe it is always busy even during the middle of the night.

- Trouble ticket: 415005

  Location: Elmwood Place, cube 35

  User: Samuel Bolivier

  The modem does not respond when the user attempts to use dial-up networking. The modem was only recently installed when dial-up networking was approved at the company.

- Trouble ticket: 415006

  Location: Elmwood Place, cube 2

  User: Maggie Palmateer

  The user receives the message The Remote Computer Did Not Respond even though it seems like it connected. She can hear the modem making the chhh sound.

What You Do	How You Do It
1. Resolve trouble ticket 415001.	a. Verify that the telephone line is connected to the line-in, Line, or Telco port on the modem.
	b. Verify that the other end of the telephone line is plugged into the wall jack.
	c. Unplug any other devices attached to the telephone line such as an answering machine or fax machine.
	d. Verify that your telephone receiver is not off the hook.
	e. Untangle the phone line, especially from power cords.

2. **Resolve trouble ticket 415002.**

 After performing each step, be sure to test the modem again to see if you have found the solution to the problem. It is possible that you will not need to perform all of the steps shown here.

a. If using an external modem, **verify that it is plugged in, turned on, and properly connected to the system.**

b. **Open the Network And Internet Connections page from Control page, and then click Phone And Modem Options.**

    Display the Modems page and verify that the correct modem make and model is listed.

c. **Select the modem and click Properties.**

d. **Display the Diagnostics page.**

e. **Click Query Modem, and then review the results of the query.**

f. **Click View Log.**

    After reviewing the log file, **close Notepad.**

g. **Click Cancel** to close the Modem Properties dialog box.

h. In the Network And Internet Connections window, **click Network Diagnostics.**

i. **Click Scan Your System.**

j. **Expand Modems and verify that the settings are accurate for the modem to connect to your network.**

k. If it is still not working, **remove the modem and reinstall it.**

3. Resolve trouble ticket 415003.

    a. Verify that the correct driver for your make and model of modem is installed.

    b. Open Phone And Modem Options, and then display the Modem Properties dialog box.

    c. Display the Advanced page, and then click Change Default Preferences.

    d. Verify that Port Speed, Data Protocol, Compression, and Flow Control match the settings needed to connect to the network.

    e. Display the Advanced page.

    f. Verify that the Hardware Settings Data Bits, Parity, Stop Bits, and Modulation are the appropriate settings to connect to the network.

    g. Click OK.

    h. Click Advanced Port Settings.

    i. Verify that Use FIFO Buffers UART settings are appropriate for your modem, and then click OK.

    j. Display the Modem page.

    k. Display the Maximum Port Speed drop-down list and lower the speed.

    l. Try the connection again.

4. **Resolve trouble ticket 415004.**

    a. **Open HyperTerminal.**

    b. **Choose File→Properties.**

    c. **Display the Settings page.**

    d. **Click ASCII Setup.**

    e. **Check Echo Typed Characters Locally.**

    f. **Click OK twice.**

    g. **Enter the command** ATX0, **and then enter the phone number.**

    h. **Straighten any kinks or tangled phone lines.**

    i. **Verify that the correct phone number is being dialed.**

    j. If dialing out of a business and an outside line access number is required, **verify that the number followed by at least one comma precedes the phone number.**

    k. **Contact the party being dialed and find out if they are having any problems with the connection hardware or software.**

5. Resolve trouble ticket 415005.

    a. Verify that the phone line is correctly connected to the modem.

    b. If this is an external modem, **verify that the modem is securely connected to the system and that the power supply is connected to the modem, plugged in, and turned on.**

    c. **Close any other open applications and try dialing again.**

    d. **Verify that the modem settings in Control page match the physical modem COM and IRQ settings.**

    e. If this is an external modem, **try another cable.**

    f. **Reset the modem through HyperTerminal with the command AT&F.**

    g. **Try dialing again.**

6. Resolve trouble ticket 415006.

    a. In the System Tray, **right-click the connection icon.**

    b. **Verify that a connection was established.**

    c. **Disconnect.**

    d. **Try the connection again.**

    e. If you still cannot connect **verify that all settings are correct for establishing the remote connection.**

Review Questions

1. A user reports that she's receiving the error message "No Dialtone" when she tries to user her modem. After asking her questions, you have determined that she was able to use the modem yesterday. What is the first step you should take to troubleshoot this problem?

    _____

    _____

2. You have been called in to troubleshoot an internal modem that is displaying the error message"Modem Not Responding." You have verified that the correct modem driver is installed. Which two Windows utilities can you use to further troubleshoot the modem?

    _____

    _____

3. You have just installed a new modem into a user's computer. The modem isn't working. What steps should you use to troubleshoot the modem?

    _____

    _____

    _____

    _____

4. A user is able to dial in to his ISP but is unable to log in. What might be the problem?

    _____

    _____

5. You have been asked to troubleshoot a modem that occasionally disconnects a user's connection to her ISP. What are two possible causes of this problem?

    _____

    _____

    _____

    _____

Exercise 8-3

Troubleshooting Power Problems

Activity Time:

20 minutes to 1 hour(s)

Objective:

To determine the proper troubleshooting approach in various power-problem scenarios, and to diagnose and resolve several power-related problems.

Scenario:

The following list of trouble tickets are power problems that have been assigned for you to resolve.

- Trouble ticket: 125001

  Location: Main building, 51B24

  User: Darlene Burley

  When the user turns on the PC, it doesn't always come on and sometimes it just shuts itself down abruptly, with no warning. The help center has determined that the user does not hear the fan when the system is turned on.

- Trouble ticket: 125002

  Location: Main building, 21K37

  User: Earle Washburn

  The user turns on the power switch, but the system does not come on. He does not hear the fan, there is no power light on, and he hears no beeps or other sounds coming from the system.

- Trouble ticket: 125003

  Location: Main building, 22F16

  User: Enrique Dominguez

  The user is having intermittent power problems. The system is powering off in the midst of his working. Often when he comes back from break, his system has been rebooted. He is using a legacy database application and his data is being corrupted. When he turns on the system again, it indicates that the system was not shut down properly. He needs a list of what he should be on the lookout for when the system is booting so he can record if any of them occur to help narrow down what is causing the power problem.

- Trouble ticket: 125004

  Location: Elmwood Place, cube 20

  User: Sylvania Rawleigh

  One of the other hardware technicians has been trying to troubleshoot a power problem. The system will not come on when the user turns on the power switch. He determined that the user has an ATX system board and power supply. You have been assigned to take over this trouble ticket.

1. **What should you do to resolve trouble ticket 125001?**

2. **Resolve trouble ticket 125002.**

    a. Verify that the power cord is securely connected to the power supply and to the electrical outlet on the UPS or surge protector.

    b. Verify that the UPS or surge protector is turned on and plugged in.

    c. Verify that the UPS or surge protector is working by plugging in a lamp with a known good light bulb and turning it on.

    d. If the lamp did not light, check to see whether any reset buttons need to be reset on the UPS or surge protector, or check the electric outlet's circuit breaker.

    e. If none of these fixed the problem, prepare to replace the power supply by powering off and removing any external power cables from power supply connections.

    f. Remove the cover, and then disconnect all connections from the power supply to internal devices including unplugging it from the system board.

    g. If necessary, remove any components needed to have complete access to the power supply.

    h. Unscrew the power supply from the back of the system case.

    i. Determine if, and in which direction, the power supply needs to be slid to remove it from the slots holding it in place, then remove it from the system.

    j. Slide the replacement power supply into place and screw it to the system case.

    k. If you removed any components to remove the power supply, reinstall those components.

8

l. Reconnect the power connections to internal and external devices.

m. Verify that all components are working properly.

3. List some of the possible clues found during the POST that the user should record in helping determine the cause of the power problem described in trouble ticket 125003.

4. Resolve trouble ticket 125004.

a. Set the multimeter for DC volts over 12V.

b. **Locate an available internal power supply connector.** If none are free, you will need to power off the system and unplug it, then remove one from a floppy drive or CD drive, then power on the system again.

c. **Insert the black probe from the multimeter into one of the two center holes on the internal power supply connector.**

d. **Insert the red probe from the multimeter into the hole for the red wire.**

e. **Verify that the multimeter reading is +5V DC.**

f. **Move the red probe into the hole for the yellow wire.**

g. **Verify that the multimeter reading is +12V DC.**

h. **If either reading is incorrect, test again. If the reading is still incorrect, replace the power supply.**

i. If the reading was correct, check the documentation for the ATX motherboard to see if there is a logic circuit switch that signals power to be turned on or off, that it is properly connected, and how it should be set.

j. **Verify that the motherboard, processor, memory and video card are all correctly installed and working.**

Review Questions

1. What two problems might you see if you suspect a line noise power problem?

_____

2. You have been asked to troubleshoot a user's computer. The computer shuts itself down with no warning. You don't hear the fan working. What should you do first to troubleshoot this problem?

_____

3. A user reports that his computer does not come on when he turns on the power switch. The computer is connected to a UPS. What should you check before opening the computer case?

_____

_____

_____

_____

4. What are two indicators you might see during the boot process that indicate a problem with the power supply?

_____

_____

_____

5. What tool can you use to test the voltage supplied by the power supply?

_____

EXERCISE 8-4

Troubleshooting Boot Problems

Activity Time:

20 minutes

Objective:

To determine the proper troubleshooting approach in various boot-problem scenarios, and to diagnose and resolve boot-related problems.

Scenario:

The following are the trouble tickets to which you have been assigned. All of the users are experiencing some type of problem when trying to boot their systems.

- Trouble ticket: 175001

    Location: Main building, 12C42

    User: Eric Spender

    The system is slow to boot. On responding to the user's trouble ticket, you find that the system contains an Intel D815EEA motherboard.

- Trouble ticket: 175002

    Location: Elmwood Place, cube 12

    User: Samantha Condello

    The user hears beeps when starting the system. She hears four beeps followed by another four beeps followed by one beep.

- Trouble ticket: 175003

    Location: Main building, 22G44

    User: Patti Lu

    One long beep followed by three short beeps sound when the user attempts to start the system. This system has AMI BIOS.

- Trouble ticket: 175004

    Location: Main building

    User: Garold Martin

When the user tries to boot, the message Non-system Disk Or Disk Error is displayed.

- Trouble ticket: 175005

  Location: Main building, 51A12

  User: Joellen Folts

  The user inherited this system from a previous employee. The previous employee set a power-on password for the system and nobody knows what it is.

---

1. **What are some potential causes and solutions to the problem described in trouble ticket 175001?**

---

2. **Search using a Web search engine such as Google for the beep code pattern indicated in trouble ticket 175002.**

   Which BIOS manufacturer uses this beep code pattern and what are some potential causes and solutions to the problem described in trouble ticket 175002?

---

3. **What are some potential causes and solutions to the problem described in trouble ticket 175003?**

---

4. **What are some potential causes and solutions to the problem described in trouble ticket 175004?**

---

5. What are some potential causes and solutions to the problem described in trouble ticket 175005?

_____

Review Questions

1. A user reports that she hears a series of four beeps when she turns on her computer. How can you determine what these beeps mean?

   _____

2. You have been asked to troubleshoot an "Operating System Not Found" error message. What is the first thing you should check?

   _____

   _____

3. A user does not remember the power-on password for his computer. What should you do?

   _____

   _____

4. Once the computer's BIOS locates the hard disk drive in a computer from which to boot, what happens next?

   _____

5. What happens first when you turn on the power to a computer?

   _____

EXERCISE 8-5

Troubleshooting Memory Problems

Activity Time:

20 minutes

Objective:

To determine the proper troubleshooting approach in various memory-problem scenarios, and to diagnose and resolve memory-related problems.

Scenario:

The following are the trouble tickets to which you have been assigned. All of the users are experiencing some type of problem related to the memory installed in their systems.

- Trouble ticket: 401001

    Location: Main building, 12B52

    User: Roger Wheaton

    The user is experiencing corrupted data in his database application. The hard drive has been checked and no problems were found with it. The application was reinstalled and the database was reindexed and all data problems have been corrected. No other users are experiencing this problem when they enter data. He has been successfully entering data until just recently.

- Trouble ticket: 401002

    Location: Elmwood Place, cube 6

    User: Rory Waldon

    The user is complaining of application crashes. He is fine if he is only running his email and word processing programs. If he also opens his graphics program at the same time, then the applications are crashing.

- Trouble ticket: 401003

    Location: Main building, 22G42

    User: Hazel Beech

    Additional memory was installed in her system and now it won't boot.

1. After troubleshooting trouble ticket 401001, you believe it is memory related. Why might the memory experience problems all of a sudden?

2. You are attempting to resolve trouble ticket 401002. Why is the user only experiencing the problem when additional applications are opened? What can you do to determine the cause?

3. Resolve trouble ticket 401003.

    a. Verify that the correct memory was installed in the system.

    b. Verify that memory was installed and configured correctly.

    c. Try swapping memory around in the memory banks.

    d. Check to see if the BIOS manufacturer has released any upgrades that would resolve the problem.

8

Review Questions

1. What two memory problems could cause a computer to appear to boot but its screen to remain blank?

2. A user has asked you to troubleshoot his computer. After questioning the user, you've determined that she just installed a new memory module she bought at a discount store. What might be the problem?

3. A user reports that his computer periodically reboots and hangs. What should you check first?

_____

4. You have installed new memory in a computer and now it won't boot. You have verified that you installed the correct memory type for the computer, and that it was installed correctly. You have swapped the memory around in the computer's memory banks but the computer still won't boot. What should you try next?

_____

EXERCISE 8-6

Troubleshooting System Board Problems

Activity Time:

10 minutes

Objective:

To determine the proper troubleshooting approach to take when presented with a problem with a system board.

Scenario:

Gene Gibson at the Training Center has been experiencing system problems. You have checked every component in the system, tried replacing the components with spares, and still his system is acting up. His department's budget does not allow for replacing the system, so this one will need to be repaired. It worked fine for over a year. When the movers moved it into his new office, the system was found to have been shipped upside down, with inadequate packing materials, and heavy items placed on top of it. This resulted in the system case being bent.

1. **What are the most common system board problems?**

2. **What would lead you to believe the system board was the problem?**

Review Questions

1. You have determined that the heat sink and fan in a server are not sufficient to keep the server's CPU from getting too hot. What other types of cooling methods should you consider?

2. What is the most common cause of system board problems?

3. You are attempting to troubleshoot a computer that won't boot. You have checked the computer's power connections and power supply, CMOS setup, CPU, memory, and all cable connections. Which component should you check next?

_____

4. True or False: Viruses can infect a computer's BIOS.

_____

Exercise 8-7

Correcting Portable System Problems

Activity Time:

30 minutes

Objective:

To determine the proper troubleshooting approach in various portable-system problem scenarios, and to diagnose and resolve problems with portable systems.

Scenario:

The following list of trouble tickets are portable system problems that have been assigned for you to resolve.

- Trouble ticket: 051001

  Location: Main building, 35A12

  User: Hazel Beech

  User has a Compaq Armada portable system. She is having problems with the monitor. She had been using an external monitor. The system went into hibernation mode and during that time, she removed the system from the docking station. Now that she is home, she can't get anything to display on the internal monitor.

- Trouble ticket: 051002

  Location: Main building, 35B43

  User: James Lindsey

  User has a laptop that enters hibernation mode while he is using it.

- Trouble ticket: 051003

  Location: Main building, 11C41

  User: Hermione Ardell

  User has charged the battery for 24 hours, but the system will still not turn on unless it is plugged in.

- Trouble ticket: 051004

  Location: Elmwood Place, cube 6

  Gene Gibson

  User added memory to his ThinkPad. When he turns it on, it beeps but nothing is displayed on screen. There is no hard drive activity either.

What You Do	How You Do It

1. Resolve trouble ticket 051001.

   a. Turn on the portable computer system.

   b. With the cover open, **press and hold the Fn key while pressing the Function key marked for the monitor.** On an Armada 7400, this would be the F4 key.

   c. If the internal monitor still doesn't work, **verify that the screen is secure in the case by pressing the bottom of the screen and case intersection.**

   d. If the internal monitor still doesn't work, **try plugging it back into the docking station and using the external monitor.**

   e. If neither monitor works, **obtain repair services from an authorized Compaq service center.**

2. **What are some of the causes you should check for in attempting to resolve trouble ticket 051002?**

3. **What would you suggest to the user as the reason for the problem shown in trouble ticket 051003?**

4.	Reseat the memory in the laptop in an attempt to resolve trouble ticket 051004.	a.	Locate the memory compartment on the laptop and open it.
		b.	Unclip the memory module and remove it.
		c.	Hold the SODIMM module at a 45 degree angle to the memory slot.
		d.	Push the module firmly into the slot.
		e.	Push the module down until it locks into the clips.
5.	If reseating the memory did not resolve trouble ticket 051004, check other possible causes for the problem.	a.	Check that the power cord is plugged in.
		b.	Verify that the SODIMM module is locked in place.
		c.	Make sure no other components were accidentally disconnected when you installed the memory.

Review Questions

1. A user reports that his laptop unpredictably goes into hibernation mode even when he is currently using the computer. What should you check?

2. A user is having a problem with her laptop battery providing only 30 minutes of battery power. You have verified that she is following the correct procedure to recharge the battery. The battery is three years old. What should you do?

3. You have installed new memory in a laptop and now the computer won't boot. What should you check?

4. A user reports that when he removes his laptop from its docking station, he is unable to see anything on the laptop's built-in monitor. What should you do?

_____

_____

EXERCISE 8-8

Diagnosing System Problems

Activity Time:

1 hour(s)

Objective:

To determine the proper troubleshooting approach in various system-level problem scenarios.

Scenario:

You are working on the help desk. The following calls are received. You need to work with the customer to determine what the problem is. After you determine what the problem is, a technician will be assigned to visit the user to actually fix the problem if it can't be fixed over the phone with the user.

8

1.   Lillian Gherhardt: "I came in this morning and my laptop is acting weird. I turn it on and it starts to come up, but then part way through coming up, it just seems to die."

What questions might you ask Lillian to help determine the exact issue she is dealing with?

You ask Lillian if she would be willing to check all connections, including checking for a loose battery, and to try booting again so you can help her troubleshoot the problem.

What part of the troubleshooting model does this correspond to? What can this step help you determine?

Is it likely that you can resolve this problem over the phone or will a desk-side technician need to visit this user to resolve the problem?

2. Jerome Fischer: "I have been working all night on this program, and now that I need to burn it to CD, I can't."

After asking Jerome questions about his attempts to burn the CD, you have determined that he does indeed have a CD-RW drive, a blank CD, has burning software installed, and has successfully burned CDs previously.

What should you do next in the troubleshooting process?

Do you think this problem can be resolved over the phone or will a desk-side technician need to visit the user to resolve the problem?

8

3. Melanie Drum: "My monitor just made a strange sound, and now it is blank. I need to finish the report I was working on for my manager within the next half hour."

What would be the most appropriate response to resolving this user's problem?

4. Toby Palantine: "I got a new digital camera. I took some pictures and plugged the camera into the PC's USB port like the documentation says to do, but I don't seem to see the camera anywhere so that I can get the pictures onto my computer. I tried looking in Explorer and My Computer, but I don't see anything about my camera anywhere. My manager wants the pictures that we took as soon as possible so that she can include them in the brochure she is creating."

Describe all of the troubleshooting process that you would use to help Toby resolve the problem he is experiencing.

Review Questions

1. What are the three phases in the troubleshooting model?

   _____

2. What are two sources of information you should use during the Collect phase of troubleshooting?

   _____

   _____

   _____

3. List two resources you can use to help you isolate a problem.

   _____

   _____

4.   Why should you make only one change at a time when correcting a problem?

_____

_____

8

Lab 8-1

Creating System Troubleshooting Plans

Activity Time:

20 minutes

Objective:

To research and document the appropriate steps to take in troubleshooting various hypothetical computer system problems.

Scenario:

You work for the R. A. Kash Computer Sales and Support company. You have shown your skills in troubleshooting specific device problems, so you have been promoted to the team responsible for troubleshooting system-wide problems.

Today, you have some trouble tickets from a customer who has problems that could not be resolved by the first-tier support technician. You plan to research and document your trouble-shooting approach to each situation in advance, so that you can use your time efficiently when you go to the client's site later in the day to clear up the problems.

 When you have finished the lab, you can refer to the Creating System Troubleshooting Plans Lab Results.txt file to check your work.

1. **One of the customer's employees cannot access the Internet. The computer was recently added to a new workgroup, and can access the other computers in the workgroup. What approach would you take to troubleshoot this problem?**

---

2. **An employee tries to dial in to the Internet so that she can access the customer's Web site from home. She can connect, but gets disconnected almost immediately every time. What approach would you take to troubleshoot this problem?**

---

3. **A computer is having intermittent system problems, including system lock-ups, memory errors, and abrupt system shutdowns. Reinstalling the operating system and applications has not corrected the situation. What components would you troubleshoot in attempting to resolve this problem?**

CHAPTER 9

Windows Tools

Activities included in this chapter:

- Exercise 9-1 Choosing the Correct Graphical Tool
- Exercise 9-2 Choosing the Correct Command-line Tool
- Lab 9-1 Identifying Graphical and Command-line Tools

Exercise 9-1

Choosing the Correct Graphical Tool

Activity Time:

10 minutes

Objective:

To identify the functions of various graphical tools.

Scenario:

As part of a job interview for an A+ technician position, you've been asked to correctly identify a list of graphical tools that you'd use to manage a Windows computer.

1. **Match the tool with its description.**

    ____ Windows Explorer

    a. Found in Windows 2000 and Windows XP, this tool contains just about every system administration or information tool you'd need to manage both operating systems.

    ____ My Computer

    b. Found in Windows 98 and Windows NT 4.0, this tools is used to connect to other computers on the network.

    ____ Control Panel

    c. This tool, found in the lower-left corner of a Windows desktop, contains all the tools you'd need to manage the computer.

    ____ Computer Management

    d. Found in Windows 98, Windows 2000, and Windows XP, this tool is used to gather information about the hardware attached to a computer.

    ____ My Network Places

    e. Opened directly from the Start menu in Windows XP, this tool contains programs used to configure the Windows operating system or the computer's hardware.

    ____ Network Neighborhood

    f. Opened from the desktop in Windows 98, Windows NT 4.0, and Windows 2000, this tool is used to manage files and folders on your computer.

    ____ Device Manager

    g. Found in Windows 2000 and Windows XP, this tool is used to connect to other computers on the network.

    ____ Start menu

    h. Opened from the Programs menu in Windows 98 and Windows NT 4.0, this tool is used to manage files and folders on your computer.

9

Review Questions

1. Which utility do you use to add, modify, and delete user and group accounts in Windows 2000?

2. Which utility enables you to connect to another computer on the network in Windows XP?

_____

3. You want to change the current user's password on a Windows 9x computer. What utility should you use?

_____

4. What is the file extension for program or application files?

_____

5. Which utility enables you to view a list of the hardware devices installed in a computer along with the status of each device?

_____

EXERCISE 9-2

Choosing the Correct Command-line Tool

Activity Time:

10 minutes

Objective:

To identify the functions of various command-line tools.

Scenario:

As the second part of a job interview for an A+ technician position, you've been asked to correctly identify a list of command-line tools that you'd use to manage a Windows computer.

1. **Match the command-line tool with its description.**

    ___ Md

    ___ Deltree

    ___ Ver
    ___ Xcopy

    ___ Dir
    ___ Mem
    ___ Attrib

    ___ Set

    a. Copies files, folders, and directory trees.
    b. Displays the operating system version.
    c. Creates a new directory.
    d. Displays the memory usage on a computer.
    e. Configures environment variables.
    f. Changes file attributes.
    g. Deletes a specified directory structure (a directory and all its subdirectories).
    h. Displays the contents of a directory.

Review Questions

1. Which command-line utility enables you to delete a directory and all of its subdirectories?

    _____

2. Which command-line utility enables you to configure environment variables?

    _____

3. Which command-line utility should you use if you want to display the contents of a text file?

    _____

4. You need to create a new partition on a hard disk. Which command-line utility should you use?

    _____

5. You want to transfer the Io.sys and Msdos.sys files from a boot disk to a hard disk so that the computer can boot from the hard disk. What utility should you use?

    _____

Lab 9-1

Identifying Graphical and Command-line Tools

Activity Time:

10 minutes

Objective:

To identify the functions of common Windows graphical and command-line tools.

Scenario:

You've been asked to help a new Windows user identify some common tools you'd use to manage a Windows computer. The user has a list of tools he's been told he should know about, and he's asked you to describe the tools to him.

9

1. **Match the tool to its description.**

___ Taskbar	a. Tool used to connect to other computers in Windows 98.
___ Start button	b. Command used to display a text file.
___ Deltree	c. Command used to display the operating system version.
___ Disk Manager	d. Tool located at the bottom of the Windows screen; contains the Start button and system tray.
___ Type	e. Command used to configure environment variables.
___ User Manager	f. Tool used to access almost any tool on a Windows computer.
___ Set	g. Tool used to manage hard disks in Windows NT 4.0.
___ Ver	h. Tool used to create user account in Windows NT 4.0.
___ Disk Management	i. Tool used to manage hard disks in Windows XP.
___ Network Neighborhood	j. Command used to delete a directory and all the files and subdirectories it contains.

CHAPTER 10

Managing Applications

Activities included in this chapter:

- Exercise 10-1 Examining the Registry
- Exercise 10-2 Examining User Profiles
- Exercise 10-3 Examining User Profile Folders
- Exercise 10-4 Installing the Windows 2000 Professional Support Tools
- Exercise 10-5 Configuring Virtual Memory in Windows 2000
- Exercise 10-6 Installing a Non-Windows Application Without a Setup Program
- Exercise 10-7 Configuring a Non-Windows Application's Memory Usage
- Exercise 10-8 Removing the Windows 2000 Support Tools
- Lab 10-1 Installing and Configuring Applications

EXERCISE 10-1

Examining the Registry

Activity Time:

10 minutes

Objective:

To identify the components of the Registry structure for a Windows operating system.

Setup:

Your user name is Admin#, where # is the number assigned to your computer. The password for this account is password.

Scenario:

You manage several Windows 2000 computers. You're planning to install new applications on those computers. You have just read an article that stated that when you install an application, that application's setup program updates the HKEY_LOCAL_MACHINE\Software key with information about that application. Before you install the new applications, you want to review the Windows 2000 Registry so that you can identify the changes installing the applications makes to the Registry.

What You Do	How You Do It
1. As a local administrator, **review the contents of the HKEY_LOCAL_MACHINE\ Software key.**	a. **Turn on the power to the computer.** The computer boots into Windows 2000 Professional by default.
	b. If necessary, in the User Name text box, **type** *Admin#* where # is your assigned student number.
	c. In the Password text box, **type** *password* **and click OK** to log on to Windows 2000.
	d. From the Start menu, **choose Run.**
	e. In the Open text box, **type** `regedt32` **and click OK** to open Registry Editor.
	f. If necessary, **choose Windows→HKEY_LOCAL_ MACHINE** to make the HKEY_LOCAL_MACHINE subtree window the current window.
	g. In the left pane, **double-click the Software key** to expand the folder. You see a list of the keys within the Software key.

| | h. **Close Registry Editor.** |

Review Questions

1. In what Registry subtree does Windows store all file association information?

   _____

2. Which Registry subtree is present in Windows 9x but not in Windows 2000?

   _____

3. Which Registry subtree contains all the configuration information for the computer's hardware?

    _____

4. In Windows 9x, what command do you use to open Registry Editor?

    _____

5. In Windows 2000, what command do you use to open Registry Editor?

    _____

Exercise 10-2

Examining User Profiles

Activity Time:

10 minutes

Objective:

To demonstrate how the user profile preserves desktop settings for each user.

Setup:

In addition to your Admin# user, you can also log in as Administrator with a password of password.

Scenario:

You have just been hired to work as a member of the Help Desk department at a company that only has Windows 2000 computers. In the past, you've supported only Windows 9x computers. One of your duties will be to respond to questions users have about configuring their desktops. You want to familiarize yourself with the Windows 2000 user profiles so that you can be prepared for users' questions.

10

1. **Verify that Windows 2000 automatically retains each user's wallpaper settings.**

    a. On the desktop, **right-click and choose Properties** to open the Display Properties dialog box.

    b. Below Select A Background Picture Or HTML Document As Wallpaper, **select a wallpaper.**

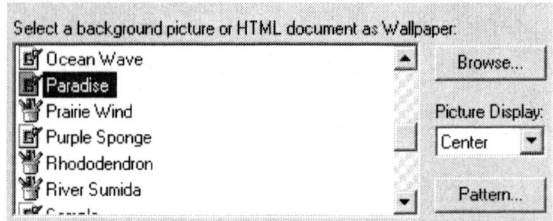

    c. **Click OK** to save your changes.

    d. If necessary, **click Yes** to enable Active Desktop.

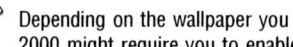 Depending on the wallpaper you select, Windows 2000 might require you to enable Active Desktop.

    e. From the Start menu, **choose Shut Down.**

    f. From the What Do You Want Your Computer To Do drop-down list, **select Log Off Admin# and click OK.**

    g. **Log on as Administrator with a password of password.** Notice that you don't see the wallpaper you selected for the other user. Windows 2000 stores the wallpaper selection as part of the user's profile.

    h. **Log off and log back on as Admin#.**

Review Questions

1. Which Windows operating systems automatically create user profiles for each user who logs on to the computer?

   _____

2. True or False: Windows 2000 stores all Web sites a user adds to the Favorites menu in Internet Explorer in the user's profile.

   _____

3. What settings do all user profiles contain at a minimum?

   _____

   _____

10

Exercise 10-3

Examining User Profile Folders

Activity Time:

10 minutes

Objective:

To examine the user profile folder structure on a Windows 2000 computer.

Scenario:

As a new technician for your company, you are responsible for managing user profiles. You think user profiles have been created on your company's Windows 2000 computers. You want to examine the folder structure so that you know where to look for profile components in case you run into any problems.

What You Do	How You Do It
1. Review the contents of the user profiles folders, including the Default User profile.	a. From the Start menu, **choose Programs→ Accessories→Windows Explorer.**
	b. **Open the D:\Documents and Settings folder** to display the profiles on the computer. You see a folder for Admin#, Administrator, and All Users.

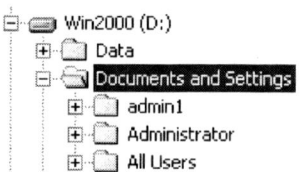

	c. **Choose Tools→Folder Options.** You must configure Windows Explorer to display hidden files in order to see the Default User profile.
	d. In the Folder Options dialog box, **select the View tab.**

e. Below Hidden Files And Folders, **select Show Hidden Files And Folders.**

   Hidden files and folders
     ○ Do not show hidden files and folders
     ◉ Show hidden files and folders

f. **Click OK** to save your changes.

g. **Review the contents of the D:\Documents and Settings folder.** You now see the Default User profile.

   ⊟ 💾 Win2000 (D:)
     ⊞ 📁 Data
     ⊟ 📁 Documents and Settings
       ⊞ 📁 admin1
       ⊞ 📁 Administrator
       ⊞ 📁 All Users
       ⊞ 📁 Default User

10

h. **Select your Admin#'s profile folder.** It contains various subfolders that define the contents of the profile.

i. **Select the Start Menu\Programs subfolder for your profile.** This enables you to identify the Start menu items that are specific to your user account.

j. **Select your user's Desktop folder.** This folder will contain the user-specific shortcuts on your desktop.

k. **Close Windows Explorer.**

Review Questions

1. With the exception of the My Documents folder, where does Windows 9x store the user profile folders by default?

2. Where does Windows 9x store the \My Documents folder by default?

_____

3. Where does Windows NT store user profiles?

_____

4. Where does Windows 2000 store user profiles?

_____

5. Which user profile do Windows 2000 and Windows XP use as a template for creating new users' profiles?

_____

EXERCISE 10-4

Installing the Windows 2000 Professional Support Tools

Activity Time:

15 minutes

Objective:

To install a Windows-based application, the Windows 2000 Professional Support Tools.

Setup:

The installation file for the Windows 2000 Professional Support Tools is in the \\2000srv\ Support folder. Your user account is defined on 2000srv and has the necessary permissions to access the Support share.

Scenario:

You would like to have a tool available to you on your Windows 2000 computer that you can use to determine if an application is compatible with the Windows operating systems. You know that the Application Compatibility Program (Apcompat.exe), which is included in a typical installation of the Windows 2000 Support Tools, can provide this information for you.

10

What You Do	How You Do It

1. **Install the Windows 2000 Professional Support Tools.**

   a. From the Start menu, **choose Settings→ Control Panel.**

   b. **Double-click Add/Remove Programs.**

   c. **Click Add New Programs.**

   d. Even though you will be installing your program from a network share, **click CD Or Floppy.**

   e. **Click Next.** The wizard will now search your local drives for an installation program. When it doesn't find such a program, it will prompt you to locate the installation program manually.

   f. In the Open text box, **enter the path \\2000srv\support\setup.exe** or browse to locate this program.

   g. **Click Finish.**

   h. In the Windows 2000 Support Tools Wizard, **click Next.**

   i. On the User Information page, **click Next** to accept the Name and Organization defined when Windows 2000 was installed on your computer.

j. **Verify that the Typical installation type is selected and click Next.**

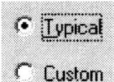

k. **Click Next** to install the tools onto your computer.

l. When the installation is complete, **click Finish.**

m. **Close Add/Remove Programs and Control Panel.**

2. Verify that the tools were installed and that you can run the Application Compatibility Tool.

a. From the Start menu, **choose Programs→ Windows 2000 Support Tools→Tools Help.** The Windows 2000 Support Tools Help window opens with an alphabetical list of all the support tools.

A

Acldiag.exe

Adsiedit.msc

Apcompat.exe

Apmstat.exe

b. In the right pane, **click the Apcompat.exe link** to display the help information about the Application Compatibility program.

c. **Click the Run Application Compatibility Tool Now link** to verify that you can run the Application Compatibility program.

Run Application Compatibility tool now.

Open command prompt now.

d. **Click Cancel** to close the Application Compatibility program.

e. **Close the Windows 2000 Support Tools Help window.**

Review Questions

1. List two methods for installing an application.

_____

_____

2. You have just finished installing an application for a user. What should you do next?

_____

A+ Certification Troubleshooting and Repair Lab Guide, Third Edition

3.   From what sources can you install an application?

_____

4.   What is the name of the file that runs automatically when you insert a CD-ROM?

_____

5.   You have determined that the only way to install a new application for a user is by double-clicking the application's installation file on its CD-ROM. What file extensions should you look for to find the installation file?

_____

Exercise 10-5

Configuring Virtual Memory in Windows 2000

Activity Time:

15 minutes

Objective:

To implement and test changes to the virtual memory configuration to support specific system memory requirements.

Scenario:

You're responsible for managing the Windows 2000-based computers for users who run AutoCAD. The current project your users are working on is quite large, and the users are receiving out-of-memory errors when they work on this project. You have an additional 128 MB of RAM on order for each computer, but you would like the users to be able to continue working on the project until you're able to upgrade their computers' RAM.

What You Do	How You Do It
1. **Increase the page file size.**	a. If necessary, **log on as Admin#.**

b. In Control Panel, **open the System Properties dialog box.**

c. **Select the Advanced tab.**

d. **Click Performance Options.**

e. In the Performance Options dialog box, **click Change.**

f. In the Drive list, **select the drive on which the page file is stored.**

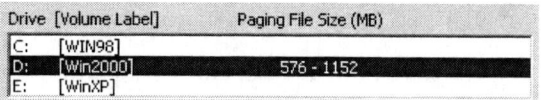

g. In the Initial Size text box, **type a value that is 128 MB greater than the current initial size.**

h. **Increase the maximum size of the page file by 128 MB.**

i. **Click Set.**

j. **Click OK three times.**

k. **Close Control Panel.**

2. **Test your changes to the virtual memory configuration.**

a. **Restart the computer.**

b. **When prompted, log on as Admin#.**

c. **In Control Panel, double-click System.**

d. **Select the Advanced tab and click Performance Options.**

e. **Verify that the settings are correct for virtual memory.**

f. **Close all open windows.**

Review Questions

1. What is the name of the file Windows 2000 uses for virtual memory?

_____

2. Where does Windows 2000 store the file it uses for virtual memory by default?

_____

3. What utility do you use to configure virtual memory in Windows 2000?

_____

4. True or False: You can configure Windows 2000 with multiple virtual memory files.

_____

EXERCISE 10-6

Installing a Non-Windows Application Without a Setup Program

Activity Time:

10 minutes

Objective:

To install a non-Windows application, AutoShop.

Data Files:

- AutoShop.exe

Setup:

You'll find the AutoShop folder and the program within it in the C:\Data folder. You have a user named User# on your computer.

Scenario:

All users at one of the Windows 2000 computers in your company need access to a small command-line utility, AutoShop, that has no setup program.

10

1.   **Install AutoShop.**

          a.   **Open Windows Explorer.**

          b.   **Copy the D:\Data\AutoShop folder and its contents to D:\.**

          c.   In the left pane, **select the D:\Documents And Settings\All Users\Desktop folder.**

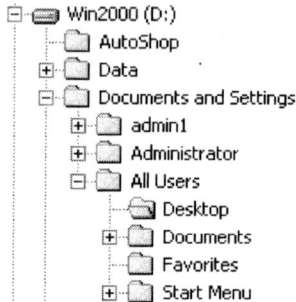

          d.   In the right pane, **right-click and choose New→Shortcut.**

          e.   In the Type The Location Of The Item text box, **type *D:\AutoShop\Autoshop.exe*** or browse to locate this file.

          f.   **Click Next.**

          g.   **Click Next** to accept the default name of AutoShop for this shortcut.

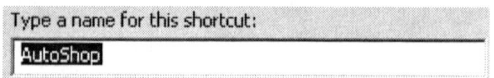

          h.   **Select an icon for the shortcut.**

          i.   **Click Finish** to create the shortcut to the AutoShop program.

          j.   **Close Windows Explorer.**

---

2.   **Verify that the installation of AutoShop was successful.**

          a.   While logged on as Admin#, **verify that you see the AutoShop shortcut on your desktop.**

          b.   **Double-click AutoShop** to verify that you can run the non-Windows application.

          c.   **Press Q** to quit AutoShop.

          d.   **Log off as Admin#.**

          e.   **Log on as User# with a password of password** (replace # with your assigned student number).

          f.   **Verify that you see the AutoShop shortcut on your desktop.**

          g.   **Double-click AutoShop** to verify that you can run the non-Windows application.

          h.   **Press Q** to quit AutoShop.

10

Review Questions

1.   How do you install a non-Windows application that does not have a setup program?

      _____

      _____

      _____

2. How do you install a non-Windows application that has a setup program?

_____

_____

_____

3. You want to create a shortcut to run a non-Windows application in Windows 2000. You want this application to be available to all users of the computer from their desktop. Where should you create the shortcut?

_____

4. You want to create a shortcut to run a non-Windows application in Windows 2000. You want this application to be available to only one user and placed on his desktop. Where should you create the shortcut?

_____

5. You want to create a shortcut to run a non-Windows application in Windows 2000. You want this application to be available to all users of the computer from their Start menus. Where should you create the shortcut?

_____

EXERCISE 10-7

Configuring a Non-Windows Application's Memory Usage

Activity Time:

10 minutes

Objective:

To configure memory usage settings as appropriate for an individual non-Windows application.

Scenario:

Users of the AutoShop MS-DOS application are reporting that they're getting out-of-memory errors when they try to run the application. After researching the problem, you've determined that you need to reserve 480 KB of conventional memory and 2048 KB of extended memory for the program to run properly.

10

What You Do	How You Do It

1. **Configure the non-Windows application.**

   a. **Log on as your Admin# account.**

   b. On the desktop, **right-click the AutoShop shortcut and choose Properties.**

   c. **Select the Memory tab.**

   d. From the Conventional Memory drop-down list, **select 480.**

   e. From the Extended (XMS) Memory drop-down list, **select 2048.**

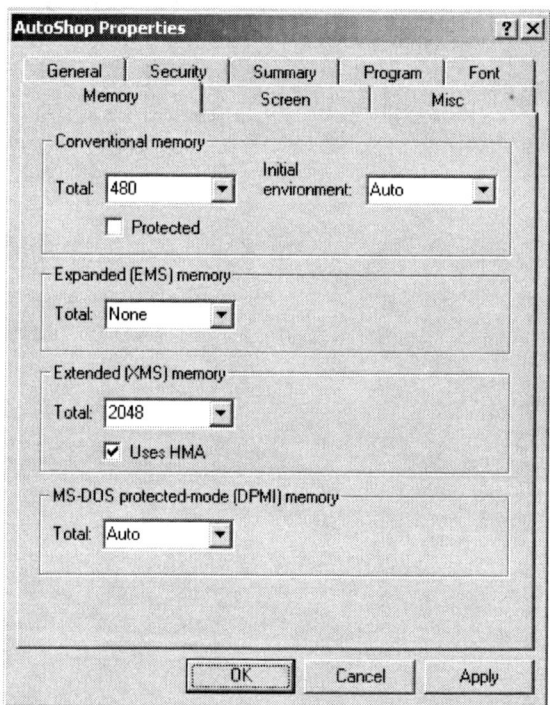

   f. **Click OK** to save your changes.

2.   **Test AutoShop.**

a.   On the desktop, **double-click AutoShop** to run the application.

b.   **Press Q** to close the AutoShop application.

Review Questions

1.   What is the name of the memory segment that consists of the first 640 KB of RAM?

   _____

2.   What is extended memory?

   _____

3.   Which environment variable does Windows use to identify the folders in which it searches for executable files?

   _____

4.   You have determined that you need to configure the memory usage for a non-Windows application in order for it to run correctly. What should you do?

   _____

   _____

5.   What utility do you use to configure environment variables in Windows 2000?

   _____

10

EXERCISE 10-8

Removing the Windows 2000 Support Tools

Activity Time:

10 minutes

Objective:

To remove a Windows-based application, the Windows 2000 Support Tools, from the computer.

Scenario:

A user is running out of disk space on her computer. You have a new hard disk on order but it won't be in until next week. The user is unable to run a critical application on her computer because it has so little free space. After examining the applications installed on her computer, you've determined that she no longer needs to run the Windows 2000 Support Tools.

What You Do	How You Do It
1. Remove the Windows 2000 Support Tools.	a. **Verify that you're logged on as Admin#.**
	b. In Control Panel, **double-click Add/Remove Programs.**
	c. **Select the Windows 2000 Support Tools and click Remove.**
	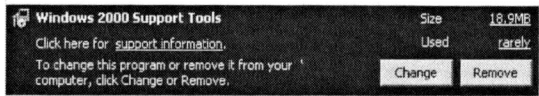
	d. **Click Yes** to confirm that you want to remove the tools from your computer.
	e. **Close Add/Remove Programs and Control Panel.**

2. **Verify that the application was removed.**

    a. From the Start menu, **choose Programs.**

    b. **Review the list of programs** to verify that the Windows 2000 Support Tools are no longer installed.

Review Questions

1. What steps should you use to remove an application in Windows 2000?

    _____

    _____

    _____

2. How can you verify that an application was removed successfully?

    _____

10

LAB 10-1

Installing and Configuring Applications

Activity Time:

30 minutes

Objective:

To install and configure Windows and non-Windows applications on a Windows 98, Windows 2000, or Windows XP computer.

Data Files:

* AutoShop.exe

Setup:

If you will be keying this lab immediately following the Managing Applications chapter, you will need access to the Windows 98 Resource Kit installation files. Complete the following tasks:

    1.   Copy the \Tools\Reskit folder and its contents from the Windows 98 installation CD-ROM to C:\Tools\Reskit on the classroom domain controller.

    2.   Share the C:\Tools\Reskit folder as Reskit.

Once the Resource Kit tools are available on the domain controller, reboot your computer to Windows 98 and begin the lab.

If you will be keying this lab outside of the pre-established classroom environment, you will need:

* A computer with a default installation of Windows 98, Windows 2000, or Windows XP.

* Access to the student data files.

* If you are using Windows 98, access to the \Tools\Reskit folder from the Windows 98 installation CD-ROM, or access to the Windows 98 Resource Kit installation CD-ROM.

* If you are using Windows 2000 or Windows XP Professional, access to the Windows 2000 Professional Resource Kit installation CD-ROM.

Scenario:

You have been called in as an A+ technician to install and configure applications on a client's Windows-based computer. The client has two applications that she wants to use: the Windows Resource Kit tools, and the AutoShop MS-DOS application. After meeting with the client, you've discovered that the tool she uses most often from the Resource Kit is Cliptray.exe. For this reason, she would like you to make it as easy as possible for her to access and run Cliptray.exe. You have also reviewed the documentation for the AutoShop application and have determined that it needs 480 KB of conventional memory and 2048 KB of extended memory in order to perform adequately.

 When you have finished the lab, you can refer to the Installing and Configuring Applications Lab Results.txt file to check your work.

1. **Install the Resource Kit.**

---

2. **Create a shortcut to the Cliptray.exe Resource Kit utility on the desktop.**

---

3. **Install the AutoShop application.**

10

---

4. **Configure the necessary memory requirements for AutoShop.**

Chapter 11

Installing Network Components

Activities included in this chapter:

- Exercise 11-1 Examining Device Manager
- Exercise 11-2 Updating a Network Card Driver
- Exercise 11-3 Configuring TCP/IP Manually
- Exercise 11-4 Configuring TCP/IP Automatically
- Exercise 11-5 Troubleshooting TCP/IP Problems
- Exercise 11-6 Installing the NetBEUI Protocol
- Exercise 11-7 Removing the NetBEUI Protocol
- Exercise 11-8 Installing NWLink IPX/SPX
- Exercise 11-9 Installing the NetWare Client
- Exercise 11-10 Removing the NetWare Client
- Exercise 11-11 Configuring a Network Connection in Windows 9x
- Lab 11-1 Configuring a Network Connection

EXERCISE 11-1

Examining Device Manager

Activity Time:

10 minutes

Objective:

To use Device Manager to determine the properties and status of a given device.

Scenario:

You've just been hired to work as a member of the Help Desk department at a company that has Windows 2000 computers. Your boss has told you that you will be primarily fielding network support calls. Because you're new to these computers, you want to familiarize yourself with their hardware so that you can be prepared for any support calls that might come your way.

What You Do	How You Do It
1. **Determine the type of network card installed in the computer and that it is working properly.**	a. If necessary, **log on as Admin#.**
	b. In Control Panel, **double-click System.**
	c. **Select the Hardware tab.**
	d. **Click Device Manager.**
	e. In the list of devices, **expand Network Adapters.**

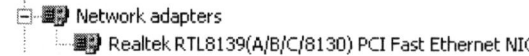

	f. **Right-click the network adapter driver and choose Properties.**
	g. **Review the Device Status portion of the dialog box** to determine if the device is working properly.

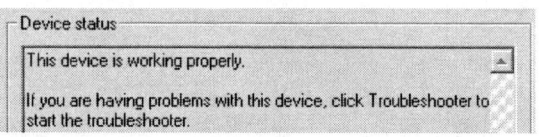

	h. **Click Cancel** to close the network driver's Properties dialog box.
	i. **Close Device Manager, System Properties, and Control Panel.**

11

Review Questions

1. How can you verify that a hardware device is working properly?

2. What feature of Windows 2000 enables it to automatically install a device driver for any new hardware you connect to a computer?

_____

3. What does it mean when a driver is signed?

_____

4. True or False: You cannot install an unsigned driver in Windows 2000.

_____

5. How do you configure driver signing options?

_____

EXERCISE 11-2

Updating a Network Card Driver

Activity Time:

10 minutes

Objective:

To use the Update Driver function to obtain the most current driver for a device.

Scenario:

You're the on-site A+ technician for a company with a large network. After researching on Microsoft's Web site, you've determined that Microsoft has posted an updated driver on their Web site for the network card in one of the Windows 2000-based computers you're responsible for supporting.

11

What You Do	How You Do It

1. **Update the network card driver.**

    a.   From the Start menu, **choose Settings→ Network And Dial-up Connections.**

    b.   **Right-click Local Area Connection and choose Properties.**

    c.   In the Local Area Connection Properties dialog box, **click Configure.**

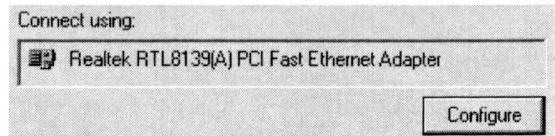

    d.   **Select the Driver tab.**

    e.   **Click Update Driver.**

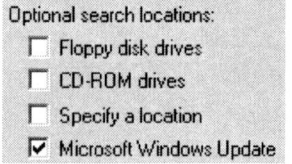

    f.   In the Upgrade Device Driver Wizard, **click Next.**

    g.   **Verify that Search For A Suitable Driver For My Device is selected and click Next.**

    h.   On the Locate Driver Files page, **check Microsoft Windows Update and uncheck all other search locations.**

Optional search locations:
- ☐ Floppy disk drives
- ☐ CD-ROM drives
- ☐ Specify a location
- ☑ Microsoft Windows Update

    i.   **Click Next.**

j. On the Driver Files Search Results page, **click Next** to install the new device driver or to continue with the wizard.

k. **Click Finish.**

l. **Click Close** to close the Properties dialog box for your network card.

m. **Click OK** to close the Local Area Connection Properties dialog box.

---

2. **Verify that the network card and driver are working properly.**

a. In Network And Dial-up Connections, **right-click Local Area Connection and choose Status.**

b. **Verify that the connection's status states Connected.**

c. **Click Close** to close the Local Area Connection Status dialog box.

d. **Close Network And Dial-Up Connections.**

11

Review Questions

1. From what locations can you install an updated network card driver?

_____

_____

2. What utility do you first open to update a network card driver?

_____

3. How can you verify that an updated driver for a network card is working properly in Windows 2000?

_____

_____

4. What permissions do you need to update a network card driver in Windows 2000?

_____

5. How can you verify that an updated driver for a network card is working properly in Windows 9x?

_____

EXERCISE 11-3

Configuring TCP/IP Manually

Activity Time:

15 minutes

Objective:

To configure a network connection with static IP addressing information.

Setup:

Use an IP address of 192.168.200.#, where # is your computer number. The subnet mask is 255.255.255.0. The preferred DNS server's address is 192.168.200.200.

Scenario:

As an A+ technician, you receive a support call from a client stating that her new Windows 2000 Professional laptop can't connect to her office's small network. When you review the computer's configuration, you determine that it's attempting to obtain an IP address from a DHCP server. Your client's network doesn't have a DHCP server. Instead, all computers are configured manually with IP addresses.

11

1. **Configure the TCP/IP protocol.**

    a. **Open Network And Dial-up Connections.**

    b. **Right-click the Local Area Connection and choose Properties.**

    c. In the list of network components, **select Internet Protocol (TCP/IP).**

    ☑ 🖳 Internet Protocol (TCP/IP)

    d. **Click Properties.**

    e. **Select Use The Following IP Address.**

    f. In the IP Address text box, **type *192.168. 200.#,*** where # is your assigned computer number.

    g. In the Subnet Mask text box, **verify that the subnet mask is 255.255.255.0.**

    h. In the Preferred DNS Server text box, **type *192.168.200.200***

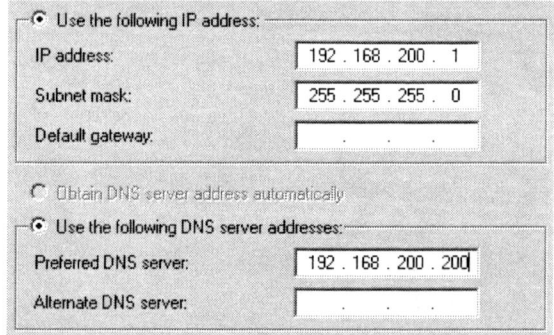

    i. **Click OK twice.**

    j. **Close Network And Dial-Up Connections.**

2. **Verify the IP addressing configuration.**

   a. From the Start menu, **choose Programs→Accessories→Command Prompt.**

   b. **Enter** *ipconfig /all*

   c. **Verify that the IP address, subnet mask, and DNS server address information are correct.**

   ```
   IP Address. . . . . . . . . . . . : 192.168.200.1
   Subnet Mask . . . . . . . . . . . : 255.255.255.0
   Default Gateway . . . . . . . . . :
   DNS Servers . . . . . . . . . . . : 192.168.200.200
   ```

3. **Test TCP/IP connectivity.**

   a. In the Command Prompt window, **type** *ping 192.168.200.200* to verify that you can communicate on the network using the TCP/IP protocol.

   b. **Close the Command Prompt window.**

Review Questions

1. What two properties of TCP/IP must you configure at a minimum?

2. You have just manually configured the TCP/IP protocol in Windows 2000. What command should you use to verify that you used the correct addressing?

3. What command enables you to test TCP/IP connectivity?

4. You have been asked to assign the IP address of 171.205.131.5 and subnet mask of 255.255.255.0 to a computer. What portion of the IP address is the network address?

5. What are the three optional addressing parameters you might use when configuring TCP/IP?

Exercise 11-4

Configuring TCP/IP Automatically

Activity Time:

5 minutes

Objective:

To configure a network connection to obtain IP addressing information automatically.

Scenario:

One of your clients, a growing company, has just implemented DHCP servers to reduce the administrative workload for assigning IP addresses. The network administrator has configured the DHCP server to provide computers with an appropriate IP address, subnet mask, and DNS server address. As an A+ technician, you've been called in to assist with configuring the client's Windows 2000 computers to use DHCP.

---

1. Configure your computer to obtain its IP address and DNS server address information automatically.

   a. Open Network And Dial-up Connections.

   b. Display the properties of the Local Area Connection.

   c. In the list of network components, **select Internet Protocol (TCP/IP).**

   d. Click Properties.

   e. Select Obtain An IP Address Automatically.

   f. Select Obtain DNS Server Address Automatically.

   g. Click OK twice.

   h. Close Network And Dial-Up Connections.

---

2. **Verify and test the IP addressing**
    configuration.

    a. **Open a Command Prompt window.**

    b. **Enter** `ipconfig /all`

    c. **Verify that your computer successfully**
        leased an IP address, subnet mask, and DNS
        server address from the DHCP server.

    d. **Enter** `ping 192.168.200.200` to test
        connectivity.

    e. **Close the Command Prompt window.**

Review Questions

1. What are the two methods for automatically assigning IP addresses?

2. What range of IP addresses is used by APIPA?

3. What command should you use to force a computer to obtain an IP address from a DHCP server or APIPA?

4. What command should you use to determine if a computer obtained its IP address through a DHCP server?

5. What command should you use to configure a computer to no longer use an IP address assigned by the DHCP server?

Exercise 11-5

Troubleshooting TCP/IP Problems

Activity Time:

15 minutes

Objective:

To identify the correct troubleshooting approach in various TCP/IP problem scenarios.

Scenario:

Your company provides technical support to a number of different clients. These clients have networks that range in size from only a few computers to as many as hundreds of computers. As an A+ technician, your job is to troubleshoot connectivity problems that your clients report.

1. One of your clients calls to report that he is unable to connect to any network resources or the Internet. After questioning him, you've determined that someone accidentally unplugged the DHCP server. The client reports that the DHCP server is up and running, but he's still unable to connect to any resources. You have the client type in `ipconfig /all`, and here's what he reports:

   - IP address: 169.254.225.48
   - Subnet mask: 255.255.0.0
   - Default gateway: None
   - DNS server: None

   After reviewing your company's documentation for this client's network, you've determined that the client's IP address should be on the 192.168.200.# network with a subnet mask of 255.255.255.0. The default gateway address is 192.168.200.1.

   What should you try next to attempt to solve the problem?

   a) Have the client open a Command Prompt window and enter `ping 127.0.0.1`.

   b) Have the client open a Command Prompt window and enter `ping 192.168.200.1`.

   c) Have the client open a Command Prompt window and enter `ipconfig /release` and `ipconfig /renew`.

   d) Have the client manually configure his IP address to one on the 192.168.200.# network, a subnet mask of 255.255.255.0, and a default gateway address of 192.168.200.1.

2. You receive a call from a client who reports that she's unable to access any Web sites in Internet Explorer. While talking with this user, you verify that she can ping the server's IP address on her network segment, the IP address of the default gateway, and the IP address of a computer on another network segment. You also determine that none of the other users on her network can connect to Web sites in Internet Explorer.

What might be the problem?

a) Her network's WINS server is down.

b) Her network's DNS server is down.

c) Her computer is configured with the wrong default gateway address.

d) Her computer is configured with the wrong subnet mask.

---

3. One of your clients reports that he is unable to see computers when he double-clicks Computers Near Me in My Network Places.

Which step should you take first?

a) Ask the client to ping another computer on his network.

b) Ask the client if any of the other users on the network are experiencing problems.

c) Ask the client to verify that the DHCP server is running.

d) Ask the client to run `ipconfig /release` and `ipconfig /renew`.

---

4. A client reports that he's unable to connect to any computers on the network or the Internet. You have him run the IPConfig command, and all his TCP/IP addressing parameters are correct. When you have him ping other computers on the network, his computer is unable to reach them. This computer is the only one that's experiencing a problem.

What should you check next?

a) That his computer's network cable is plugged in to both the network card and the wall jack.

b) That the router is on and functioning properly.

c) That the hub is on and functioning properly.

d) That the DHCP server is on and functioning properly.

---

5. Your client tells you that she has just installed a new server on her network. This server has a CD-ROM tower in it that she wants to share with all users on the network. No users can connect to this computer. All of her users can connect to other resources on the network and the Internet.

Which configuration parameter might be the cause of this problem?

a) The server's IP address

b) The users' IP addresses

c) The users' subnet masks

d) The server's default gateway address

Review Questions

1. What symptom would you expect to see if a computer's subnet mask is incorrect?

2. What symptom would you expect to see if you configure a computer with an IP address that's already in use on another computer?

3. What utility should you use to verify that a computer can connect to a DNS server and successfully find an IP address for a host name?

4. How should you use the ping command if you want to troubleshoot name resolution?

5. You have been asked to troubleshoot a computer that is unable to connect to any Internet Web site by name but is able to connect to a Web site by its IP address. You suspect that the computer does not have the correct DNS server address. What command can you use to view the DNS server address configured on the computer?

Exercise 11-6

Installing the NetBEUI Protocol

Activity Time:

15 minutes

Objective:

To install the NetBEUI network protocol as an additional protocol on a networked computer.

Scenario:

Your client, a non-profit agency, has just received a donation of a legacy CD-ROM tower that supports only the NetBEUI protocol. He would like you to configure his network's Windows 2000 computers so that they can access this CD-ROM tower. Currently, your client uses only the TCP/IP protocol on the network.

11

What You Do	How You Do It
1. **Install NetBEUI.**	a. **Display the Properties of the Local Area Connection.**
	b. **Click Install** to install a new network component.
	c. In the Select Network Component Type dialog box, **select Protocol.**

	d. **Click Add.**
	e. In the Network Protocol list, **select NetBEUI Protocol.**

	f. **Click OK** to install the NetBEUI protocol.
	g. **Click Close** to close the Local Area Connection Properties dialog box.
	h. **Close Network And Dial-up Connections.**

2. **How do you verify connectivity after installing the NetBEUI protocol?**

Review Questions

1. Which Windows operating systems support the NetBEUI protocol by default?

   _____

2. What utility do you use to install NetBEUI?

   _____

   _____

3. What permissions do you need to install NetBEUI in Windows 2000 and Windows NT?

   _____

4. How can you verify that the NetBEUI protocol is working properly in Windows 2000?

   _____

   _____

Exercise 11-7

Removing the NetBEUI Protocol

Activity Time:

15 minutes

Objective:

To remove the NetBEUI protocol from a networked computer.

Scenario:

Your client is an elementary school. The principal would like to make sure that the students cannot access the administrative computers. All of the computers are running Windows 2000 Professional. The students' computers are running the NetBEUI protocol. The administrative computers are running both the NetBEUI protocol and the TCP/IP protocol so that they can access the Internet.

What You Do	How You Do It
1. Remove the NetBEUI protocol.	a. Display the properties of the Local Area Connection.
	b. In the list of network components, select **NetBEUI Protocol**.
	c. **Click Uninstall** to remove the protocol.
	d. **Click Yes** to confirm that you want to remove the protocol.
	e. **Click Yes** to confirm that you want to restart the computer.
	f. **Log back on as Admin#.**

2. **Verify that the NetBEUI protocol is no longer installed.**

    a. **Display the properties of the Local Area Connection.**

    b. **Verify that you don't see the NetBEUI protocol listed.**

    c. **Close all open windows.**

Review Questions

1. You think that a user removed the NetBEUI protocol from his Windows 2000 computer. How can you know for sure?

_____

_____

11

EXERCISE 11-8

Installing NWLink IPX/SPX

Activity Time:

10 minutes

Objective:

To install NWLink IPX/SPX as an additional protocol on a networked computer.

Scenario:

Your client has a custom database application that runs only on a Novell NetWare 3.12 server. You're in the process of configuring new Windows 2000-based computers for your client's network.

What You Do	How You Do It
1. **Install the NWLink IPX/SPX protocol.**	a. **Display the properties of the Local Area Connection.**
	b. **Click Install** to install a new network component.
	c. In the Select Network Component Type dialog box, **select Protocol.**
	d. **Click Add.**
	e. In the Network Protocol list, **select NWLink IPX/SPX/NetBIOS Compatible Transport Protocol.**
	NetBEUI Protocol Network Monitor Driver NWLink IPX/SPX/NetBIOS Compatible Transport Protocol
	f. **Click OK** to install the protocol.
	g. **Click Close** to close the Local Area Connection Properties dialog box.
	h. **Close Network And Dial-up Connections.**

2. **How can you verify that the NWLink IPX/SPX protocol is installed successfully?**

Review Questions

1. What is the default frame type selected when you install NWLink IPX/SPX?

_____

_____

2.   Which versions of NetWare servers use IPX/SPX as their default protocol?

_____

3.   Which versions of NetWare servers use TCP/IP as their default protocol?

_____

4.   In what scenario would you change the default frame type for NWLink IPX/SPX?

_____

_____

_____

5.   How can you verify that the NWLink IPX/SPX protocol is functioning correctly in Windows 2000?

_____

_____

Exercise 11-9

Installing the NetWare Client

Activity Time:

15 minutes

Objective:

To install the Client Service for NetWare as an additional network client.

Scenario:

One of your clients has ordered a custom application from a software programming company. This application runs only on a Novell NetWare server. As part of their contract, the software programming company is going to install and configure a Novell NetWare server on which to run the custom application. Your client has asked you to prepare his users' Windows 2000 computers so that they can access the NetWare server when the software programming company delivers it. The NetWare server has not been delivered yet.

11

1. **Install Client Service For NetWare.**	a. **Open the properties for the Local Area Connection.**
	b. **Click Install.**
	c. **Verify that Client is selected and click Add.**
	d. **Select Client Service For NetWare and click OK.**

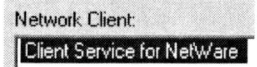

e. Wait until you see the Select Netware Logon dialog box (the Shutdown dialog box may appear first). **Verify that <None> is selected in the Preferred Server drop-down list.**

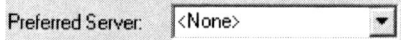

f. **Click OK** to close the Select NetWare Logon dialog box.

g. **Click Yes** to restart the computer.

h. **Log back on to the computer as Admin#.**

i. **Close all open windows.**

Review Questions

1. You are installing the Client Service For NetWare. When should you use the Preferred Server configuration parameter?

_____

_____

2. You are installing the Client Service For NetWare. When should you use the Default Tree And Context configuration parameter?

_____

3. You just installed the Client Service For NetWare on a user's computer. He is complaining that each print job he sends to the NetWare printers has an extra blank sheet of paper at the end. What should you do?

_____

_____

4. What protocol must you install before you can install the Client Service For NetWare?

_____

11

EXERCISE 11-10

Removing the NetWare Client

Activity Time:

15 minutes

Objective:

To uninstall the Client Service for NetWare when the client is no longer needed.

Scenario:

A client just called to say that she has migrated all of her users' data and applications from the NetWare server to the Windows 2000 server. She configured the Windows 2000 server to use only the TCP/IP protocol. She plans to remove the NetWare server from the network, and she would like you to make sure that the users' Windows 2000 computers have only the network components installed that are necessary for accessing the Windows 2000 server.

What You Do	How You Do It
1. Remove the NetWare Client and NWLink IPX/SPX protocol.	a. Display the properties for the Local Area Connection.
	b. Select Client Service For NetWare and click Uninstall.
	c. Click Yes to confirm that you want to uninstall Client Service For NetWare.
	d. Click Yes to restart the computer.
	e. When prompted, log on as Admin#.
	f. Remove the NWLink IPX/SPX protocol.

Review Questions

1. What steps should you use to remove the Client Service For NetWare from a computer?

_____

_____

_____

2. You had installed both NWLink IPX/SPX and the Client Service For NetWare so that a user could access a NetWare server on her network. The network administrator has replaced the NetWare server with a Windows 2000 server that uses only the TCP/IP protocol. What software should you remove from the user's computer?

_____

11

Exercise 11-11

Configuring a Network Connection in Windows 9x

Activity Time:

25 minutes

Objective:

To configure all the required components of a network connection on a Windows 98 computer.

Setup:

The Windows 98 installation files are in C:\Win98.

Scenario:

Your client, a non-profit organization, has just received a donation of a Windows 98 computer. They have asked you to make sure that the computer works properly and to configure it to work on their network. The network consists of Windows 2000 and NetWare 3.12 servers. All users obtain their IP addresses from a DHCP server. In addition, the network has a shared CD-ROM tower that supports only the NetBEUI protocol. Although the client does not yet want the Windows 98 computer to log on to the Windows 2000 domain, they plan to later configure the computer to do so.

1. **Update the network card driver.**

    a. **Reboot the computer.** From the boot menu, **select Microsoft Windows** to load the Windows 98 operating system.

    b. **Log on as Admin#.**

    c. From the Start menu, **choose Settings→ Control Panel.**

    d. **Double-click System.**

    e. **Select the Device Manager tab.**

    f. In the list of devices, **expand Network Adapters.**

    ```
    ⊟──▣ Network adapters
         │── ▣ Dial-Up Adapter
         └── ▣ Realtek RTL8139/810X Family PCI Fast Ethernet NIC
    ```

    g. **Select the network card driver and click Properties.**

    h. **Select the Driver tab.**

    i. **Click Update Driver.**

    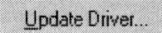

    j. In the Update Device Driver Wizard, **click Next.**

    k. **Verify that Search For A Better Driver Than The One Your Device Is Using Now is selected and click Next.**

l.   **Check Microsoft Windows Update.**

☑ Microsoft Windows Update

m.   **Click Next.**

n.   If the Wizard found an updated driver, **click Next and then click Continue, otherwise click Next.**

o.   **Click Finish** to close the Update Device Driver Wizard.

p.   **Click Close** to close the Properties dialog box for the network card.

q.   **Click Close** to close System Properties.

r.   **Close Control Panel.**

2. **Verify that TCP/IP is configured to obtain an IP address automatically.**

a. **Open Control Panel.**

b. **Double-click Network.**

c. In the network components list, **select TCP/IP→network card name.**

d. **Click Properties.**

e. **Verify that Obtain An IP Address Automatically is selected.**

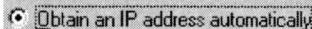

f. **Select the Gateway tab.**

g. **Verify that the Installed Gateways list is empty.**

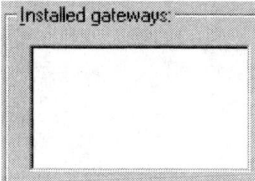

h. **Select the DNS Configuration tab.**

i. **Verify that Disable DNS is selected.**

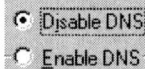

j. Select the WINS Configuration tab.

k. Verify that neither Disable WINS Configuration nor Enable WINS Configuration is selected.

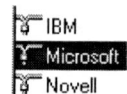

l. **Click OK** to save your changes.

---

3. **Install the NetBEUI protocol.**

a. In the Network dialog box, **click Add.**

b. **Select Protocol and click Add.**

c. In the Manufacturers list, **select Microsoft.**

d. In the Network Protocols list, **select NetBEUI.**

e. **Click OK** to install the protocol.

---

4. **Install the IPX/SPX-compatible Protocol.**

a. In the Network dialog box, **click Add.**

b. **Select Protocol and click Add.**

c. In the Manufacturers list, **select Microsoft.**

d. In the Network Protocols list, **select IPX/SPX-compatible Protocol.**

e. **Click OK** to install the protocol.

f. **Click OK** to close the Network dialog box.

g. When prompted, **click Yes** to restart the computer.

h. From the boot menu, **choose Microsoft Windows.**

i. **Log back on as Admin#.**

j. **Close Control Panel.**

Chapter 11: Installing Network Components   **337**

5. **Set the primary network logon.**

a. In the Network dialog box, from the Primary Network Logon drop-down list, **select Client For Microsoft Networks.**

b. **Click OK** to save your changes.

c. In the Insert Disk message box, **click OK.**

d. In the Copying Files dialog box, **enter** *C:\Win98* **and click OK.**

e. **Click Yes** to restart the computer.

f. From the boot menu, **choose Microsoft Windows.**

g. **Log back on as Admin#.**

6. **Test TCP/IP connectivity.**

    a. From the Start menu, **choose Run.**

    b. In the Open text box, **type** *winipcfg*

    c. **Click OK.**

    d. In the IP Configuration dialog box, **click More Info** to display all the IP addressing information.

    e. If necessary, from the drop-down list, **select the computer's network card.**

    f. **Review the IP addressing information** to verify that the computer received the correct IP address, subnet mask, and, optionally, default gateway and WINS server addresses from the DHCP server.

    g. **Click OK** to close the IP Configuration dialog box.

Review Questions

1. Which primary network logon type should you use in Windows 98 if the computer logs on to a Windows 2000 domain?

    _____

2. Which primary network logon type should you use in Windows 98 if the computer logs on to a NetWare server?

    _____

3. You are configuring a Windows 98 computer for a home user. Your client would like his children to log on with their own user names. To make this task easier, the client has asked that you configure Windows 98 so that it displays a list of all users on the computer when the computer boots. What should you do?

    _____

4. You are configuring a Windows 98 computer for a user. Your client would like Windows 98 to prompt her for a username and password when the computer boots. The Windows 98 computer is not on a network. What should you do?

    _____

5. You have been asked to troubleshoot TCP/IP on a Windows 98 computer. You would like to review the IP addressing configuration. What utility should you use?

    _____

Lab 11-1

Configuring a Network Connection

Activity Time:

30 minutes

Objective:

To configure a working network connection on a Windows-based computer.

Setup:

If you will be keying this lab immediately following the Installing Network Components chapter, you should boot into Windows XP and begin the lab.

If you will be keying this lab outside of the pre-established classroom environment, you will need:

- A networked computer with a default installation of Windows 98, Windows 2000, or Windows XP.
- A second networked computer so that you can test the network configuration.
- A DHCP server.
- Access to the Internet.

Scenario:

One of your clients has just purchased a new laptop. This laptop came with a Windows operating system already installed. Your client would like you to configure this computer so that he can connect to all of the resources on his network. He reports that he is experiencing some problems with his computer and is getting error messages referring to the network card. After interviewing the client, you've determined that:

- His network is using a DHCP server for providing IP addresses.
- Your client plans to access a Novell NetWare 3.12 server periodically. This server is using the default Ethernet frame type of 802.2.

When you have finished the lab, you can refer to the Configuring a Network Connection Lab Results.txt file to check your work.

1. **Update the network card driver.**

---

2. **Configure TCP/IP.**

---

3. Test the TCP/IP configuration.

4. Install the appropriate NetWare-compatible protocol.

5. Install the appropriate NetWare client.

CHAPTER 12

Implementing Local Security in Windows 2000/NT/XP

Activities included in this chapter:

- Exercise 12-1 Creating Local Accounts
- Exercise 12-2 Deleting a Local Account
- Exercise 12-3 Modifying User Account Properties
- Exercise 12-4 Setting Domain Membership
- Exercise 12-5 Configuring File and Folder Security
- Exercise 12-6 Encrypting Files and Folders
- Lab 12-1 Implementing Local Security

EXERCISE 12-1

Creating Local Accounts

Activity Time:

20 minutes

Objective:

To create and test local user accounts.

Setup:

There are two administrative user accounts on the computer: the default Administrator account and an account named Admin# which was created when the computer was installed.

Scenario:

You have been called in to configure a client's new Windows 2000 computer. After interviewing the client, you've determined that she needs accounts on the computer for the following users:

- Susan Williams (the client)
- Jeff Bernard
- Sally Thomas

After talking to the network administrator, you discover that he uses the following naming convention for naming all user accounts: the user's first name plus the first initial of their last names. In addition, the network administrator prefers that you assign each user a password of password, and that each user not be able to change his or her password.

What You Do	How You Do It
1. Create the local accounts.	a. Restart Windows 2000 Professional.
	b. Log on as Admin#.
	c. Open Control Panel.
	d. Double-click Administrative Tools.
	e. Double-click Computer Management.

f.   **Expand Local Users And Groups.**

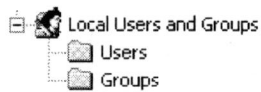

g.   **Select the Users folder.**

h.   **Right-click Users and choose New User.**

i.   In the User Name text box, **type** *SusanW*

j.   In the Full Name text box, **type** *Susan Williams*

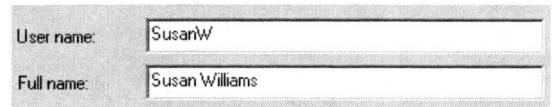

k.   In the Password text box, **type** *password*

l.   In the Confirm Password text box, **type** *password*

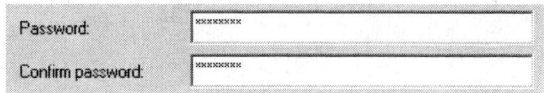

m.   **Uncheck User Must Change Password At Next Logon.**

n.   **Check User Cannot Change Password.**

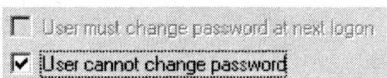

o.   **Click Create** to create Susan Williams' account.

p.   **Enter the account information for the user Jeff Bernard.**

User name:	JeffB
Full name:	Jeff Bernard
Description:	
Password:	xxxxxxxx
Confirm password:	xxxxxxxx

☐ User must change password at next logon
☑ User cannot change password

q.   **Click Create.**

r.   **Enter the account information for the user Sally Thomas.**

s.   **Click Create.**

t.   **Click Close** to close the New User dialog box.

u.   In the details pane, **verify that you see the three new user accounts.**

JeffB   Jeff Bernard
SallyT   Sally Thomas
SusanW   Susan Williams

v.   **Close Computer Management and Administrative Tools.**

---

2. **Verify that you can log on with each new user account.**

   a. **Press Ctrl+Alt+Delete.**

   b. **Click Log Off.**

   c. **Click Yes** to confirm that you want to log off.

   d. In the User Name text box, **type** *SusanW*

   e. In the Password text box, **type** *password*

   f. **Click OK** to log on as SusanW.

   g. **Repeat these steps to log off as each user and then log on as JeffB and SallyT.**

3. **What would happen if you attempted to log on as JeffB to the class.com domain?**

Review Questions

12

1. How do you open the Computer Management utility in Windows 2000 by using Control Panel?

2. What two users are created automatically when Windows 2000 is installed?

3. What four users are created automatically when Windows XP is installed?

4. Which user account is disabled by default?

5. You would like to give a user the necessary permissions to back up and restore files on a computer. To what built-in group should you add the user?

6. You have just created a new user account in Windows 2000. To what group is the user added by default?

_____

EXERCISE 12-2

Deleting a Local Account

Activity Time:

15 minutes

Objective:

To delete an unneeded local user account and associated files.

Scenario:

The user Sally Thomas no longer works for your client's company. Your client has asked you to make sure that Sally can no longer access her computer and to prevent her user profile from using up disk space.

12

What You Do	How You Do It
1. Delete the local user account.	a. **Log on as Admin#.**
	b. **Open Computer Management.** (On your desktop, right-click My Computer and choose Manage.)
	c. **Expand Local Users And Groups.**
	d. **Select the Users folder.**
	e. **Right-click SallyT and choose Delete.**

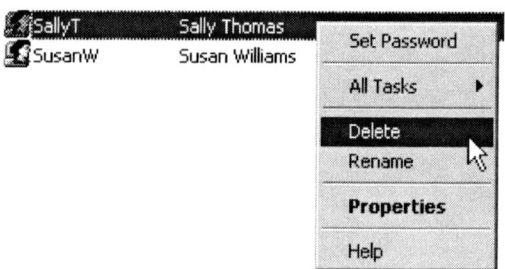

f. **Click Yes** to confirm that you want to delete the account.

g. **Close Computer Management.**

2. **Delete any unnecessary user profiles.**

a. If necessary, **log on as Admin#.**

b. **Open the System Properties dialog box.**
    (Right-click the My Computer icon and choose
    Properties.)

c. **Select the User Profiles tab.**

d. **Select a user profile with the name of
    Account Unknown.**

e. **Click Delete.**

f. **Click Yes** to confirm that you want to delete
    the profile.

g. **Click OK** to close the System Properties dialog
    box.

h. **Close the Control Panel.**

12

3. **Verify that the profile was removed
    from the hard disk.**

a. **Open Windows Explorer.**

b. **Expand the drive on which Windows 2000 is
    installed.**

c. **Expand Documents And Settings.**

d. **Verify that you don't see any folders for
    users who no longer have accounts on the
    server.**

e. **Close Windows Explorer.**

Review Questions

1. What utility do you use to delete a user account in Windows NT?

   _____

2. What utility do you use to delete a user account in Windows 2000?

   _____

3. You have just deleted a user account from Windows 2000. How do you delete the user's profile?

   _____

   _____

4. Why should you delete a user's profile after deleting their user account?

   _____

EXERCISE 12-3

Modifying User Account Properties

Activity Time:

15 minutes

Objective:

To configure and test the appropriate properties for a local user account.

Setup:

You have created a user named SusanW.

Scenario:

Your client, Susan Williams, calls to tell you that she just got married and would like her account name to reflect her new last name of Hill. In addition, she would like sufficient permissions so that she can perform all administrative tasks on her computer.

12

What You Do	How You Do It
1. **Change the account's user name and full name.**	a. **Open Computer Management** (on the desktop, right-click the My Computer icon and choose Manage).
	b. **Expand Local Users And Groups.**
	c. **Select the Users folder.**
	d. **Right-click SusanW and choose Rename.**

	e. **Enter *SusanH* and press Enter.**
	f. **Double-click SusanH** to open the Properties dialog box.
	g. In the Full Name text box, **change the user's name to Susan Hill.**
	h. **Click OK** to save your changes.

A+ Certification Troubleshooting and Repair Lab Guide, Third Edition

2. **Add the user to the Administrators group.**

a. In the details pane, **double-click SusanH.**

b. In the SusanH Properties dialog box, **select the Member Of tab.**

c. **Click Add.**

d. **Select the Administrators group and click Add.**

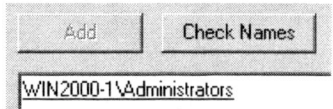

e. **Click OK** to close the Select Groups dialog box.

f. **Click OK.**

g. **Close Computer Management.**

3. **Rename Susan Hill's profile folder** to reflect her new user account name.

a. **Open Windows Explorer.**

b. **Select D:\Documents And Settings.**

c. In the right pane, **right-click the SusanW folder and choose Rename.**

d. **Enter** *SusanH*

e. **Close Windows Explorer.**

12

4. **Test Susan Hill's administrative privileges.**

    a. **Log on as SusanH.**

    b. **Open Computer Management.**

    c. **Expand Local Users And Groups.**

    d. **Right-click Users and choose New User.**

    e. **Create a new user named TestUser with a password of password.** By creating a new user, you verify that Susan Hill has administrative privileges on the computer.

    f. **Close the New User dialog box.**

    g. **Close all open windows.**

Review Questions

1. How do you rename a user account in Windows 2000?

    _____

    _____

2. How do you rename a user's profile folder in Windows 2000?

    _____

    _____

3. What problem can you encounter if you reset a user's password in Windows XP?

    _____

4. What utility should you use to reset a user's password in Windows NT?

    _____

5. You would like to prevent a user from changing her password. What should you do?

    _____

EXERCISE 12-4

Setting Domain Membership

Activity Time:

15 minutes

Objective:

To configure a Windows client computer as a member of a domain and test the domain membership.

Setup:

You have an Active Directory domain on your network. The domain name is class.com. In the domain, you have a domain user account named Admin#. This account is a member of the Domain Admins group, which gives you the necessary authority to add computers to the domain. The password for the Admin# domain user account is also password.

Scenario:

You've been called in on a contract basis to assist a large company with configuring its Windows 2000 client computers to access a Windows 2000 Active Directory domain. (The company is in the midst of migrating its servers from Novell NetWare 4.12 to Windows 2000.) The Windows 2000 computers are all currently members of the default workgroup (WORKGROUP).

What You Do	How You Do It
1. Join the Class.com domain.	a. Log on as Admin#.
	b. Open Control Panel.
	c. Double-click System.
	d. Select the Network Identification tab.
	e. Click Properties.
	f. Below Member Of, **select Domain**.

g. In the Domain text box, **type *class.com* and click OK.**

h. In the Name text box, **type *Admin#***

i. In the Password text box, **type *password***

j. **Click OK** to log on to the class.com domain.

k. **Click OK** to close the Network Identification message.

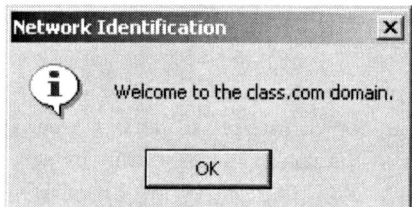

l. **Click OK** to close the second Network Identification message.

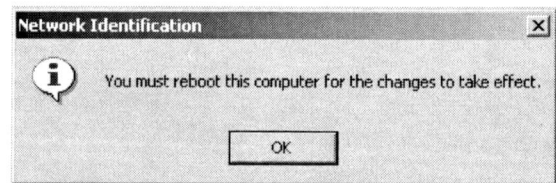

m. **Click OK** to close the System Properties dialog box.

n. **Close Control Panel.**

o. **Click Yes** to confirm that you want to reboot the computer.

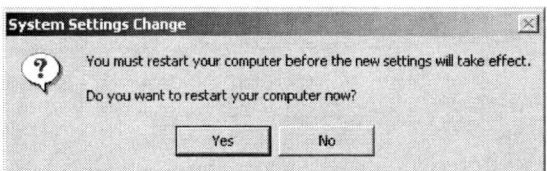

p. From the boot menu, **select Windows 2000 Professional.**

---

2. **Verify that you can log on to the domain.**

a. When the Welcome To Windows dialog box is displayed, **press Ctrl+Alt+Delete.**

b. In the User Name text box, **type** *Admin#*

c. In the Password text box, **type** *password*

d. **Click the Options >> button.**

e. From the Log On To drop-down list, **select Class.**

f. **Click OK** to log on to the domain.

g. In the Getting Started With Windows 2000 wizard, **uncheck Show This Screen At Startup.**

h. **Close the Getting Started With Windows 2000 wizard.**

 When you log on for the first time, Windows 2000 automatically displays a Click On The Start Button message bubble. You can close this message bubble by clicking anywhere in the bubble.

Review Questions

1. Which Microsoft network model groups computers together for organizational purposes?

   _____

2. Which Microsoft network model groups computers together for security and centralized administration?

   _____

3. What is the default workgroup name?

   _____

4. True or False: You can change a computer's workgroup membership at any time.

   _____

5. Which Control Panel applet should you use to add a computer as a member of a domain?

   _____

6. Besides the domain name, what other information will you need in order to add a computer as a member of a domain?

   _____

   _____

EXERCISE 12-5

Configuring File and Folder Security

Activity Time:

20 minutes

Objective:

To configure and test the appropriate security settings for local file resources.

Data Files:

- D:\Data\Personnel

- D:\Data\Proposals

Setup:

In addition to the Administrator and Admin# user accounts, you have two local user accounts: SusanH and JeffB. SusanH is a member of the built-in Administrators group. JeffB is a member of the built-in Users group.

Scenario:

Your client, Susan Hill, would like to occasionally let another user (Jeff Bernard) use her Windows 2000 computer to work on sales proposals. She has asked you to make sure that Jeff can't access any of the files and folders in the D:\Data\Personnel folder. In addition, she would like Jeff to be able to create, modify, and delete proposals in the D:\Data\Proposals folder, but she doesn't want any other users to have access to this folder. Susan doesn't want to prevent members of the Administrators group from accessing either the D:\Data\Personnel or D:\Data\ Proposals folders. The \Proposals folder contains a file named Template for New Proposals.doc. As a precaution, Susan would like this file to be read-only to prevent her or Jeff from overwriting it.

12

What You Do	How You Do It

1. **Assign the necessary permissions for the D:\Data\Personnel folder.**

   a.   **Open Windows Explorer.**

   b.   **Expand the D drive.**

   c.   **Select the D:\Data folder.**

   d.   **Right-click the D:\Data\Personnel folder and choose Properties.**

   e.   **Select the Security tab.**

   f.   **Uncheck Allow Inheritable Permissions From Parent To Propagate To This Object.**

   g.   **Click Remove** to remove the previously inherited permissions from the folder.

   h.   **Click Add.**

   i.   **From the Look In drop-down list, select WIN2000-#** to look for users and groups defined on the local computer.

⚠ Make sure you select the Administrators group, not the Administrator user.

   j.   In the Name list, **select Administrators.**

   k.   **Hold down the Control key and select JeffB.**

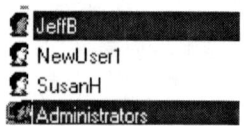

A+ Certification Troubleshooting and Repair Lab Guide, Third Edition

l.   **Click Add.**

m.   **Click OK.**

n.   In the Name list, **select the Administrators group.**

o.   In the Permissions list, **check Allow next to Full Control** to assign Full Control permissions to members of the Administrators group.

p.   In the Name list, **select Jeff Bernard.**

q.   In the Permissions list, **check Deny next to Full Control** to deny all permissions to this user.

r.   **Click OK** to save your permissions assignments.

s.   **Click Yes** to confirm that you want to deny permissions to JeffB.

2. Assign the necessary permissions for the D:\Data\Proposals folder.

a. Right-click the D:\Data\Proposals folder and choose Properties.

b. Select the Security tab.

c. Uncheck Allow Inheritable Permissions From Parent To Propagate To This Object.

d. Click Remove to remove the previously inherited permissions from the folder.

e. Click Add.

f. From the Look In drop-down list, select WIN2000-#.

⚠ Make sure you select the Administrators group, not the Administrator user.

g. In the Name list, select Administrators.

h. Hold down the Control key and select JeffB.

i. Click Add.

j. Click OK.

k. In the Name list, select the Administrators group.

l. In the Permissions list, check Allow next to Full Control.

m. In the Name list, select Jeff Bernard.

n. In the Permissions list, check Allow next to Modify (which will also assign the Write permission to the user).

Permissions:	Allow	Deny
Full Control	☐	☐
Modify	☑	☐

o. **Click OK** to save your permissions assignments.

3. **Assign the Read-Only attribute to Template for New Proposals.doc.**

a. In Windows Explorer, **select the D:\Data\ Proposals folder.**

b. In the right pane, **right-click Template for New Proposals.doc and choose Properties.**

c. **Check Read-Only.**

☑ Read-only

d. **Click OK** to save your changes.

e. **Close Windows Explorer.**

4.   Test the permissions assignments.

   a. **Log off and log back on to your computer as SusanH,** not the domain.

   b. **Open Windows Explorer.**

   c. **Verify that you can open and change the files within the D:\Data\Personnel and D:\Data\Proposals folders.**

   d. **Close Windows Explorer.**

   e. **Log off and log back on as JeffB.**

   f. **Verify that you can open and change all files but the Template for New Proposals file within the D\Data\Proposals folder.**

   g. **Attempt to make changes to the Template for New Proposals file.**

   h. **Verify that you can't access the D\Data\Personnel folder.**

Review Questions

1. Which file system in Windows 2000 enables you to set file and folder permissions?

   _____

2. You have created a template folder on a computer that is shared by two users. You want both users to be able to read files in this folder but not change them. What permissions should you assign to the two users?

   _____

3. You have installed a non-DOS application into a folder on a computer that is shared by two users. You want the users to be able to run the application but not modify any of its files. What permissions should you assign to the two users?

   _____

4. Which file attribute should you assign if you don't want users to be able to change the contents of a file?

   _____

5. Which Windows 2000 utility enables you to configure file and folder permissions?

_____

6. You want to assign users permissions to a folder on your computer. Where should you go to assign the permissions?

_____

7. To what accounts can you assign permissions in Windows 2000?

_____

12

EXERCISE 12-6

Encrypting Files and Folders

Activity Time:

10 minutes

Objective:

To implement and test encryption on files and folders.

Data Files:

- Salary.doc

Scenario:

Your client, Susan Hill, occasionally permits other users at her company to use her computer to access the Internet or look at reports. Because she is the accountant for the company, she keeps many of the confidential records for the company. For example, she has a document listing employee names and their salaries. This file is named Salary.doc and it's stored in the D\Data\Personnel folder. She has asked you to make sure that no user (not even an administrator) other than herself can open the file, even if she accidentally copies the file to a folder in which other users have permissions.

What You Do	How You Do It
1. **Encrypt the Salary.doc file.**	a. **Log on as SusanH.**
	b. **Open Windows Explorer.**
	c. **Select the D\Data\Personnel folder.**
	d. In the right pane, **right-click Salary and choose Properties.**
	e. On the General page, **click Advanced.**
	f. **Check Encrypt Contents To Secure Data.**
	☑ Encrypt contents to secure data
	g. **Click OK** to close the Advanced Attributes dialog box.
	h. **Click OK.**
	i. In the Encryption Warning dialog box, **select Encrypt The File Only.**
	⦿ Encrypt the file only
	j. **Click OK.**
	k. **Close Windows Explorer.**
2. **Test the encryption.**	a. **Log on as Admin#.**
	b. In Windows Explorer, **attempt to open the D\Data\Personnel\Salary.doc file.**

12

c. **Click OK** to close the error message.

> ⚠ Access to E:\Data\PERSON~1\Salary.doc was denied.
>
> [OK]

d. **Close Windows Explorer.**

Review Questions

1. What permissions do you need to a file before you can encrypt it?

_____

2. You want to encrypt a file. What steps should you use to accomplish this task in Windows 2000?

_____

_____

_____

_____

_____

3. True or False: When you encrypt a folder, Windows 2000 automatically encrypts all files, subfolders, and their files and well.

_____

_____

4. How do you decrypt a file?

_____

_____

_____

_____

LAB 12-1

Implementing Local Security

Activity Time:

40 minutes

Objective:

To configure security settings on a Windows 2000 or Windows XP-based computer.

Setup:

If you will be keying this lab immediately following the Implementing Local Security in Windows 2000/NT/XP chapter, you should boot into Windows XP and begin the lab.

If you will be keying this lab outside of the pre-established classroom environment, you will need a computer with the default installation of Windows 2000 or Windows XP.

Scenario:

As an A+ technician, you have been called in by one of your clients, Consulting Architects, Inc., to configure a new user's computer. The network administrator for your client's network tells you that this new user is named William Murphy, and that he would like you to assign a password of *password* to the user account. He would like the system to prompt the new user to change his password when he first logs on to the computer. Mr. Murphy works for the Design department at Consulting Architects, Inc. All the computers within this department are members of a workgroup named Design.

The network administrator also tells you that this new user should be able to install applications on the computer, but that he should not have the full privileges of an administrator. In addition, the new user will be working on sensitive proposals, so the network administrator wants you to make sure that no users other than Mr. Murphy will be able to access his data files.

12

 When you have finished the lab, you can refer to the Implementing Local Security Lab Results.txt file to check your work.

1. **Configure the computer as a member of the Design workgroup.**

---

2. **Create William Murphy's user account.**

---

3. **Add the new user account to the appropriate group.**

---

4. Implement encryption on the new user's My Documents folder.

_____

5. Configure the user account to prompt for a password change.

_____

CHAPTER 13

Managing File and Print Resources in Windows 2000/NT/XP

Activities included in this chapter:

Exercise 13-1

Sharing a Folder

Activity Time:

20 minutes

Objective:

To configure a shared folder with appropriate permissions and test access to the shared folder.

Setup:

Your computer is a member of the class.com domain. You have an Admin# and a DomainUser# account in the domain. The password for all user accounts is password. The Admin# user account is a member of Domain Admins.

Setup:

You will work with a partner in this exercise. You will each create and secure a shared folder for your partner to access.

Scenario:

As a member of your company's Help Desk, you find that you frequently need to share some of your report files with other members of the department. You would like this folder to be accessible by other Help Desk staffers plus the domain administrators, but no other users in the Active Directory domain. When the other Help Desk staffers and the administrators access the files on your computer, they will need to be able to make any changes required to the files. The manager of the IT department has asked that department members name shares with names that correspond to their computer names (for example, WIN2000–1 should use \SharedDocs1).

What You Do	How You Do It
1. As the Admin# user, **create an D:\SharedDocs# folder.**	a. **Log on to the class.com domain as Admin#.**
	b. **Open Windows Explorer.**
	c. **Select the D drive.**
	d. **Choose File→New→Folder.**
	e. **Type** *SharedDocs#* **and press Enter.**
2. **Share the folder with the desired permissions.**	a. **Right-click SharedDocs# and choose Sharing.**
	b. **Select Share This Folder.** The default share name is SharedDocs#.

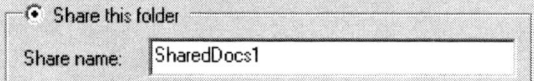

	c. **Click Permissions.**
	d. **Add the Administrators group from the local computer to the permissions list.**
	e. In the Name list, **verify that the Administrators group is selected.**
	f. In the Permissions list, **check the Allow box for Full Control.**
	g. In the Name list, **select Everyone and click Remove.**
	h. **Click OK twice.**
3. **Test access to the shared folder on your partner's computer as an authorized and an unauthorized user.**	a. From the Start menu, **choose Run.**

b. **Enter the UNC path to your partner's SharedDocs# folder.**

Open: \\win2000-2\SharedDocs2

c. **Click OK.** The shared folder window on your partner's computer opens.

d. **Log off and log back on as your User# account.** This account doesn't have permission to use the SharedDocs folder.

e. From the Start menu, **choose Run.**

f. **Enter the UNC path to your partner's SharedDocs# folder.**

g. **Click OK.** You should receive an Access is Denied message.

h. **Click OK** in the message box.

Review Questions

1. You have been asked to set up a shared folder on a user's computer. The user would like other users in her department to be able to open files from this folder. She doesn't want other users to be able to modify the files in this folder. What share permissions should you assign?

2. A user has asked you to share a folder on his computer. He would like to limit the number of people who can connect to the shared folder at the same time. What should you do?

3. True or False: You can share a folder multiple times, each with a different share name.

4. You have shared a folder and given the group Everyone the Full Control share permissions. A user reports that when he connects to this shared folder, he can't create any new files. What should you check?

_____

_____

5. How does Windows 2000 determine a user's effective permissions if the user has both share and NTFS permissions for the same folder?

_____

_____

EXERCISE 13-2

Connecting to a Network Printer

Activity Time:

10 minutes

Objective:

To install a network printer as the default printer.

Scenario:

You're working with another technician from your company to install an HP Laser Jet 5si MX printer on the print server for one of your clients. The print server and all client computers are members of an Active Directory domain. The other technician shared the printer as NetPrint. Your job is to set up the Windows 2000 computers on the client's network so that the computers' users can print to this printer. The IT director for the company would like this printer to be the default printer for all users. Because this company has mostly temporary workers, your client configured each user to use a user name of User#, where # is the unique number assigned to the user's computer.

What You Do	How You Do It

1. **Install the network printer.**

    a. **Log on to the class.com domain as User#.**

    b. From the Start menu, **choose Settings→ Printers.**

    c. **Double-click Add Printer.**

    d. **Click Next.**

    e. On the Local Or Network Printer page, **select Network Printer.**

        ○ Local printer
            ☐ Automatically detect and install my Plug and Play printer
        ◉ Network printer

    f. **Click Next.**

    g. On the Locate Your Printer page, **verify that Find A Printer In The Directory is selected and click Next.**

        ◉ Find a printer in the Directory

    h. In the Find Printers dialog box, **click Find Now.**

    i. In the Name list, **select the HP Laser Jet 5si MX printer and click OK.**

        Name
        HP LaserJet 5si MX

    j. **Click Finish.** The printer object appears in the Printers folder. The check mark indicates that this is the default printer for the computer.

Because this is the first printer installed on the computer, you are not prompted as to whether you want to make this printer the default printer.

      k.   Close the Printers window.

Review Questions

1.   How do you start the Add Printer Wizard Windows 2000?

2.   What permissions do you need to connect to a network printer?

3.   What type of printer should you select (local or network) if you want to configure a Windows 2000 computer to connect to a network-attached printer?

4.   You are attempting to connect to a network-attached printer in Windows 2000. The printer is using TCP/IP and has its own IP address. How do you specify the IP address of the network-attached printer?

5.   How can you verify that a network printer is installed correctly?

EXERCISE 13-3

Capturing a Printer Port

Activity Time:

10 minutes

Objective:

To capture a network printer to a printer port for printing through a DOS application.

Data Files:

* D:\Data\MyReport.txt

Scenario:

A client calls to report that she has just upgraded her computer to Windows 2000. She still runs the Edit MS-DOS application that was developed for her company. Your client reports that she's unable to print whenever she uses Edit, but she's able to print to the network printer named \\2000srv\NetPrint whenever she uses any of her Windows applications. She doesn't have a local printer attached to her computer.

What You Do	How You Do It
1. **Capture the printer port.**	a. If neccessary, **log in as Admin#.**
	b. From the Start menu, **choose Programs→ Accessories→Command Prompt.**
	c. **Enter** net use lpt1 \\2000srv\netprint
	You should see a message stating that the command completes successfully.

13

2. **Test the capture of the printer port.**

   a. In the Command Prompt window, **enter `edit D:\Data\MyReport.txt`** to open the Edit MS-DOS application. You can use the Edit program to verify that you're able to print.

   b. **Press Alt+F to display the File menu.**

   c. **Press P to print to the captured printer port.**

   d. **Press Enter to confirm that you want to print the complete document.**

   e. **Press Alt+F.**

   f. **Press X to exit the Edit program.**

   g. **Enter `net print \\2000srv\netprint`** to view the accumulated print jobs.

   h. **Close the Command Prompt window.**

Review Questions

1. What is the syntax of the command you use to capture a printer port?

   _____

2. Where do you run the command to capture a printer port?

   _____

3. How can you view the status of captured print jobs?

   _____

4. For what type of applications might you need to capture a printer port?

   _____

5. What is the syntax of the command you use to disconnect a captured printer port?

   _____

EXERCISE 13-4

Installing a Local Printer

Activity Time:

10 minutes

Objective:

To install and share a local printer.

Scenario:

One of your clients has just ordered a new Hewlett-Packard Color Laserjet 5. He would like to use this printer on his Windows 2000 computer as his default printer. Your client's computer has a single parallel port. He has also asked that you make the printer available to other users in the company. Even though your client hasn't yet received the printer, he would like you to configure his computer so that all he will need to do is plug in the printer when it arrives.

13

What You Do	How You Do It
1. **Install and share the printer.**	a. From the Start menu, **choose Settings→ Printers.**
	b. **Double-click the Add Printer icon.**
	c. **Choose Local Printer.**
	d. **Uncheck Automatically Detect And Install My Plug And Play Printer.**
	e. **Click Next.**
	f. Below Use The Following Port, **verify that LPT1 is selected.**

g. **Click Next.**

h. Below Manufacturers, **select HP.**

i. Below Printers, **select HP Color Laserjet 5.**

j. **Click Next.**

k. **Accept the default printer name of HP Color Laserjet 5.**

l. Below Do You Want Your Windows-based Programs To Use This Printer As The Default Printer, **verify that Yes is selected.**

m. **Click Next.**

n. **Select Share As.**

o. **Accept the default share name of HPColorL.**

○ Do not share this printer
● Share as: HPColorL

p. **Click Next.**

q. Optionally, **enter a Location and Comment.**

r. **Click Next.**

s. Below Do You Want To Print A Test Page, **select No.**

t. **Click Next.**

u. **Click Finish.** You now see the HP Color Laserjet 5 in the Printers folder; the hand icon underneath the printer indicates that it's shared.

HP Color
LaserJet 5

Review Questions

1.   When you install a local printer on a Windows 2000 computer, who has the necessary permissions to manage the printer?

     _____

2.   You are looking at the contents of a user's Printers folder on a Windows 2000 computer. How can you tell by looking at the list of printers which printer is the user's default printer?

     _____

3.   You are looking at the contents of a user's Printers folder on a Windows 2000 computer. How can you tell by looking at the list of printers if a printer is shared?

     _____

4.   True or False: You can skip printing a test page when you install a local printer.

     _____

5.   When you share a printer, which print permission enables a user to delete his print job from the print queue?

     _____

EXERCISE 13-5

Troubleshooting Printing Problems

Activity Time:

15 minutes

Objective:

To determine the proper troubleshooting approach for various print problem scenarios.

Scenario:

You're contracted as an A+ technician to work on-site at one of your client's locations. The client has asked you to manage all of the printers on the network. You're responsible for responding to any problems that arise with printing. While you were out at lunch, you received three trouble tickets relating to printing problems.

Trouble Ticket #1

1. Mary reports that she's unable to print from Microsoft Excel. After talking with her on the phone, you've determined that everything is okay with the printer hardware.

    When you get to her desk, what step should you take next to troubleshoot the problem?

13

Trouble Ticket #2

2. Andy reports that he's attempting to print to his local printer, but none of the print jobs are printing. When you arrive at his desk, you check out the printer hardware and everything seems to be fine. When you double-click the printer in the Printers folder, you see Andy's jobs listed.

    What should you try next?

Trouble Ticket #3

3. Suzanne's computer is configured to print to both a local and a network printer. She just installed a non-Windows application and executed the command `net use lpt1 \\2000srv\netprint` so that she can print from the non-Windows application. Suzanne reports that all her print jobs now print to the network printer.

   What might be the problem and how can you fix it?

Review Questions

1. You have been asked to troubleshoot a problem where a user is unable to print to his local printer. What should you check first?

_____

2. You have verified that a user's printer is functioning properly, but the user is still unable to print. What should you do next?

_____

3. You are troubleshooting a shared printer. A user is unable to print to the printer, but other users can successfully print to the same printer. You have already verified that the printer's hardware is functioning correctly. What should you check next?

_____

4. You have reviewed a printer's print queue in Windows 2000 and you see that jobs are accumulating in the print queue. What should you do?

_____

5. A user reports that when she tries to print to a printer she just installed, she gets nothing but garbled characters on the page. You have verified that the printer's hardware is functioning correctly. What should you check?

_____

LAB 13-1

Managing File and Print Resources

Activity Time:

40 minutes

Objective:

To configure shared file and print resources using a Windows 2000 or Windows XP-based computer.

Setup:

If you will be keying this lab immediately following the Managing File and Print Resources in Windows 2000/NT/XP chapter, boot into Windows XP and begin the lab.

If you will be keying this lab outside of the pre-established classroom environment, you will need:

- A networked computer with the default installation of Windows 2000 or Windows XP.
- A domain controller. Follow the steps outlined in the "For the Classroom Domain Controller" setup procedure in the Class Setup section.

Scenario:

As a member of the IS department for your company, Classroom Management, you have been asked to configure a new user's Windows-based computer. This user, Sarah Vance, will be logging on to your company's Windows 2000 domain, class.com. In addition, Sarah will be creating templates for documents such as reports and proposals on her computer; these templates must be accessible by all authorized users in your company. However, the network administrator has told you that no one should be able to modify the templates other than Sarah. The network administrator would like you to name this folder \Templates and store it on the drive containing Windows.

Sarah will need the ability to print from her computer. Your company has a network printer named \\2000srv\netprint. She will also be printing to this printer from an MS-DOS application.

 When you have finished the lab, you can refer to the Managing File and Print Resources Lab Results.txt file to check your work.

1. **Configure the computer as a member of the class.com domain.**

2. Create and share a folder for storing the templates.

_____

3. Connect to the network printer.

_____

4. Capture the lpt1 port to the network printer.

_____

CHAPTER 14

Managing File and Print Resources in Windows 9x

Activities included in this chapter:

- Exercise 14-1 Setting the Domain Membership to the Class.com Domain
- Exercise 14-2 Configuring User-level Security
- Exercise 14-3 Sharing a Folder with User-level Security
- Exercise 14-4 Installing a Network Printer
- Exercise 14-5 Troubleshooting Printing Problems in Windows 9x
- Exercise 14-6 Enabling User Profiles on a Windows 98 Computer
- Lab 14-1 Managing File and Print Resources in Windows 98

EXERCISE 14-1

Setting the Domain Membership to the Class.com Domain

Activity Time:

15 minutes

Objective:

To configure the network membership for a Windows 98 computer.

Scenario:

Your company has many Windows 9x computers connected to its network. To enable your users to easily browse other company computers for shared resources, you want all computers to be a member of your company's Class.com domain. In addition, you want all users to log on by using a domain user account.

What You Do	How You Do It
1. Set the membership of your computer to the Class.com domain.	a. Reboot the computer to Windows 98 and log on as Admin#.
	b. Choose Start→Settings→Control Panel.
	c. Double-click Network.
	d. Select the Identification tab.
	e. In the Workgroup text box, **type** *Class*
	f. Click OK.
	g. In the Copy Files From text box, **type** *C:\Win98* and click OK.
	h. Click Yes to restart the computer.
	i. Log back on to the computer.

A+ Certification Troubleshooting and Repair Lab Guide, Third Edition

Review Questions

1. Which Network Properties tab enables you to specify a workgroup or domain name?

   _____

2. What two types of names might be assigned to a computer?

   _____

3. Can Windows 9x computers truly be members of a domain?

   _____

4. Where does a user get authenticated when logging in to the domain?

   _____

5. What is the NetBIOS equivalent name for the DNS name of myserver.xyz.com?

   _____

14

EXERCISE 14-2

Configuring User-level Security

Activity Time:

10 minutes

Objective:

To enable user-level access control on a Windows 98 computer.

Setup:

The Admin# account is a domain user account in the Active Directory domain. The Windows 98 installation files are in C:\Win98.

Scenario:

Your company has many Windows 9x computers connected to its network. The users of these computers need to share computer resources such as folders and local printers with other network users. You want to make sure that these shares are as secure as possible. All the users of these computers have an individual user account with the company's Windows domain, class.com.

What You Do	How You Do It

1. **Set the security level of your computer to user-level.**

    a.   **Choose Start→Settings→Control Panel.**

    b.   **Double-click Network.**

    c.   **Click the Access Control tab.**

    d.   In the Control Access To Shared Resources Using box, **select User-level Access Control.**

    e.   In the Obtain List Of Users And Groups From text box, **type** *class*

    f.   **Click OK.**

    g.   In the Copy Files From text box, **type** *C:\Win98* **and click OK.**

    h.   **Close the Control Panel window.**

    i.   **Click Yes** to restart the computer.

    j.   When prompted, **log back on to the computer.**

14

Review Questions

1.   What are the two security level settings that can be specified for Windows 9x computers?

2. Which security level has you assign a password to each shared resource?

_____

3. Can you have both security level settings enforced on a single Windows 9x computer?

_____

4. When using user-level security, where does the list of users and groups come from?

_____

5. In a network of all Windows 9x computers what security-levels can be used?

_____

Exercise 14-3

Sharing a Folder with User-level Security

Activity Time:

15 minutes

Objective:

To assign share permissions on shared folder on a Windows 98 computer to specific user accounts, and to test the shared folder permissions.

Scenario:

An employee in the Human Resources Department wants you to create a folder on her computer in which all users in your company can read, but not change, the files contained in the folder. The employee has stated that it is important that no one but company employees be able to read the files. The user has a Windows 98 computer and per company policy, it is configured with user-level security using the company's domain, class.com, to obtain its user list.

14

What You Do	How You Do It

1. **Create and share the folder with the desired permissions.**

a. If necessary, **log on as Admin#.**

b. Using Windows Explorer, **create a folder named C:\HRDocs.**

c. **Right-click C:\HRDocs.**

d. **Choose Sharing.**

e. **Select Shared As.**

f. In the Share Name text box, **type *HR Documents***

g. **Click Add.**

h. In the Name list box, **select Domain Users.**

i. **Click Read Only.**

j. **Click OK.**

k. **Click OK.**

A+ Certification Troubleshooting and Repair Lab Guide, Third Edition

l. **Look at the folder.** Windows 98 displays a hand under the folder to indicate that the folder is shared.

HRDocs

m. **Close Windows Explorer.**

2. **Verify that your partner can access your shared folder.**

a. From the Start menu, **choose Run.**

b. In the Open text box, **enter the UNC path to your partner's HR Documents shared folder.**

Open: \\win98-2\hr documents

c. **Click OK** to connect to your partner's shared folder. Because the folder is currently empty, you will not see any files.

d. **Close the window.**

Review Questions

14

1. What access permission is required in Windows 98 to open and view a file?

2. Is there a permission that will allow a user to view the contents of a file but not be allowed to copy it?

3. When you share a folder in Windows 98, do the folder name and the share name have to be the same?

4. What are the custom access permissions in Windows 98?

5. In Windows 98, what share-level access type should you use if you want some users to have full control and others to have read-only?

_____

EXERCISE 14-4

Installing a Network Printer

Activity Time:

10 minutes

Objective:

To install a network printer so that it is available for printing from a Windows 98 computer.

Setup:

The company's network printer is named NetPrint. The Windows 98 installation files are stored on each computer in the C:\Win98 folder.

Scenario:

Your company recently installed an HP Laser Jet 5si MX printer, called \\2000srv\NetPrint, to service all company employees' print needs. The technician who installed the printer on the server did not install any additional drivers for legacy Windows clients. This printer will be the default printer for all company computers. All applications used in the company are Windows-based.

14

What You Do	How You Do It

1. **Install the network printer on your computer.**

    a. From the Start menu, **choose Settings→ Printers.**

    b. **Double-click Add Printer.**

    c. **Click Next.**

    d. **Select Network Printer.**

    e. **Click Next.**

    f. In the Network Path Or Queue Name text box, **browse to find the NetPrint printer on the classroom server.**

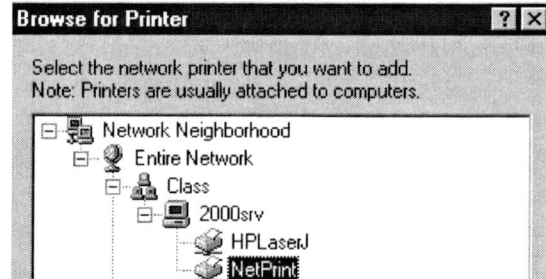

    g. **Click OK** to select the printer.

    h. Below Do You Print From MS-DOS-based Programs, **select No.**

    i. **Click Next.**

    j. In the Printer Name text box, **type *Network Printer***

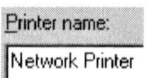

k. **Click Next.**

l. Below Would You Like To Print a Test Page, **select No.**

m. **Click Finish.**

n. **Click OK** to close the Insert Disk message box.

o. In the Copy Files From text box, **type** *C:\Win98* **and click OK.**

p. **Close the Printers window.**

Review Questions

1. Who or what supplies the print driver during a new network printer installation in Windows 98?

   _____

2. What are two methods you can use to select the network printer you want to install?

   _____

3. What would you click to navigate to the location for configuring a network printer?

   _____

14

4. During the installation of a network printer, how could you confirm that the configuration settings will work?

   _____

5. Why would a Windows 9x computer not prompt you to make a network printer your default network printer during installation?

   _____

EXERCISE 14-5

Troubleshooting Printing Problems in Windows 9x

Activity Time:

15 minutes

Objective:

To deterimine the proper troubleshooting approach for various printing problems on Windows 9x computers.

Scenario:

You have been placed in charge of the printers for your company. This job includes not only printer installations, but troubleshooting problems as well. You've received three trouble tickets relating to printing problems.

Trouble Ticket #1

1. John has a local printer attached to his computer. He calls to say that he can't print documents from any of his Microsoft Office applications. You arrive at John's desk and check the hardware and everything seems fine. You try printing a test page from Notepad, but it also fails to print. You restart the computer in Safe Mode Command Prompt Only and enter the command `copy c:\windows\mouse.txt lpt1`. The mouse.txt file prints successfully.

   What do you suspect the problem is and how would you correct it?

Trouble Ticket #2

2. Sarah has both a local printer and a connection to a network printer, an HP LaserJet 5si. She calls to say that she can print to her local printer but not to the network printer. Sarah tells you that the IT support person recently came by and installed a Windows 9x update on her computer. You stop by the network printer and see that it is online and printing jobs from other users. You try printing a test page from Notepad, but it fails to print. You restart the computer in Safe Mode Command Prompt Only and enter the command `copy c:\windows\mouse.txt lpt1`. The mouse.txt file also fails to print. You check the printer's properties and they are set per the manufacturer's specifications.

    What do you suspect the problem might be and how do you fix it?

Trouble Ticket #3

3. Gail has both a local printer and a connection to a network printer. She calls to say that she can print to the network printer, but not to her local printer. You arrive at Gail's desk and check the local printer's hardware and everything seems fine. You try printing a test page from Notepad, but it fails to print. You restart the computer in Safe Mode Command Prompt Only and enter the command `copy c:\windows\mouse.txt lpt1`. The mouse.txt file also fails to print. You check the printer's properties and they are set per the manufacturer's specifications. You then remove and re-install the printer's driver, but still local print jobs fail to print.

What do you suspect the problem might be and how do you fix it?

14

Review Questions

1. What is the IEEE specification for bi-directional printing?

2. If your cable does not support the IEEE specification for bi-directional printing what should you do?

_____

3. In Safe Mode Command Prompt Only, what command would you type to confirm that the hardware and its physical connection is correct for a non-USB laser printer?

_____

4. What utility can you use to guide you through the diagnosis of a printer problem?

_____

5. Does Windows 9x support printing to postscript printer?

_____

EXERCISE 14-6

Enabling User Profiles on a Windows 98 Computer

Activity Time:

15 minutes

Objective:

To enable and test user profiles.

Scenario:

You work for a company that runs three different 8-hour shifts. Each Windows 98 computer is used by three different users during a 24-hour period. Each user has a unique user account that they log in with to connect to network resources. Many of the users have complained that when they come in for their shift, their work environment isn't as they left it; documents on the Start→Documents menu aren't the ones they opened, items have been added or deleted from their Start menu, Active Desktop items have been changed and someone keeps changing the wallpaper! They ask you to make sure "their stuff" isn't changed during the other shifts.

What You Do	How You Do It
1. Enable user profiles.	a. From the Start menu, **choose Settings→ Control Panel.**
	b. **Double-click Passwords.**
	c. **Select the User Profiles tab.**
	d. **Select Users Can Customize Their Preferences And Desktop Settings.**

Users can customize their preferences and desktop settings. Windows switches to your personal settings when you log on.

| | e. In the User Profile Settings box, **check Include Desktop Icons And Network Neighborhood** |

**Contents In User Settings and Include Start
Menu And Program Groups In User Settings.**

User profile settings

☑ Include desktop icons and Network Neighborhood
contents in user settings.

    f.   **Click OK.**

    g.   **Close Control Panel.**

    h.   **Click Yes** to restart Windows 98.

---

2. **Test to verify user profiles are working
correctly.**

    a.   **Log on to the computer as TestUser.**

    b.   **Click Yes** to confirm that you want the com-
puter to retain your individual settings.

       The user profile for your TestUser is created.

    c.   **Make a change to the display properties of
the desktop.**

    d.   **Log off as TestUser.**

    e.   **Log on as Admin#.**

    f.   **Click Yes** to confirm that you want the com-
puter to retain your individual settings.

    g.   **Log on as TestUser.** The Windows 98 Desktop
display changes from the default were retained
for the TestUser.

    h.   **Log off TestUser.**

    i.   **Log on as Admin#.**

Review Questions

1. Where are user profiles saved on a Windows 9x computer?

   _____

2. In Control Panel, which icon would you double-click to enable user profiles?

   _____

3. What folder name is a user's profile saved under?

   _____

4. What Internet Explorer data is maintained under a user profile?

   _____

5. Can you configure User Profiles so that only certain users can maintain them?

   _____

   _____

14

LAB 14-1

Managing File and Print Resources in Windows 98

Activity Time:

50 minutes

Objective:

To share a folder and a printer on a Windows 98 computer, and to configure the appropriate security on the system and on the shared resources.

Setup:

If you will be keying this lab immediately following the Managing File and Print Resources in Windows 98 chapter, you should boot into Windows 98 and begin the lab.

If you will be keying this lab outside of the pre-established classroom environment, you will need:

- A networked computer with a default installation of Windows 98.
- A second networked computer with default installation of Windows 98 so that you can test the share permissions on the first computer's resources.

Scenario:

You've been hired by AlphaBeta Company to move one of their older Windows 98 computers to the production floor. On the production floor, many engineers will be logging in, running diagnostic programs and then storing the report files in the local My Documents folder. The engineers have expressed a desire to have a personalized work environment when they work on the production floor computer. They complain that things get moved around all the time on them and when they are in a hurry, it takes too much time to re-adjust to the modified environment.

The engineers also need access to the files in this folder from their office computers so that they can pull data from the report files into other database and statistical programs. All the office computers are members of a workgroup called Production. Security is not a large concern at AlphaBeta, but they would like to restrict access to the share on this computer. They would like to give managers the ability to read the reports, and only allow those who run the reports full control of the folder. They would like you to change the name displayed in Network Neighborhood from My Documents to Prod Reports, so they don't confuse the folder with their local My Documents folder.

In addition, there is an HP Laser Jet 4si they'd like to print the reports on. Many times it is inconvenient to run down to the production floor computer to print, so they'd like you to make it so they can print the reports on this printer from their office computers. Because the reports are a high priority, they don't want other employees to use the printer.

When you have finished the lab, you can refer to the Managing File and Print Resources in Windows 98 Lab Results.txt file to check your work.

1. **Set the computer's workgroup to Production.**

2. **Enable user profiles on the computer.**

3. **Verify security is set to share-level.**

4. **Share the My Documents folder with two passwords: one for ReadOnly access and the other for Full access.**

5. On the computer, **install the HP LaserJet 4si printer.**

6. **Share the printer and protect it with a password.**

7. **Test the share permissions on the file and the printer.**

14

CHAPTER 15

Managing Disk Resources in Windows 2000/NT/XP

Activities included in this chapter:

- Exercise 15-1 Creating an Extended Partition
- Exercise 15-2 Deleting a Partition
- Exercise 15-3 Creating a Primary Partition
- Exercise 15-4 Converting a FAT Partition to NTFS
- Exercise 15-5 Compressing Files
- Exercise 15-6 Defragmenting a Hard Disk
- Lab 15-1 Managing Disk Resources

EXERCISE 15-1

Creating an Extended Partition

Activity Time:

15 minutes

Objective:

To create, format, and test an extended partition and logical drive.

Setup:

Restart the computer and choose Windows 2000 Professional from the boot menu.

Scenario:

One of your clients has a computer configured to boot Windows 98, Windows 2000, and Linux; the client uses this computer to test custom applications he develops. The computer has a single hard disk, and each operating system is configured with its own primary partition. The client has asked you to make the 1 GB of free space remaining on the disk available to both Windows 98 and Windows 2000. Your client would like you to assign the drive letter of S (for "shared") to this partition.

What You Do	How You Do It
1. Given that your client wants the partition to be accessible to both Windows 98 and Windows 2000, what type of partition must you create (given the current configuration of the hard disk)? Why?	
2. What file system(s) can you use on this partition? Why?	

3. **Create an extended partition.**	a. **Log on to the Local computer as Admin#.**
	b. **Open Computer Management and select Disk Management** (right-click My Computer and choose Manage to open Computer Management).
	c. On Disk 0, **right-click the available free space and choose Create Partition.**
	d. **Click Next.**
	e. **Select Extended Partition and click Next.**
	f. In the Amount Of Disk Space To Use text box, **type *1024*** to create an extended partition that is 1 GB in size.

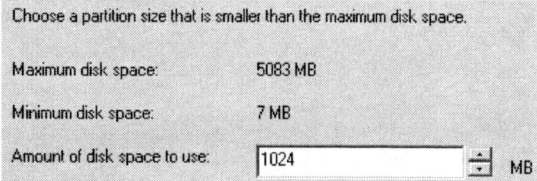

	g. **Click Next.**
	h. **Click Finish.**

---

4. **Create and format a logical drive within the extended partition.**	a. **Right-click the extended partition and choose Create Logical Drive.**
	b. **Click Next.**
	c. On the Select Partition Type page, **click Next** to accept the default of Logical Drive.
	d. **Click Next** to create the logical drive to use all the available space within the extended partition.

15

e. From the Assign A Drive Letter drop-down list, **select S:.**

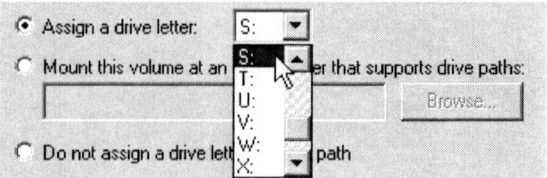

f. **Click Next.**

g. From the File System To Use drop-down list, **select FAT32.**

h. **Check Perform A Quick Format.**

i. **Click Next.**

j. **Click Finish.**

k. When the format is complete, **close Computer Management.**

5. **Verify that the new drive is accessible.**

a. **Open Windows Explorer.**

b. **Access the S drive.**

c. **Close Windows Explorer.**

Review Questions

1. What is a partition?

2. What are the two types of partitions you can create?

3. Which type(s) of partitions can be marked as Active?

_____

4. How many extended partitions can you create on a single hard disk?

_____

5. When formatting a partition on a Windows 2000 computer, which file systems can you use?

_____

15

EXERCISE 15-2

Deleting a Partition

Activity Time:

10 minutes

Objective:

To delete an unused extended partition and logical drive to recover the disk space.

Scenario:

A client calls to ask for your help with her Windows 2000 computer. She has installed a hard disk given to her by a friend into the Windows 2000 computer. When she accesses this hard disk, she finds that it has an S: partition on it. She would like to get rid of the S: partition and create a new one so that she can be sure that all her friend's old data is no longer on the disk.

A+ Certification Troubleshooting and Repair Lab Guide, Third Edition

What You Do	How You Do It

1. **Delete the S: partition.**

    a. **Open Computer Management and select the Disk Management folder.**

    b. **Right-click the S: partition and choose Delete Logical Drive.**

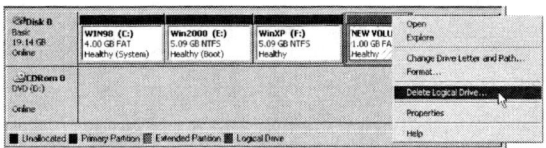

    c. **Click Yes** to confirm that you want to delete the logical drive.

    d. **Right-click the extended partition and choose Delete Partition.**

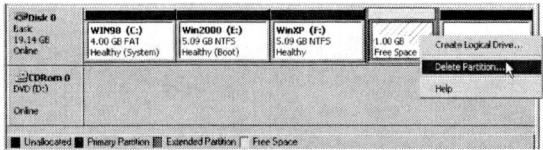

    e. **Click Yes** to confirm that you want to delete the extended partition.

    f. **Close Computer Management.**

2. **Verify that the S: partition is no longer accessible.**

    a. **Open Windows Explorer.**

    b. **Check the list of drives.**

    c. **Close Windows Explorer.**

15

Review Questions

1. Where do you navigate to delete a partition under Windows 2000?

   _____

2. What utility do you use to delete a partition in Windows NT?

   _____

3. After deleting a partition under Windows NT what else must you do to complete the process?

   _____

4. Prior to being able to delete an extended partition on a Windows 2000 machine what must you do?

   _____

5. What happens to the drive letter of a deleted partition?

   _____

Exercise 15-3

Creating a Primary Partition

Activity Time:

10 minutes

Objective:

To create, format, and test a new primary partition.

Scenario:

One of your clients reports that she's running out of disk space on her computer. After examining her computer, you've determined that she has two partitions, one primary and one extended. Your client also has free space left over on the hard disk. She uses her computer to run both Windows and non-Windows applications. One of her non-Windows applications cannot access the NTFS file system. All hard disk space must be accessible by all applications. Your client has asked you to assign the letter Z to the partition if possible.

15

What You Do	How You Do It

1. **Create a primary partition in the free space.**

    a.   **Open Computer Management and select Disk Management.**

    b.   **Right-click the free space on Disk 0 and choose Create Partition.**

    c.   **Click Next.**

    d.   **Verify that Primary Partition is selected.**

Select the type of partition you want to create:

       ⊙ Primary partition

       ○ Extended partition

    e.   **Click Next.**

    f.   In the Amount Of Disk Space To Use text box, **type 100** to configure the new partition with 100 MB of disk space.

    g.   **Click Next.**

    h.   From the Assign A Drive Letter drop-down list, **select Z:** to assign Z as the drive letter for the new partition.

       ⊙ Assign a drive letter: Z: ▾

    i.   **Click Next.**

    j.   **Verify that Format This Partition With The Following Settings is selected.**

    k.   From the File System To Use drop-down list, **select FAT.**

                                A+ Certification Troubleshooting and Repair Lab Guide, Third Edition

l.   Check Perform A Quick Format.

☑ Perform a Quick Format

m.   Click Next.

n.   Click Finish.

o.   Close Computer Management.

2.   Verify that the new drive is accessible.

a.   Open Windows Explorer.

b.   Access the Z drive.

c.   Close Windows Explorer.

Review Questions

1.   How many primary partitions can be created on a Windows 2000 basic disk?

_____

2.   How many primary partitions can be created on a Windows 9x system?

_____

3.   How do you know which partition is active on a Windows NT system?

_____

4.   How do you know which partition is active on a Windows 2000/XP computer?

_____

5.   You would like to have a partition that can be used by DOS, Windows 9x, and Windows 2000. What format must you use?

_____

EXERCISE 15-4

Converting a FAT Partition to NTFS

Activity Time:

10 minutes

Objective:

To convert a FAT-formatted partition to the NTFS file system.

Scenario:

A client just called to ask you how to set folder permissions on her hard disk. She is sharing her computer temporarily, and would like to prevent other users from accessing her confidential files. The confidential files are all stored on the Z drive.

What You Do	How You Do It
⚠ Do not convert the C drive to NTFS.	
1. **Verify the volume label and file system on the Z drive.**	a. In Windows Explorer, **display the properties for the Z drive.**
	b. **Record the volume label:** _____
	c. **Record the file system:** _____
	d. **Close Windows Explorer.**

2. **Convert the Z drive to NTFS.**

   a. **Open a Command Prompt window** (from the Start menu, choose Programs→Accessories→ Command Prompt).

   b. **Enter** `convert z: /fs:ntfs`

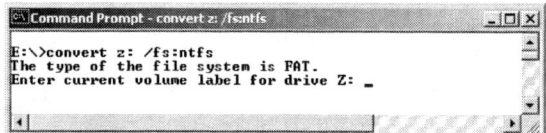

```
E:\>convert z: /fs:ntfs
The type of the file system is FAT.
Enter current volume label for drive Z: _
```

   c. When prompted, **enter the volume label.**

```
The type of the file system is FAT.
Enter current volume label for drive Z: NEW VOLUME
```

   d. **Close the Command Prompt window.**

3. **Verify that the Z drive is using the NTFS file system.**

   a. In Computer Management, **display the properties for the Z drive.**

   b. **Verify that the file system is now NTFS.**

   c. **Close Computer Management.**

Review Questions

1. What is the syntax of the command used to convert a FAT partition to an NTFS partition?

2. Can you convert an NTFS partition to the FAT file system?

3. Which operating systems can use the NTFS file system?

4. Do you have to restart the computer after converting a partition to NTFS?

15

5. Why would you want to convert a FAT partition to NTFS rather than just reformat it using NTFS?

_____

_____

Exercise 15-5

Compressing Files

Activity Time:

15 minutes

Objective:

To compress files and folders to save disk space.

Data Files:

- D:\Data\NASA

Scenario:

One of your clients, a contractor with the Stennis Space Center, is responsible for downloading and presenting space-related images. Because these images are so large, they are using up much of her computer's disk space. She would like you to take whatever steps you can to minimize the amount of disk space required for these images. Your client downloads these images to the D:\Data\NASA folder.

15

What You Do	How You Do It
1. Compress the D:\Data\NASA folder.	a. Open Windows Explorer.
	b. Right-click the D:\Data\NASA folder and choose Properties.
	c. Record the value for Size On Disk:
	_____
	Size on disk: 9.85 MB (10,334,208 bytes)
	d. Click Advanced.
	e. Check Compress Contents To Save Disk Space.
	☑ Compress contents to save disk space
	f. Click OK.
	g. Click OK to close the Properties dialog box.
	h. Select Apply Changes To This Folder, Subfolders And Files.
	⦿ Apply changes to this folder, subfolders and files
	i. Click OK.
	j. Right-click the D:\Data\NASA folder and choose Properties.
	k. Compare the Size On Disk to what you recorded in step C. You should see that compressing the D:\Data\NASA folder reduced the amount of disk required for the folder.

Size on disk: 5.92 MB (6,211,326 bytes)

l. **Click Cancel** to close the Properties dialog box.

2. **Configure Windows Explorer to display compressed files in a different color.**

    a. In Windows Explorer, **choose Tools→Folder Options.**

    b. **Select the View tab.**

    c. **Check Display Compressed Files And Folders With Alternate Color.**

    ☑ Display compressed files and folders with alternate color

    d. **Click OK.**

    e. **Examine the folder list in Windows Explorer.** You can now easily see which files are compressed and which are not.

    f. **Close Windows Explorer.**

3. **What will happen if your client downloads a new file to the D:\Data\NASA folder?**

15

4. **What will happen if your client moves one of the files from the D:\Data\NASA folder to another folder on the same partition?**

5. **What will happen if your client copies one of the files from the D:\Data\NASA folder to another uncompressed folder on the same partition?**

Review Questions

1. What are the pre-requisites for compressing a folder?

   _____

2. Can you compress a single file?

   _____

3. How can you tell if a file is currently compressed?

   _____

4. A Windows 9x client wants to connect to a share on your Windows 2000 computer. The share is compressed on an NTFS partition. Will the Windows 9x client be able to access the file?

   _____

5. You are interested in how much space will be saved by compressing a folder. How can you determine the space savings?

   _____

Exercise 15-6

Defragmenting a Hard Disk

Activity Time:

10 minutes to 60 minutes

Objective:

To defragment a disk to improve disk performance.

Scenario:

One of your clients is complaining that his hard disk in his Windows 2000 computer is very slow. He says that he can hear the hard disk "crunching away" whenever he attempts to save a file to the D drive. He's asked you to do what you can to resolve the problem.

15

What You Do	How You Do It
1. **Analyze the fragmentation on the hard disk.**	a. From the Start menu, **choose Programs→ Accessories→System Tools→Disk Defragmenter.**
	b. In the Volume list, **select the D drive.**
	c. **Click Analyze.**
	d. In the Disk Defragmenter message box, **click View Report.**
	e. In the Volume Information area, **scroll to the Volume Fragmentation statistics.** You can determine the overall fragmentation percentage here.

```
Volume fragmentation
    Total fragmentation                    = 7 %
    File fragmentation                     = 14 %
    Free space fragmentation               = 0 %
```

| | f. In the Most Fragmented Files list, **click the Fragments column heading** to sort by this column. The larger files have the greatest amount of fragmentation. |
| | g. **Click Close.** |

2. **Based on the analysis you see in the report, should you defragment this disk?**

3. **Defragment the disk.**

    a. **Click Defragment.** The information displayed in Disk Defragmenter and the status bar changes as the defragmentation progresses.

        If you don't want to take the time for defragmentation to complete, click Stop.

    b. **Close Disk Defragmenter.**

Review Questions

1. Why would you defragment a hard drive?

2. When is it recommended to defragment a hard disk?

3. What does the process of defragmenting physically do to the files on disk?

4. What causes fragmentation?

5. Where is the Disk Defragmenter utility located in Windows 2000?

15

Lab 15-1

Managing Disk Resources

Activity Time:

30 minutes

Objective:

To create and manage a disk partition on a Windows 2000 or Windows XP-based computer.

Setup:

If you will be keying this lab immediately following the Managing Disk Resources in Windows 2000/NT/XP chapter, you will need to delete the Z drive created during the chapter. You should then boot into Windows XP and begin the lab.

If you will be keying this lab outside of the pre-established classroom environment, you will need:

- A computer with a 4 GB or larger hard disk that contains one 3 GB partition with a default installation of Windows 2000 or Windows XP, and the rest of the disk left as free space.

Scenario:

You have been asked by a client to manage the hard disks on some Windows computers. After reviewing the configuration of the computers, you have determined that whoever installed Windows did not use all available disk space. The company representative tells you that the company is very concerned about two things: the security of the users' files, and making sure that users have enough available disk space. When asked, the company representative also tells you that according to his knowledge, the computers' hard disks have never been defragmented.

 When you have finished the lab, you can refer to the Managing Disk Resources Lab Results.txt file to check your work.

1. **Create a new partition from the remaining free space on the hard disk.**

---

2. **Format the new drive to NTFS.**

---

3. **Compress the new drive.**

---

4. **Defragment the hard disk.**

CHAPTER 16

Managing Disk Resources in Windows 9x

Activities included in this chapter:

- Exercise 16-1 Creating an Extended Partition on a Windows 98 Computer
- Exercise 16-2 Compressing a Drive on a Windows 98 Computer
- Exercise 16-3 Uncompressing a Drive on a Windows 98 Computer
- Exercise 16-4 Converting an Existing Windows 98 FAT Partition to FAT32
- Exercise 16-5 Defragmenting a Hard Disk in Windows 98
- Lab 16-1 Managing Disk Resources in Windows 98

Exercise 16-1

Creating an Extended Partition on a Windows 98 Computer

Activity Time:

20 minutes

Objective:

To create, format, and test an extended partition.

Setup:

In Windows 2000, open Computer Management and delete the Z drive.

Scenario:

When the Windows 98 computers in AlphaBeta Company were set up, the primary partition that Windows 98 was installed on didn't take up the entire space available on the hard disk—1 GB of free space was left. Over the years, users have utilized much of the space on the existing primary partition. The Administrative Assistant at AlphaBeta has asked you to make the extra space on her computer usable for storing additional files.

What You Do	How You Do It
1. Restart Windows 98 in MS-DOS mode.	a. **Restart the computer and choose Microsoft Windows from the boot menu** to load Windows 98.
	b. **Log on as Admin#.**
	c. **Choose Start→Shut Down.**
	d. In the Shut Down Windows dialog box, **select Restart In MS-DOS Mode.**
	e. **Click OK.**

2. **Create a 1 GB extended partition on the computer.**

a. At the C:\Windows prompt, **enter** `fdisk`

b. **Enter N** to bypass enabling large disk support and use 16-bit FAT as the file system on your computer.

c. **Enter N** to bypass treating all NTFS partitions as large disks (you see this message only because you have NTFS partitions on the computer).

d. **Enter 1** to select Create A DOS Partition Or Logical DOS Drive.

e. **Enter 2** to select Create An Extended DOS Partition.

f. **Enter 1024.**

```
Enter partition size in Mbytes or percent of disk space (%) to
create an Extended DOS Partition...............................:[ 1024]
```

g. **Press Esc.**

h. **Press Enter** to confirm that you want to create a logical drive within your computer's extended partition. The logical drive information is displayed. You might see that Fdisk adjusted the size of the partition slightly.

```
Enter logical drive size in Mbytes or percent of disk space (%)...[ 1028]
```

16

i. **Press Esc** to return to the Fdisk main menu.

j. **Press Esc** to exit out of Fdisk.

k. **Press Esc again.**

l. **Press Ctrl+Alt+Delete** to reboot the computer.

m. **Choose Microsoft Windows from the boot menu** to load Windows 98.

3. **Format the D drive.**

a. **Log on as Admin#.**

b. **Open Windows Explorer.**

c. **Right-click on D: and choose Format.**

d. In the Format – (D:) dialog box, **verify that Quick (Erase) is selected for the Format Type.**

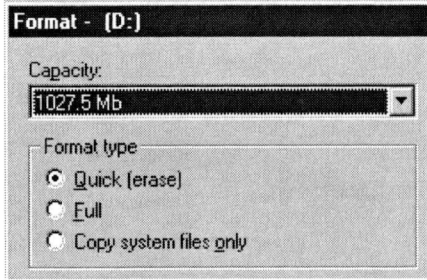

e. **Click Start** to begin the format.

f. **Click OK** to confirm that you want to format this drive.

g. **Click OK** again to confirm the format.

h. **Click Close** to close the Format Results dialog box.

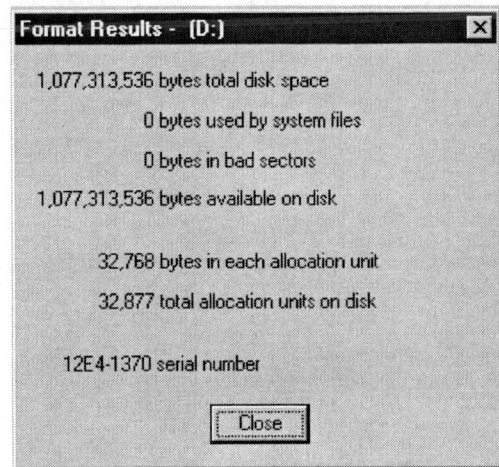

		i.	**Click OK** to close the ScanDisk message box.
		j.	**Close Windows Help.**
		k.	**Click Close.**

4.	**Verify that you can access the D drive.**	a.	In Windows Explorer, **select D:**. You don't see any files because the drive is empty.

Review Questions

1. What is the largest partition size FAT32 can accommodate?

   _____

2. Which Windows operating systems can access a FAT32 partition?

   _____

3. What utility is used to create a partition on Windows 9x computers?

   _____

4. You logged in to a Windows 9x computer but Fdisk is not running correctly. What might the problem be?

   _____

5. How many partitions can Fdisk create on a single hard drive?

   _____

Exercise 16-2

Compressing a Drive on a Windows 98 Computer

Activity Time:

20 minutes

Objective:

To install compression software and compress a drive to save disk space.

Setup:

You have created a D drive that is 1 GB in size. The Windows 98 installation files are in C:\Win98.

Scenario:

Your client, AlphaBeta Company, has many older Windows 98 computers with small hard disks. Users are complaining that they don't have enough room on their computers to store their files. They often have to do a bit of cleanup by deleting files or moving them to other media before they can save new ones on their D drives. With the downturn in the economy, AlphaBeta can't afford to replace the hard disks with larger ones. They've asked you to try to gain them more space on the hard disks without replacing them.

16

What You Do	How You Do It

1. Determine how much free space is on the D drive of your computer.

    a. Open Win98-#.

    b. Select the D drive.

    c. Record the free space listed in the left pane:_____

(D:)
Local Disk

Capacity: 1.00 GB

Used: 0 bytes

Free: 1.00 GB

    d. Close Win98-#.

2. If necessary, **install DriveSpace 3.**

a. In Control Panel, **double-click Add/Remove Programs.**

b. **Select the Windows Setup tab.**

c. In the Components list, **select System Tools and click Details.**

d. **Check Disk Compression Tools and click OK.**

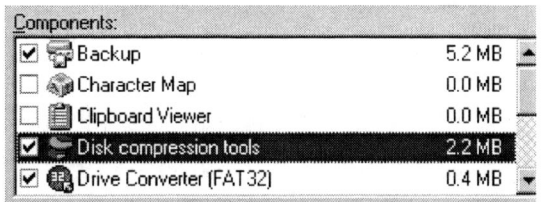

e. **Click OK.**

f. In the Insert Disk message box, **click OK.**

g. In the Copying Files dialog box, **enter** *c:\win98* **and click OK.**

h. **Click OK.**

i. **Close Control Panel.**

3. **Compress the D drive on your
    computer.**

    ⚠ Do not compress the C drive.

a. **Choose Start→Programs→Accessories→
    System Tools→DriveSpace.**

b. In the DriveSpace dialog box, **select Drive D.**

c. **Choose Drive→Compress.** Notice that you will
    nearly double the size of the D drive by com-
    pressing it.

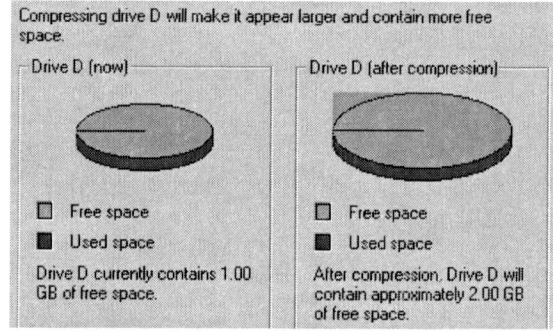

d. **Click Options.**

e. **Click OK** to accept the default host drive let-
    ter and free space size.

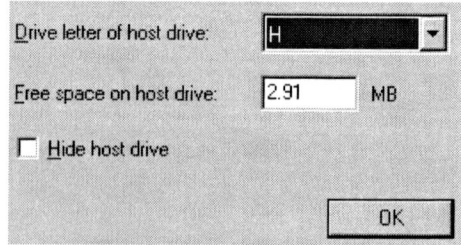

f. **Click Start.**

g. **Click No** to skip creating a Windows 98 Startup
    disk.

 A Windows 98 compressed drive is also not accessible in Windows 2000 or Windows XP.

h.   **Click OK** to close the message box stating that a Windows 98 compressed drive is not accessible in Windows NT.

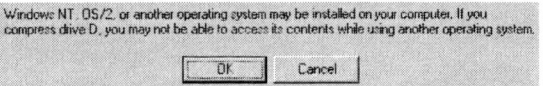

Windows NT, OS/2, or another operating system may be installed on your computer. If you compress drive D, you may not be able to access its contents while using another operating system.

[OK]   [Cancel]

i.   If neccessary, **click Compress Now.**

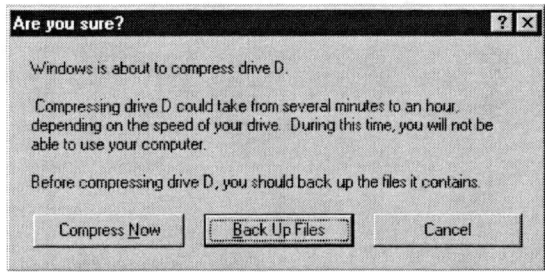

Are you sure?   ? X

Windows is about to compress drive D.

Compressing drive D could take from several minutes to an hour, depending on the speed of your drive. During this time, you will not be able to use your computer.

Before compressing drive D, you should back up the files it contains.

[Compress Now]   [Back Up Files]   [Cancel]

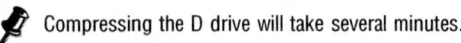 Compressing the D drive will take several minutes.

j.   **Click Cancel** to close the message stating that the hard disk is full (you receive this error message because the host file created on the D drive uses almost all of the available disk space).

k.   **Click Close** to close the Compress A Drive dialog box.

l.   **Close DriveSpace.**

m.   When prompted, **click Yes** to restart the computer.

16

4. **Verify the free space on D.**

a. When the computer restarts, **choose Microsoft Windows** from the boot menu.

b. **Log on as Admin#.**

c. In Win98-#, **check the free space on D.** You should see that you now have 2 GB of free space (instead of 1 GB).

d. **Close My Computer.**

Review Questions

1. You are running low on disk space and want to free up some space. Which of the following should free up disk space on your computer: defragmenting the drive, compressing the drive, running Scandisk on the drive, or adding a new disk.

   _____

2. What must be installed before you can compress a drive on a Windows 9x system?

   _____

3. Why should you not compress the C drive on a Windows 9x/Windows NT dual boot computer?

   _____

   _____

4. Can you compress a single file on a Windows 98 system?

   _____

5. You want to compress an 8 GB drive on a Windows 9x computer but are not able to. What is the problem?

   _____

EXERCISE 16-3

Uncompressing a Drive on a Windows 98 Computer

Activity Time:

15 minutes

Objective:

To uncompress a compressed drive.

Scenario:

Your client, AlphaBeta Company, has many older Windows 98 computers with small hard disks. Users complained that they didn't have enough room on their computers to store their files, so their D drives were compressed using DriveSpace. The company has decided to replace the hard disks with larger ones and wants to make sure when they transfer the data to the new drive no compression information gets copied.

16

1. Uncompress the D drive on your computer.

    a. Choose Start→Programs→Accessories→ System Tools→DriveSpace.

    b. In the DriveSpace dialog box, **select the D drive.**

    c. **Choose Drive→Uncompress.**

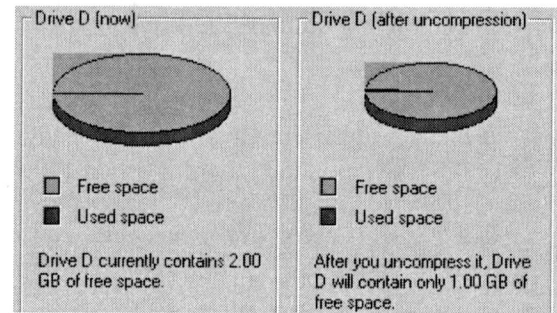

    d. **Click Start.**

    e. If neccessary, **click Uncompress Now.**

        Uncompressing the D drive will take several minutes.

    f. **Click Yes** to remove the compression driver from memory.

    g. **Click Close.**

    h. **Close DriveSpace.**

    i. When prompted, **click Yes** to restart the computer.

2. **Verify that the D drive is no longer compressed.**

a. From the boot menu, **choose Microsoft Windows.**

b. **Log on as Admin#.**

c. In Win98-1, **check the free space on D.** You should see that you now have only 1 GB of free space.

d. **Close Win98-1.**

Review Questions

1. When uncompressing a drive, how can you be sure everything will fit on the drive when uncompressed?

_____

2. To be safe, prior to compressing or uncompressing a drive, what should you do?

_____

3. Because drive compression saves space, why would you not want to compress all the drives on your computer?

_____

_____

_____

4. What utility is used on a Windows 98 computer to uncompress a drive?

_____

5. Will Fdisk recognize a Windows 9x compressed drive?

_____

_____

16

EXERCISE 16-4

Converting an Existing Windows 98 FAT Partition to FAT32

Activity Time:

15 minutes

Objective:

To convert a FAT-formatted drive to the FAT32 file system to improve file system performance.

Scenario:

The AlphaBeta Company has many Windows 98 computers where space has become an issue. As a consultant, you interviewed many of the users and found that while they store a lot of files on the D drives of their hard disks, the size of the files they typically store is fairly small. You believe the cluster size being used on the FAT16 partition may be increasing the amount of space each file consumes. You want to reduce the cluster size in hopes of regaining quite a bit of unused space on each computer for your client.

What You Do	How You Do It
1. Convert the D drive to FAT32.	a. Choose Start→Programs→Accessories→ System Tools→Drive Converter (FAT32).
Do not convert the C drive to FAT32.	b. Click Next.
	c. In the Drives list box, **select the D drive.**

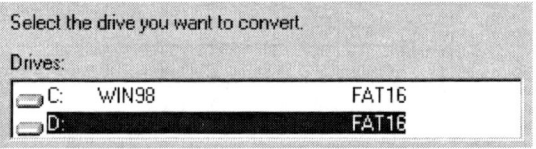

	d. Click Next.
	e. If necessary, **click OK** to close any anti-virus messages.

f. **Click OK** to verify you understand the warning regarding OS limitations with FAT32 while dual-booting a computer.

 If you are running a previous version of MS-DOS, Windows, or Windows NT, you will not be able to access a FAT32 drive while running those operating systems.

g. **Click Next twice** to advance the Disk Converter wizard.

h. **Click Next** to restart your computer in MS-DOS mode and begin the conversion.

i. From the boot menu, **choose Microsoft Windows.**

j. **Log on as Admin#.**

k. **Click Finish** to close the Drive Converter (FAT32) wizard.

The conversion was successful.

---

2. **Verify the drive has been converted to FAT32.**

a. **Open Windows Explorer.**

b. **Right-click the D drive and choose Properties.** The File System reads FAT32.

Type: Local Disk
File system: FAT32

c. **Click OK.**

d. **Close Windows Explorer.**

16

Review Questions

1. After converting a 1.5 GB FAT partition to FAT32, you notice that there is more free space. How can this be?

   _____

   _____

   _____

2. What is the name of the Drive Converter(FAT32) executable file?

   _____

3. Why does Drive Converter scan your programs and utilities prior to converting a drive to FAT32?

   _____

4. With all the performance benefits of FAT32, what are some reasons why you might not want to convert to FAT32?

   _____

   _____

5. Why would you convert a drive to FAT32 instead of reformatting it using FAT32?

   _____

   _____

EXERCISE 16-5

Defragmenting a Hard Disk in Windows 98

Activity Time:

10 minutes to 60 minutes

Objective:

To defragment a hard disk to improve disk performance.

Scenario:

Some of the users at your client, AlphaBeta Company, have been complaining that their Windows 98 computers have slowed down to a crawl. They say that it takes forever to load the operating system at startup. Some application startup times are much slower than others, and the computer takes a long time to respond to their input. After interviewing the users, you discover that the computers get passed from an exiting employee to their replacement. Preparation of the computer for the new employee only includes deleting personal files of the exiting employee and removing any unnecessary or unauthorized programs applications. You suspect that the hard disks are very fragmented causing inefficient storage of files. Each computer has a single C partition on its hard disk.

16

1. **Defragment your computer.**	a. **Choose Start→Programs→Accessories→ System Tools→Disk Defragmenter.**
	b. In the Select Drive dialog box, the C drive is selected by default. **Click OK** to start the defragmentation process.
	c. **Click Show Details** to graphically display the defragmentation process.
	d. **Click Legend** to display the legend for the various graphics you see in the Show Details window.

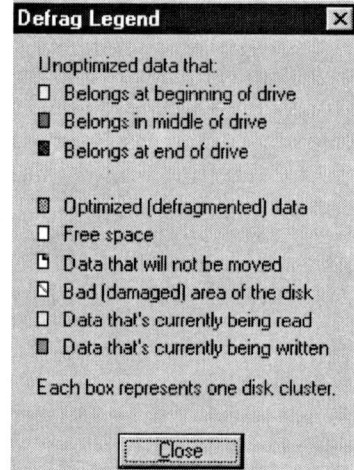

	e. **Click Close** to close the Defrag Legend dialog box.
	f. **Click Yes** to close Disk Defragmenter when defragmentation is finished.

Review Questions

1. Which System Tool is used to defragment a hard drive on a Windows 9x computer?

   _____

2. While watching Disk Defragmenter you notice a bunch of symbols being moved around but don't know what they mean. How can you find out?

   _____

3. Is it possible that after running Disk Defragmenter you might see extra free space on the drive?

   _____

4. You are defragmenting a drive but don't see the graphical display of the process going on. What should you do?

   _____

5. What do the little boxes represent as they move around the Disk Defragmenter Details screen?

   _____

16

Lab 16-1

Managing Disk Resources in Windows 98

Activity Time:

1 hour(s)

Objective:

To perform common disk-management tasks on a Windows 98 computer with multiple disk partitions.

Setup:

You cannot key this lab immediately following the Managing Disk Resources in Windows 9x chapter. To key this lab outside of the pre-established classroom environment, you will need:

- A computer with a 3 GB or larger hard disk that contains one 2 GB partition with a default installation of Windows 98 and the rest left as free space.

Scenario:

You've been called to AlphaBeta Company to help get more life out of some older Windows 98 computers. The users have been complaining that they just don't have enough space to store their files. However, the company can't afford to upgrade the components in the computers at this time. When you examine the computers in question, you see that the hard disks are larger than 2 GB in size, but Windows 98 was installed using FAT and the extra disk space was never partitioned and formatted for use. When asked, the company representative also tells you that according to his knowledge, the computers' hard disks have never been defragmented.

 After you have finished the lab, you can refer to the Managing Disk Resources in Windows 98 Lab Results.txt file to check your work.

1. **Create a new extended partition from the remaining free space on the hard disk.**

---

2. **Create a logical drive within the extended partition that uses all the available disk space.**

---

3. **Format the new partition to FAT32.**

---

4. **Convert the existing partition to FAT32.**

---

5. **Defragment the hard disk.**

___

16

CHAPTER 17

Connecting to Internet and Intranet Resources

Activities included in this chapter:

- Exercise 17-1 Creating a Dial-up Connection on a Windows 2000 Computer
- Exercise 17-2 Creating a Virtual Private Networking Connection on a Windows 2000 Computer
- Exercise 17-3 Configuring a Web Browser on a Windows 2000 Computer
- Exercise 17-4 Configuring Outlook Express on a Windows 2000 Computer
- Exercise 17-5 Troubleshooting Internet/Intranet Connection Problems
- Lab 17-1 Connecting to Internet and Intranet Resources

Exercise 17-1

Creating a Dial-up Connection on a Windows 2000 Computer

Activity Time:

15 minutes

Objective:

To install modem drivers, and create and configure an outbound dial-up connection.

Setup:

Restart the computer to Windows 2000.

Setup:

Smith Sales and Service's remote access server is running the TCP/IP protocol exclusively. The phone number for access is (585)555–5555.

Scenario:

You work for Smith Sales and Service in the IT department. Many of Smith's employees work from their homes across the United States and dial in to the company's Remote Access Server (RAS) for access to company email and network resources. Jane is a new employee who needs her desktop computer configured for dial-in access from her home in the 315 area code to the company's RAS server. A Cirrus Logic Cirrus Data Fax Voice MDK1414EC2 modem has been installed in her computer, but Windows 2000 did not recognize it and the drivers aren't installed yet. Jane tells you that her phone service is tone and she doesn't dial anything special to dial out.

What You Do	How You Do It
1. Install the Cirrus Logic MDK1414EC2 modem's drivers on your computer.	a. Log on as Admin#.
	b. Open Control Panel.
	c. Double-click Phone And Modem Options.
	d. In the Location Information dialog box, **enter** *315* as the area code.
	e. Verify that Tone Dialing is selected.
	f. Click OK.
	g. Select the Modems tab.
	h. Click Add.
	i. Check Don't Detect My Modem, I Will Select It From A List.

☑ Don't detect my modem; I will select it from a list.

j. Click Next.

k. In the Manufacturers list box, **select Cirrus Logic.**

l. In the Models list box, **select Cirrus Data Fax Voice MDK1414EC2.**

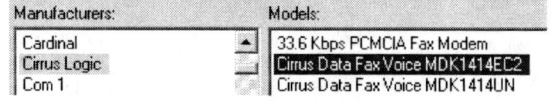

m. Click Next.

17

n. In the Select The Port To Use With This Modem list box, **select one of the available COM ports.**

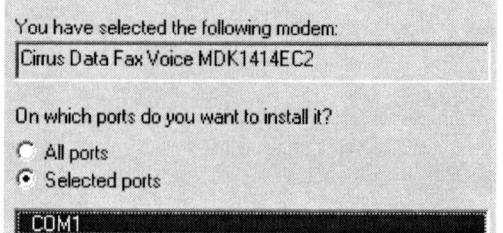

You have selected the following modem:

Cirrus Data Fax Voice MDK1414EC2

On which ports do you want to install it?

○ All ports
● Selected ports

COM1

o. **Click Next.**

p. **Click Finish.**

q. **Click OK** to close the Phone and Modem Options dialog box.

r. **Close Control Panel.**

2. **Create a new connection object to the RAS server.**

    a. Choose Start→Settings→Network and Dial-Up Connections. Double-click Make New Connection.

    b. Click Next.

    c. **Select Dial-Up To Private Network.**

○ **Dial-up to private network**
Connect using my phone line (modem or ISDN).

    d. Click Next.

    e. If necessary, on the Select A Device page, **check the modem you want this connection to use and click Next.**

    f. **Check Use Dialing Rules.**

    g. **Enter *585*** for the area code of the remote access server.

    h. **Enter *555-5555*** as the telephone number for the remote access server.

    i. **Select the United States of America (1).**

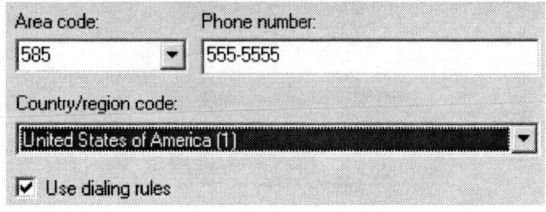

    j. **Click Next.**

    k. **Verify that Create This Connection For All Users is selected.**

Create this connection:
    ○ For all users

17

		l.	**Click Next.**
		m.	Enter *Smith Remote Access* as the name for your connection.
		n.	**Click Finish.**
		o.	**Click Cancel** to close the Connect Smith Remote Access dialog box.

3.	Configure the Smith Remote Access connection to use only the TCP/IP protocol.	a.	**Right-click your connection object and choose Properties.**
		b.	**Select the Networking tab.**
		c.	In the Components Checked Are Used By This Connection box, **verify that only Internet Protocol (TCP/IP) and Client For Microsoft Networks are checked. Uncheck any other protocols.**
		d.	**Click OK** to save your changes.

Review Questions

1. Which option would you select in the Network Connection Wizard if you wanted to dial in to a remote RAS network from a Windows 2000 computer?

_____

2. During setup of a Windows 2000 dial-up connection, you did not see a screen to select a modem. Why not?

_____

3. How can you specify an area code and/or location when setting up a Windows 2000 dial-up connection?

_____

4. When dialing in to a RAS server, will you be able to connect to other computers on the remote network or just the RAS server?

_____

_____

5. When might you select to use the SLIP protocol rather than PPP?

_____

17

Exercise 17-2

Creating a Virtual Private Networking Connection on a Windows 2000 Computer

Activity Time:

10 minutes

Objective:

To create and test an oubound VPN connection.

Setup:

The company's VPN Server's IP address is 192.168.200.200.

Scenario:

You work for Smith Sales and Service in the IT department. Many of Smith's employees work from their homes across the United States and connect to company email and network resources through their Internet Service Providers using a cable modem. Jane is a new employee who needs her desktop computer configured for VPN access from her home to the company's VPN server. Her Internet Service Provider has installed a network card and a cable modem on her desktop.

What You Do	How You Do It
1. Create a new VPN connection object.	a. Double-click Make New Connection. b. Click Next. c. Select Connect To A Private Network Through The Internet.

⦿ **Connect to a private network through the Internet**
Create a Virtual Private Network (VPN) connection or 'tunnel' through the Internet.

	d. Click Next. e. Select Do Not Dial This Initial Connection. f. Click Next. g. Enter *192.168.200.200* as the host name or IP Address for the VPN server.

Host name or IP address (such as microsoft.com or 123.45.6.78):
| 198.168.200.200 |

	h. Click Next. i. Verify that Create This Connection For All Users is selected. j. Click Next. k. Enter *Smith VPN Connection* as the name for your connection. l. Click Finish.

17

2. **Test the VPN connection.**

a. In the Connect Smith VPN Connection dialog box, in the User Name text box, **enter** *Admin#*

b. In the Password dialog box, **enter** *password*

c. **Click Connect.**

d. **Click OK** to close the Connection Complete message box.

e. In the taskbar, **right-click the Smith VPN Connection and choose Disconnect.**

Review Questions

1. What does VPN stand for?

_____

2. What two protocols are available for establishing a VPN connection in a Windows-based environment?

_____

3. When configuring a VPN connection on Windows 2000, what is the Dial Another Connection First check box used for?

_____

_____   _____

4. How will an L2TP connection be secured as data travels across the network?

_____

5. How do you specify which server you want to connect to through a VPN connection?

_____

Exercise 17-3

Configuring a Web Browser on a Windows 2000 Computer

Activity Time:

15 minutes

Objective:

To set up an Internet connection and configure the properties of Internet Explorer.

Data Files:

- C:\Data\Internet Security Policy.htm

Scenario:

The management at AlphaBeta Company has recently realized that the value of allowing their employees to access critical business information located on the Internet outweighs the risks of personal Web browsing on company time. They have hired you to configure all their Windows 2000 computers for Internet access on their company LAN. However, they have created an Internet policy statement that they want presented to the user each time they run Internet Explorer, so all employees are aware of the company's Internet access policy. They have provided the file, Internet Security Policy.htm, to you. The network does not have a proxy server, and the company does not currently have any email accounts.

17

1. Set up an Internet Connection on your computer.	a. Choose Start→Programs→Accessories→ Communications→Internet Connection Wizard.
	b. Select I Want To Set Up My Internet Connection Manually, or I Want To Connect Through A Local Area Network (LAN).
	c. Click Next.
	d. Select I Connect Through A Local Area Network (LAN).

> How do you connect to the Internet?
>
> ○ I connect through a phone line and a modem
>
> ● I connect through a local area network (LAN)

	e. Click Next.
	f. Uncheck Automatic Discovery Of Proxy Server (Recommended) to bypass using a proxy server.
	g. Click Next.
	h. Click No to bypass setting up an Internet Mail account.
	i. Click Next.
	j. Uncheck the To Connect To The Internet Immediately check box, so that Windows 2000 won't attempt to connect to the Internet immediately.
	k. Click Finish.

2. **Set the home page of Internet Explorer to Internet Security Policy.htm**

    a. **Right-click Internet Explorer on the desktop and choose Properties.**

    b. **On the General page, in the Home Page box, in the Address text box, type** *C:\Data\Internet Security Policy.htm*

    c. **Click OK.**

    d. **Open Internet Explorer.** The home page is set to the Internet Security Policy.htm file.

    e. **Close Internet Explorer.**

Review Questions

1. When setting up an Internet connection, which option should you choose if the network you're on is already connected to the Internet?

_____

2. How can you tell if your current Internet connection is using SSL?

_____

3. While typing in some information in Internet Explorer, you notice that a drop down box shows you possible matches to what you are typing. What is causing this?

_____

4. In the Internet Explorer Internet Options dialog box, which Properties tab is used to configure your cookies settings?

_____

17

5. Does a client have to register a certificate in order to support SSL?

_____

_____

Exercise 17-4

Configuring Outlook Express on a Windows 2000 Computer

Activity Time:

15 minutes

Objective:

To configure and test an email account on Outlook Express.

Scenario:

The AlphaBeta Company has grown to a large enough size that it is critical for them to have email capabilities for all their employees. They feel this will allow them to respond much quicker to each other and their customers. They have hired you to install and configure Outlook Express on all their Windows 2000 computers so that all employees can send and receive email.

What You Do	How You Do It
1. **Obtain the email account information.**	
Full name:	
Email address:	
Incoming mail server type:	
Incoming mail server name (if necessary):	
Outgoing mail server name (if necessary):	
Account password:	
2. **Configure Outlook Express to send and receive email.**	a. **Choose Start→Programs→Outlook Express.** Outlook Express prompts you to set up an email account.

17

b.   In the Display Name text box, **type the name for the email account.**

c.   **Click Next.**

d.   In the E-Mail Address text box, **type the user's email address.**

e.   **Click Next.**

f.   From the My Incoming Mail Server Is A _____ Server drop-down list box, **select the incoming mail server type.**

My incoming mail server is a | HTTP | ▼ | server.
POP3
My HTTP mail service provide IMAP ▼
HTTP
Incoming mail (POP3, IMAP or HTTP) server:

g.   If necessary, in the Incoming Mail (POP3, IMAP, or HTTP) Server: text box, **type the name of the incoming server.**

h.   If necessary, in the Outgoing Mail (SMTP) Server: text box, **type the name of the outgoing server.**

i.   **Click Next.**

j.   In the Account Name text box, **enter the user's email address.**

k. In the Password text box, **enter the user's password.**

Account name:	Grace_Williams1@hotmail.com
	For example: someone@microsoft.com
Password:	×××××××××
	☑ Remember password

l. **Click Next.**

m. **Click Finish.**

3. **Test that you can send and receive mail.**

🖈 Work with a partner.

a. **Click the New Mail button.**

b. In the To: text box, **type your partner's email address.**

c. In the Subject text box, **type *Test Email***

d. **Click Send.** When the email from your partner arrives in your inbox, you have verified you can both send and receive emails.

e. **Close Outlook Express.**

Review Questions

1. What are the commonly used email protocols?

2. Which protocol is used to send email?

17

3. You are going to be checking your email from multiple computers, each with different operating systems and software. What type of client email software would be the best to use?

_____

_____

_____

_____

4. What is the free email client installed with Windows products?

_____

5. What information is typically required to configure email client software?

_____

_____

EXERCISE 17-5

Troubleshooting Internet/Intranet Connection Problems

Activity Time:

25 minutes

Objective:

To determine the proper troubleshooting approach for various Internet or intranet connectivity problem scenarios.

Scenario:

AlphaBeta Company has recently implemented Internet/intranet connectivity on all their Windows 2000 computers. Each computer is running Outlook Express as its default mail client and Internet Explorer as its default Web browser. Because this is a new implementation, several problems have cropped up. You receive your first trouble ticket submitted by John.

---

1. John has called to complain that he can't access the cnn.com site from Internet Explorer.

    What questions would you ask to define the problem?

17

2.	John tells you that last night before he left he could access Internet sites through Internet Explorer. Today he can't access any sites. When he tries to send email, that fails as well. No one has made any changes to the configuration of his computer between last night and this morning.

You arrive at John's desk and attempt to ping an external Internet site by name. You receive an unknown host message. You attempt to ping an external site by IP address. You receive three request timed out messages.

What do you suspect is the problem?

_____

3.	**What are your next steps for troubleshooting John's computer?**

_____

4.	Ken is working in email. He has several items in his Outbox. When he clicks the Send/Receive mail button in his email client, Ken gets new messages from the mail server, but the messages in his Outbox won't transfer to the mail server. Karen, who sits next to Ken, sends Ken an email and it arrives in his Inbox just fine.

What do you suspect is the problem?

_____

5.	Carolyn, who works for Human Resources, has been accessing payroll data on the HR department's intranet Web server. She clicks a link entitled Performance Reviews and receives a message "You Are Not Authorized To View This Page."

What do you suspect is the problem?

_____

Review Questions

1. What is a Proxy Server?

   _____

   _____

2. What TCP/IP-based command can help determine if a computer on the network is accessible?

   _____

3. What might be the problem if you can successfully ping the IP Address of a remote host but you cannot successfully ping the name of the same remote host?

   _____

   _____

4. Using Outlook Express, you are able to send email but are not able to receive it. What might you check?

   _____

5. A user is experiencing network connectivity problems where she is unable to connect to anything on the network including the Internet. Everyone else's computers are working fine. What should you check first?

   _____

17

LAB 17-1

Connecting to Internet and Intranet Resources

Activity Time:

1 hour(s)

Objective:

To connect to Internet and intranet resources from a Windows 98, Windows 2000, or Windows XP computer.

Data Files:

- ABhome.htm

Setup:

If you will be keying this lab immediately following the Connecting to Internet and Intranet Resources chapter, you should boot into Windows 98 and begin the lab.

If you will be keying this lab outside of the pre-established classroom environment, you will need:

- A networked computer with a default installation of Windows 98, Windows 2000, or Windows XP.

- An email account. This might be an account on a private email server, such as Microsoft Exchange Server, or an account from a free Internet email service that supports Outlook Express, such as Hotmail.

- Internet access, if your mail account is Internet-based.

- Access to the student data files.

Scenario:

AlphaBeta Company is a small, not-for-profit company. They've been operating without Internet access, on donated Windows computers. They recently received a grant so that they can get all their client computers Internet access and email. The staff members, who all work from their homes, are very excited to start using Outlook Express to communicate with each other, and Internet Explorer to do some of their initial research tasks. AlphaBeta purchased a Creative Labs Modem Blaster 28.8 modem for each of the home-based users. The modems have been physically installed in the computers, but Windows does not recognize them and the drivers aren't installed yet.

 You do not need to have an actual modem attached to your computer to perform this lab.

AlphaBeta Company's new remote access server is running the TCP/IP protocol exclusively, with server-assigned addressing information. The phone number for access is (985) 555-5555. The home-based staff members all have tone-based dialing, and don't do anything special to dial out. You've created a simple local home page called ABHome.htm, so that when Internet Explorer opens, it doesn't need to make the dial-in connection to load the home page.

When you've finished the lab, you can refer to the Connecting to Internet and Intranet Resources Lab Results.txt file to check your work.

1. **Manually install the modem driver.**

2. **Create the dial-up connection.**

3. **Set up an Internet connection.**

4. **Configure Outlook Express for your user's email access.**

5. **Configure Internet Explorer to use Outlook Express as its default mail client, and to use the ABHome.htm file as the home page.**

17

CHAPTER 18

Implementing Virus Protection

Activities included in this chapter:

- Exercise 18-1 Installing Norton AntiVirus 2003 on a Windows 98 Computer
- Exercise 18-2 Installing McAfee VirusScan version 7.0 on a Windows 2000 Computer
- Exercise 18-3 Configuring Norton AntiVirus 2003 on a Windows 98 Computer
- Exercise 18-4 Configuring McAfee VirusScan on a Windows 2000 Computer
- Exercise 18-5 Creating a Norton AntiVirus Rescue Disk Set in Windows 98
- Exercise 18-6 Creating a McAfee Virus Scan Emergency Disk in Windows 2000
- Exercise 18-7 Manually Updating Norton AntiVirus Definition Files on a Windows 98 Computer
- Exercise 18-8 Manually Updating McAfee VirusScan Definition Files on a Windows 2000 Computer
- Exercise 18-9 Removing Viruses from Your Computer
- Lab 18-1 Implementing Virus Protection

EXERCISE 18-1

Installing Norton AntiVirus 2003 on a Windows 98 Computer

Activity Time:

30 minutes to 45 minutes

Objective:

To install anti-virus software and perform a virus scan.

 You'll be keying either the Norton AntiVirus or the McAfee VirusScan activities depending on your classroom setup.

Setup:

The installation files for Norton AntiVirus 2003 reside on the company's corporate server, 2000SRV, in the share called AntiVirus.

Scenario:

The company you work for, Jake's Snack Shack, recently implemented Internet connectivity on the few Windows 98 computers it has. Prior to this point, the owner, Jake, wasn't concerned about virus protection on his computers because the threat was so minimal. However, employees now have the ability to download information from the Internet, as well as send and receive email—all of which increases the susceptibility of Jake's company computers. He would like you to protect his computers against this threat and has purchased licenses for Symantec's Norton AntiVirus 2003 for all his company's computers. There is no need to register the individual copies due to the license agreement Jake has signed with Symantec. You do not need to create a rescue disk set at this time, but you do need to scan for viruses when the installation is complete.

What You Do	How You Do It

1. **Install Norton AntiVirus 2003 on your computer.**

a. **Restart the computer and choose Microsoft Windows from the boot menu.**

b. If necessary, **log on as Admin#.**

c. **Access the \\2000SRV\AntiVirus share.**

d. **Double-click Setup.exe.** Setup updates the operating system files.

e. If prompted, **restart your computer.** From the boot menu, **choose Microsoft Windows.**

f. In the Norton AntiVirus 2003 Setup wizard, **click Next.**

g. **Click I Accept The License Agreement.**

 ⊙ I accept the license agreement

h. **Click Next.**

i. **Click Next** to accept the default destination folder.

j. **Click Next** to begin the installation.

k. **Read the text of the Readme Information and click Next.**

```
Norton AntiVirus 2003 for Windows 98/ME/2000/XP
Copyright 2002 Symantec Corporation.
All rights reserved.
README.TXT                              August 2002
```

18

l. **Click Finish.**

m. **Click Yes** to restart your computer.

n. **Log on as Admin#.** The Norton AntiVirus Infor-
    mation Wizard automatically starts.

2. **Scan for viruses.**

    a. In the Norton AntiVirus Information Wizard, click **Next.**

    b. **Click Skip** to skip registering your product.

    c. **Click Yes** to confirm that you want to skip registering Norton AntiVirus.

    d. Your displayed subscription service expiration date is one year from your installation date. **Click Next.**

Start Date:	Expiration Date:
1/14/03	1/15/04

    e. **Uncheck Run LiveUpdate and Create A Rescue Disk Set.**

    ☐ Run LiveUpdate
       Uses your Internet connection to download the latest virus protection and program updates.

    ☐ Create a Rescue Disk Set
       Copies your computer's critical setup data and startup files to a set of removable disks.

    f. **Click Next.**

    g. **Click Finish.** The virus scan begins.

    h. In the Scan: Summary dialog box, **click Finished.**

Summary	No Infection found
Scan time	9 minute(s) 33 second(s)

Action:	Files	Master Boot Record	Boot Record
Scanned:	20035	1	2
Infected:	0	0	0
Repaired:	0	0	0
Quarantined:	0	-	-
Deleted:	0	-	-

    More Info

    | Finished | More Details |

18

i. The Norton AntiVirus System Status dialog box opens. **Identify any items that need your immediate attention** (they are marked in red).

System Status: Attention ⚠

Security Scanning Features		
✓ Auto-Protect	On	
✓ Email Scanning	On	
✓ Script Blocking	On	
✓ Full System Scan	1/14/03	

Virus Definition Service		
⚠ Virus Definitions	8/19/02	
✓ Subscription Service	1/15/04	
✓ Automatic LiveUpdate	On	

j. **Close the Norton AntiVirus window.**

Review Questions

1. On what operating systems can you install Norton AntiVirus 2003?

2. How much RAM do you need in a Windows 2000 computer in order to install Norton AntiVirus 2003?

3. List three examples of a malicious code attack.

4. During installation, how does Norton AntiVirus make sure that your software has a copy of the latest virus definitions?

_____

5. What is a Trojan Horse?

_____

_____

_____

18

Exercise 18-2

Installing McAfee VirusScan version 7.0 on a Windows 2000 Computer

Activity Time:

30 minutes to 45 minutes

Objective:

To install anti-virus software and perform a virus scan.

Setup:

The installation files for McAfee VirusScan version 7.0 reside on the company's corporate server, 2000SRV, in the share called VirusScan.

Scenario:

The company you work for, Jake's Snack Shack, recently implemented Internet connectivity on all its Windows 2000 computers. Prior to this point, the owner, Jake, wasn't concerned about virus protection on his computers because the threat was so minimal. However, employees now have the ability to download information from the Internet, as well as send and receive email—all of which increase the susceptibility of Jake's company computers. He would like you to protect his computers against this threat and has purchased licenses for McAfee VirusScan Professional for all his company's computers. He does not feel that the personal firewall program is necessary, however, because he has a network firewall installed.

What You Do	How You Do It
1. Install McAfee VirusScan Professional on your computer.	a. Access the \\2000SRV\VirusScan share.
	b. Double-click Setup.
	c. In the McAfee Consumer Products Installation dialog box, click Install VirusScan Professional.
	d. In the McAfee VirusScan Professional Edition dialog box, click Next.

e. In the McAfee End User License Agreement dialog box, from the drop-down list box, **select your country.**

f. **Click Accept.**

g. **Select Custom Installation.**

h. **Click Next.**

i. **Click Next** to accept the default destination directory for McAfee VirusScan program files.

j. **Uncheck Install McAfee Firewall.**

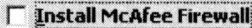

k. **Click Next twice.**

l. **Click Install.**

> Click Install to begin.
>
> If you want to review or change any of your installation settings, click Back. Click Cancel to exit the wizard.

m. **Click Next.**

n. On the Product Registration page, **click Cancel** to skip registering McAfee VirusScan.

o. **Click Finish** to complete the installation and start McAfee VirusScan.

18

p. If the Emergency Disk Wizard starts, **click Cancel.**

q. After the initial scan is done, **click OK** to close the McAfee Virus Scan window.

Review Questions

1. On what operating systems can you install McAfee VirusScan Professional Version 7.0?

   _____

2. How much RAM must a Windows 2000 computer have to support McAfee VirusScan Professional?

   _____

3. What is a worm?

   _____

   _____

   _____

   _____

4. You would like to install McAfee VirusScan on a user's computer, but you don't want to create an emergency disk during the installation. What should you do?

   _____

   _____

5. What installation step must you complete before you can download the virus definition updates for McAfee VirusScan?

   _____

Exercise 18-3

Configuring Norton AntiVirus 2003 on a Windows 98 Computer

Activity Time:

10 minutes

Objective:

To configure anti-virus software with the appropriate options.

Scenario:

You have installed Norton AntiVirus 2003 software on all the Windows 98 computers at Jake's Snack Shack. Users have noticed that since you have installed Norton AntiVirus 2003 on their computers, the computers' performance has slowed down considerably. After researching the configuration options, the IT Director has decided that setting protection to a lower level and disabling the options users do not need will improve performance. The IT Director would like you to make the following changes:

- Disable the Auto-Protect system tray icon.
- Disable Scan Floppy Disk In A: For Boot Viruses When Shutting Down.
- Disable outgoing mail scans.
- Disable the alert when scanning email attachments for worms.
- Change the setting for automatic virus protection updates to notification.

18

What You Do	How You Do It
1. **Make the desired System option changes to Norton AntiVirus on your computer.**	a. From the Start menu, **choose Programs→ Norton AntiVirus→Norton AntiVirus 2003.**
	b. **Click Options.**
	c. Under System, **click Auto-Protect.**
	d. Under How To Stay Protected, **uncheck Show The Auto-Protect Icon In The Tray.**

How to stay protected

☑ Enable Auto-Protect (recommended)
☑ Start Auto-Protect when Windows starts up (recommended)
☐ Show the Auto-Protect icon in the tray

	e. Under System, **click Advanced.**
	f. Under What Activities To Monitor When Using Floppy Disks, **uncheck Scan Floppy Disk In A: For Boot Viruses When Shutting Down.**

What activities to monitor when using floppy disks

☑ Scan floppy disk for boot viruses every time it is mounted
☐ Scan floppy disk in A: for boot viruses when shutting down
☐ Scan all additional floppies on shutdown

2.	**Make the desired Internet option changes to Norton AntiVirus on your computer.**

a.	Under Internet, **click Email.**

b.	Under What To Scan, **uncheck Scan Outgoing Email (Recommended).**

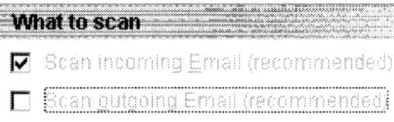

c.	Under Internet, **click LiveUpdate.**

d.	Under How To Keep Your Virus Protection Updated, **select Notify Me When Updates Are Available.**

e.	**Click OK** to save your configuration changes.

f.	**Close Norton AntiVirus.**

Review Questions

1.	Which Norton AntiVirus option configures the software to check your computer's programs for viruses as you run them and monitors your computer for activity that is typical of a virus?

2.	True or False: You cannot configure Norton AntiVirus 2003 to protect instant messenger programs such as AOL Instant Messenger.

18

3.	Which Norton AntiVirus option monitors changes to system files on Windows 98 computers?

4. A user reports that even though he has Norton AntiVirus installed, he did not receive a notification from the software when he received an infected email. What should you check?

_____

5. A user tells you that she doesn't think Norton AntiVirus has the most recent virus definitions. After looking at her software, you've determined that she's right. What should you check to make sure that her definitions are never out of date?

_____

EXERCISE 18-4

Configuring McAfee VirusScan on a Windows 2000 Computer

Activity Time:

10 minutes

Objective:

To configure anti-virus software with the appropriate options.

Scenario:

You have installed McAfee VirusScan software on all the Windows 2000 computers at Jake's Snack Shack. Users have noticed that since you have installed McAfee VirusScan Professional on their computers, the computers' performance has slowed down considerably. After researching the configuration options, the IT Director has decided that setting protection to a lower level and disabling the options users do not need will improve performance. The IT Director would like you to make the following changes:

- Disable scan on outbound files.
- Disable scan floppies: for viruses when shutting down.

In addition, the IT Director is concerned about email. He wants you to make sure that the email system won't carry in any viruses.

18

What You Do	How You Do It

1. **Make the desired System Scan option changes to McAfee Virus Scan on your computer.**

a. From the Start menu, **choose Programs→ McAfee→VirusScan Professional Edition.**

b. Under Tasks, **click Configure Automatic Protection Settings.**

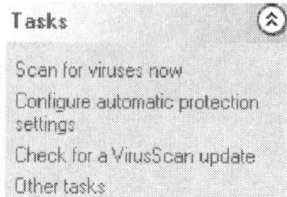

c. **Click Advanced.**

d. On the Detection page for System Scan, in the Scan box, **uncheck Outbound Files.**

e. On the Detection page for System Scan, in the Scan Floppies On box, **uncheck Shutdown.**

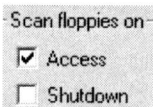

2. **Make the desired E-Mail Scan option changes to McAfee Virus Scan on your computer.**

   a. On the left side of the System Scan Properties dialog box, **click E-Mail Scan.**

   b. **Check Enable Scanning of E-mail Attachments In Microsoft Outlook.**

   ☑ Enable Scanning of e-mail attachments

   c. **Click OK.**

   d. **Close the VirusScan Professional Edition dialog box.**

Review Questions

1. A programmer has asked you to prevent McAfee VirusScan from scanning the folders in which he stores the programs he's developing. What should you do?

   _____

2. Which feature in McAfee VirusScan enables you to prevent scripts from running?

   _____

18

EXERCISE 18-5

Creating a Norton AntiVirus Rescue Disk Set in Windows 98

Activity Time:

30 minutes

Objective:

To create and test an anti-virus rescue disk set.

Setup:

To create a rescue disk set, you will need 8 floppy disks.

Scenario:

You have installed and configured Norton AntiVirus 2003 on all the Windows 98 computers at Jake's Snack Shack. Unfortunately, you've had a problem already with a master boot record virus on one of the computers. You were forced to re-install Windows 98 because you didn't have a set of rescue disks for the computer. You've decided to create a set of rescue disks for each computer.

What You Do	How You Do It
1. Create a rescue disk set for your computer.	a. **Open Norton AntiVirus.**
	b. In the Norton AntiVirus window, **click Rescue.**
	c. **Select drive A.**
	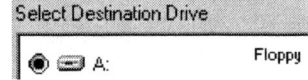
	d. **Click Create.**
	e. If necessary, **click Yes** to disable virus scanning.
	f. From the Basic Rescue Disk List, **select Basic Rescue Boot Floppy Disk and click OK.**
	g. **Label the disks as prompted and click OK.**
	h. **Insert the disks as prompted.**
	i. When finished, **remove the final disk.**

18

2. **Test your rescue disk set.**

    a. **Insert the rescue disk labeled Basic Rescue Boot Floppy Disk into the A drive.**

    b. **Click Restart.** The computer should restart using the rescue boot floppy and display the Rescue Disk screen.

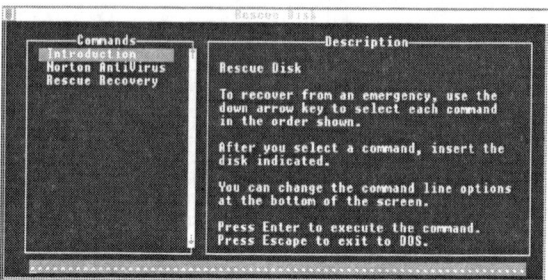

    c. **Press Esc to exit to MS-DOS.**

    d. **Remove your Basic Rescue Boot Floppy Disk from the A drive.**

    e. **Restart your computer.** From the boot menu, **choose Microsoft Windows.**

    f. **Log on as Admin#.**

Review Questions

1. What steps should you use to create a Norton AntiVirus Rescue Disk Set?

    _____

    _____

    _____

    _____

    _____

2.   What information is contained on a Norton AntiVirus Rescue Disk Set?

_____

_____

_____

3.   What information is contained on a Norton Emergency Disk Set?

_____

_____

_____

4.   How can you test a Norton AntiVirus Rescue Disk Set?

_____

_____

18

EXERCISE 18-6

Creating a McAfee Virus Scan Emergency Disk in Windows 2000

Activity Time:

20 minutes

Objective:

To create and test a virus scan emergency disk.

Setup:

To create an emergency disk, you will need a floppy disk.

Scenario:

You have installed and configured McAfee VirusScan on all the Windows 2000 computers at Jake's Snack Shack. Unfortunately, you've had a problem already with a virus on one of the computers that prevented you from booting into Windows 2000. You were forced to re-install Windows 2000 because you didn't have an emergency disk for the computer. You've decided to create an emergency disk for each computer.

What You Do	How You Do It

1. Create an emergency disk for the computer.

    a. Open McAfee VirusScan Professional.

    b. Under Tasks, click Other Tasks.

    c. Click McAfee Emergency Disk.

 McAfee Emergency Disk

    d. In the Emergency Disk Wizard, click Next.

    e. Click Next to format your emergency disk with NAI-OS.

> Your emergency disk will be formatted using the NAI-OS. The NAI-OS will give you full protection from boot sector viruses on NTFS and FAT-32 partitions as well as file scanning capabilities on FAT-16 partitions.

    f. Click Next.

    g. Insert a blank high-density disk in drive A.

    h. Click Next.

    i. When the disk is created, click Finish.

> **An Emergency Disk has been created.**
>
> - Label it -"*McAfee Emergency Boot Disk*".
>
> - Write protect it. To write protect the disk, open the write-protect notch in the upper corner of the disk.
>
> - To test your Emergency Disk, restart your computer with the disk in the A: drive. When you get to the A: prompt, type C: and press the ENTER key to access your hard drive. If you can access your hard drive in this test your Emergency Disk is functioning properly.
>
> - Store the disk in a safe place.

18

j. Remove the disk, label it, and write-protect it.

k. Close the VirusScan Professional window.

2. **Test your emergency disk.**

   a. **Close all open programs.**

   b. **Insert the emergency disk into the A drive.**

   c. **Shut down and power off the computer.**

   d. **Turn on your computer.** The computer restarts using the emergency disk and the McAfee Virus Removal Tool opens.

   e. **Enter Y** to confirm that you performed a cold boot of the computer.

```
[==============================================================]
|                NETWORK ASSOCIATES VIRUS REMOVAL TOOL         |
|                                                              |
|  THIS DISKETTE IS USED TO SIMPLIFY THE TASK OF REMOVING A    |
|  VIRUS FROM YOUR COMPUTER.  IT IS IMPORTANT TO ENSURE THAT   |
|  YOU COLD BOOTED YOUR MACHINE BEFORE USING THIS DISKETTE.    |
|  A COLD BOOT MEANS THAT THE POWER TO THE COMPUTER IS TURNED  |
|  OFF AND THEN TURNED ON WITH THIS DISKETTE IN THE A: DRIVE.  |
[==============================================================]
Did you cycle the power off and on (Y/N)?
```

   f. **Press any key** to continue. When virus scanning begins, the disk is working properly.

   g. **Turn off the computer** to stop the virus scanning.

   h. **Remove your emergency disk from the A drive.**

   i. **Restart your computer.**

   j. From the boot menu, **choose Windows 2000 Professional.**

   k. **Log on as Admin#.**

18

Review Questions

1. What information is contained on a McAfee Emergency Disk Set?

   _____

   _____

   _____

2. What is the purpose of BOOTSCAN.EXE?

   _____

   _____

3. What steps do you use to create a McAfee Emergency Disk Set?

   _____

   _____

   _____

4. How can you test a McAfee Emergency Disk Set?

   _____

A+ Certification Troubleshooting and Repair Lab Guide, Third Edition

Exercise 18-7

Manually Updating Norton AntiVirus Definition Files on a Windows 98 Computer

Activity Time:

15 minutes

Objective:

To peform a manual update to obtain the latest virus definition files for anti-virus software.

Scenario:

You've just read about a new virus threat on Symantec's Web site at http://securityresponse.symantec.com. Symantec has updated their virus definition files to scan for this virus. You want to make sure that all the Windows 98 computers at Jake's Snack Shack are protected from this nasty virus immediately.

18

What You Do	How You Do It
1. Manually update your Norton AntiVirus definition files.	a. Open Norton AntiVirus.

b. In the Norton AntiVirus window, **click the LiveUpdate icon** (at the top of the window).

c. **Click Next** to check for updates.

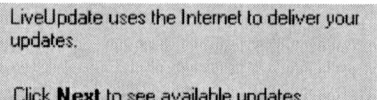

d. **Click Next** to download and install updates.

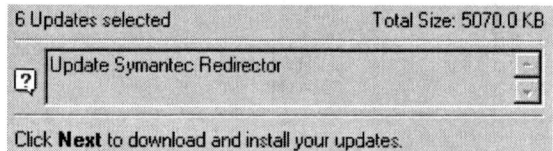

e. **Close the Norton AntiVirus window.**

f. **Click Finish.**

g. **Click OK** to reboot the computer.

Review Questions

1. In what scenario might you manually update the virus definition files in Norton AntiVirus?

   _____

   _____

2. How do you manually update virus definitions in Norton AntiVirus?

   _____

3. Where does Symantec publish information about new virus threats?

   _____

EXERCISE 18-8

Manually Updating McAfee VirusScan Definition Files on a Windows 2000 Computer

Activity Time:

15 minutes

Objective:

To peform a manual update to obtain the latest virus definition files for anti-virus software.

Scenario:

You've just read about a new virus threat on McAfee's Web site at **http://www.webimmune.net**. McAfee has updated their virus definition files to scan for this virus. You want to make sure that all the Windows 2000 computers at Jake's Snack Shack are protected from this nasty virus immediately.

18

What You Do	How You Do It
1. Manually update your McAfee VirusScan definition files.	a. **Open McAfee VirusScan Professional Edition.**
	b. **Under Tasks, click Check For A VirusScan Update.** The McAfee Instant Updater dialog box opens.

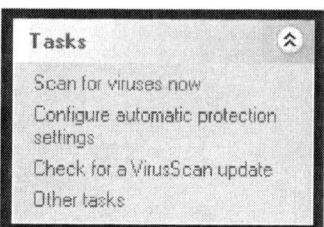

c. If any updates are found, **click Update** to download and install the available updates.

d. **Click Finish.**

e. When the automatic scan is complete, **close the McAfee Instant Updater dialog box.**

Review Questions

1. How do you manually update virus definitions in McAfee AntiVirus?

_____

2. Where does McAfee publish information about new virus threats?

_____

EXERCISE 18-9

Removing Viruses from Your Computer

Activity Time:

15 minutes

Objective:

To determine the proper procedures to follow to disinfect computers that have been attacked by viruses.

Scenario:

You've installed virus protection software on all the computers at Jake's Snack Shack. You feel confident that the computers are protected. However, support calls have come in reporting viruses. You need to respond and get the users back up and working.

---

1. Naomi calls the Help Desk to tell you that she was trying to read an email attachment she received. She now has a Norton AntiVirus alert on her Windows 98 system telling her there has been a change in her system files.

   What is your response?

---

2. Steve calls the Help Desk to tell you he downloaded a program from an Internet site and now his Windows 2000 computer won't boot. He assures you he was running his Norton AntiVirus program all along.

   What is your response?

---

3. Hank calls the Help Desk to tell you that McAfee VirusScan found a virus on his computer and he chose to clean the file. His Windows 2000 computer is functioning just fine.

   What is your response?

18

---

4. Pat calls the Help Desk to report he's getting a McAfee VirusScan alert. You get to Pat's Windows XP computer and choose to clean the infected file. VirusScan reports that the file cannot be cleaned, so you quarantine the file. You look on McAfee's **www.webimmune.net** site, but you can't find any information on this virus. What is your response?

Review Questions

1. What feature do you use in Norton AntiVirus to remove a virus?

2. Where does Norton AntiVirus place files that it detects as infected with a virus?

3. What step should you take first if Norton AntiVirus displays an alert stating that a file is infected?

4. What options does McAfee VirusScan give you when it alerts you to an infected file?

5. If you suspect that a file is infected with a new, unknown virus and you're using McAfee VirusScan, what should you do?

Lab 18-1

Implementing Virus Protection

Activity Time:

1 hour(s)

Objective:

To implement typical virus-protection measures on a Windows 98, Windows 2000, or Windows XP computer.

Data Files:

- FixKlez.com

- W32_Klez Removal Tool.doc

- W32_Klez_E@mm.doc

Setup:

If you will be keying this lab immediately following the Implementing Virus Protection chapter, boot into Windows 98 and begin the lab.

If you will be keying this lab outside of the pre-established classroom environment, you will need:

- A computer with a default installation of Windows 98, Windows 2000, or Windows XP.

- A copy of Norton AntiVirus 2003.

- Access to the student data files.

- Internet access, so that you can obtain the latest virus definition files from the Symantec security Web site.

Scenario:

AlphaBeta Company was hit hard by the W32.Klez.E@mm worm. They've called you for assistance in recovering their Windows computers. They have purchased licenses for Norton AntiVirus 2003. The company has asked you to check each computer for the worm, remove the worm if you find it, and install Norton AntiVirus 2003 on all the computers. They want to make sure that their clients are automatically getting protection updates at least every week to help prevent an attack of this scope in the future.

18

You have already searched for information regarding this worm on Symantec's Security Response Web site. You found and downloaded two reference documents: W32_Klez_E@mm. doc and W32_Klez Removal Tool.doc; and a search and removal tool, FixKlez.com.

When you've finished the lab, you can refer to the Implementing Virus Protection Lab Results.txt file to check your work.

1. **Read the W32_Klez_E@mm.doc file for general information on the Klez worm.**

2. **Read the W32_Klez Removal Tool.doc file for instructions on using the FixKlez.com tool.**

3. Following the directions in the W32_Klez Removal Tool.doc file, **run FixKlez.com.**

 If you actually find the W32_Klez_E@mm worm, observe the way the tool repairs the problem.

4. **Install Norton AntiVirus 2003.**

5. **Obtain the latest virus definiton files.**

6. **Scan the computer for viruses.**

7. **Enable LiveUpdate.**

CHAPTER 19

Preparing for Disaster Recovery

Activities included in this chapter:

- Exercise 19-1 Creating Boot Disks
- Exercise 19-2 Creating an Emergency Repair Disk
- Exercise 19-3 Installing the Recovery Console
- Exercise 19-4 Backing Up Data in Windows 2000
- Exercise 19-5 Backing Up the System State Data
- Exercise 19-6 Backing Up a Registry Key with Registry Editor
- Exercise 19-7 Preparing an ASR Backup Set
- Lab 19-1 Preparing for Disaster Recovery

Exercise 19-1

Creating Boot Disks

Activity Time:

1 hour(s)

Objective:

To create and test an MS-DOS boot disk, a Windows 98 startup disk, and a Windows 2000 boot disk.

Setup:

You will need three floppy disks to complete this activity.

The Windows 98 installation files are in the C:\Win98 folder on your computer's hard disk.

Scenario:

As an A+ technician, you want to be prepared for any emergency such as computers that won't boot. To be prepared, you need to have boot disks that you can use to boot any operating system, including MS-DOS, Windows 98, Windows 2000, Windows XP, or Windows NT. On the MS-DOS boot disk, you would like to include the files necessary for changing file attributes, formatting partitions, editing files, creating or deleting partitions, scanning disks for errors, and for transferring the operating system files.

What You Do	How You Do It
1. In Windows 98, **create an MS-DOS boot disk.**	a. **Restart the computer and choose Microsoft Windows from the boot menu.**
	b. **Log on as Admin#.**
	c. **Open Windows Explorer.**
	d. **Insert a floppy disk into the floppy disk drive.**
	e. **Right-click 3 1/2 Floppy (A:) and choose Format.**

f. Below Other Options, **check Copy System Files Only.**

```
Other options
Label:
[                              ]

☐ No label
☑ Display summary when finished
☑ Copy system files
```

g. **Click Start.**

h. When the format is complete, **click Close** to close the Format Results dialog box.

i. **Click Close** to close the Format dialog box.

j. **Select the C:\Windows\Command folder.**

k. **Choose View→Folder Options.**

l. **Select the View tab.**

m. Below Hidden Files, **choose Show All Files.**

```
📁 Hidden files
   ○ Do not show hidden files
   ○ Do not show hidden or system files
   ⦿ Show all files
```

n. **Uncheck Hide File Extensions For Known File Types.**

```
☐ Hide file extensions for known file types
```

19

o. **Click OK.**

p. From C:\Windows\Command, **copy the follow-**

ing files to the boot disk:

- Attrib.exe
- Edit.com
- Edit.hlp
- Fdisk.exe
- Format.com
- Scandisk.exe
- Scandisk.ini
- Sys.com

    q.   **Close Windows Explorer.**

 If your computer is configured to boot from hard disk before a floppy disk, you won't be able to test the boot disk. Reconfigure the computer to support booting from floppy disk before attempting to boot from a hard disk.

2.   **Test the MS-DOS boot disk.**

    a.   **Verify that you have the boot disk in the floppy drive.**

    b.   From the Start menu, **choose Shutdown.**

    c.   **Select Restart.**

    d.   **Click OK.**

    e.   When the computer restarts, **you will see an MS-DOS prompt displayed** if the boot disk you created works properly.

    f.   **Remove the boot disk from the floppy drive.**

    g.   **Label the floppy disk "MS-DOS boot disk"**

---

3.   **Create a Windows 98 Startup disk.**

a.   **Restart the computer and choose Microsoft Windows from the boot menu.**

b.   **Log on as Admin#.**

c.   **In the Control Panel, double-click Add/ Remove Programs.**

d.   **Select the Startup Disk tab.**

e.   **Click Create Disk.**

f.   **When prompted to insert the Windows 98 CD-ROM, click OK.**

g.   **In the Copy Files From text box, type C:\Win98 and click OK** to install the necessary files from the copy of the Windows 98 CD-ROM on your hard disk.

h.   **Insert a floppy disk into the floppy disk drive.**

i.   **Click OK.**

j.   **When Windows 98 completes creating the Startup disk, click OK to close the Add/ Remove Programs Properties dialog box.**

k.   **Close Control Panel.**

19

4. **Test the Windows 98 Startup disk.**

    a.   **Verify that you have the Startup disk in the floppy drive.**

    b.   **Restart the computer** (from the Start menu, choose Shutdown. Select Restart and click OK).

    c.   From the Startup menu, **choose Start Computer With CD-ROM Support.**

    d.   **You will see an MS-DOS prompt** if the computer boots successfully with the Startup disk.

    e.   **Remove the boot disk from the floppy drive.**

    f.   **Label the floppy disk "Windows 98 Startup disk"**

5.   **Create a Windows 2000 boot disk.**

a.   **Restart the computer and choose Windows 2000 Professional from the boot menu.**

b.   **Log on as Admin#.**

c.   **Open Windows Explorer.**

d.   **Insert a floppy disk into the floppy disk drive.**

e.   **Right-click 3 1/2 Floppy (A:) and choose Format.**

f.   **Check Quick Format** to reduce the amount of time required to format the floppy disk.

g.   **Click Start.**

h.   **Click OK** to confirm that you want to format the disk.

i.   When the format is complete, **click OK.**

j.   **Click Close** to close the Format A:\ dialog box.

k.   In Windows Explorer, **select the C drive.**

l.   **Choose Tools→Folder Options.**

m.   **Select the View tab.**

n.   Below Hidden Files And Folders, **select Show Hidden Files And Folders.**

o.   **Uncheck Hide File Extensions For Known File Types.**

19

p. **Uncheck Hide Protected Operating System Files (Recommended).**

q. **Click Yes** to confirm.

r. **Click OK.**

s. From C:\, **copy the following files to the boot disk:**
   - Boot.ini
   - Bootsect.dos (if it exists)
   - Ntbootdd.sys (if it exists)
   - Ntdetect.com
   - Ntldr

t. **Close Windows Explorer.**

---

6. **Test the Windows 2000 boot disk.**

a. **Verify that the boot disk is in the floppy disk drive.**

b. From the Start menu, **choose Shut Down.**

c. From the drop-down list, **select Restart and click OK.**

d. From the boot menu, **choose Windows 2000 Professional.** The computer boots successfully from the boot disk if Windows 2000 loads properly.

e. **Remove the boot disk from the floppy drive.**

f. **Label the boot disk "Windows 2000 boot disk"**

Review Questions

1. You want to create a boot disk in Windows 98 that will also enable you to partition and format hard disks. What should you do?

   _____

   _____

   _____

   _____

2. What Control Panel applet do you use to create a Windows 98 startup disk?

   _____

3. What files must you copy to a boot disk for Windows 2000?

   _____

4. How do you create an MS-DOS boot disk in Windows XP?

   _____

   _____

5. How do you verify that a boot disk works?

   _____

19

Exercise 19-2

Creating an Emergency Repair Disk

Activity Time:

15 minutes

Objective:

To create an ERD for a Windows 2000 computer.

Scenario:

One of your clients is an elementary school. You're responsible for keeping all the Windows 2000 computers at the school up and running. All the computers are configured identically. You want to be prepared for any emergency, including a computer that has corrupted files that require repair.

What You Do	How You Do It
1. Create an emergency repair disk.	a. **Verify that you're logged on to Windows 2000 as Admin#.**
	b. From the Start menu, **choose Programs→ Accessories→System Tools→Backup.**
	c. **Insert a blank floppy disk into the floppy disk drive.**
	d. **Click Emergency Repair Disk.**

Emergency Repair Disk
This option helps you create an Emergency Repair Disk that you can use to repair and restart Windows if it is damaged. This option does not back up your files or programs, and it is not a replacement for regularly backing up your system.

e. **Check Also Backup The Registry To The Repair Directory** to store a backup copy of the emergency repair disk information on the computer's hard disk.

☑ Also backup the registry to the repair directory. This backup can be used to help recover your system if the registry is damaged.

f. **Click OK** to create the disk.

g. **Click OK** to close the Emergency Repair Diskette message box.

h. **Close Backup.**

i. **Remove the floppy disk, label it, and store it in a safe place.**

Review Questions

1. What utility do you use in Windows 2000 to create an Emergency Repair Disk?

_____

2. In what folder does Windows 2000 store a backup copy of the necessary repair information when you create an Emergency Repair Disk?

_____

3. What other disks might you need to create if you need to perform an emergency repair on a computer?

_____

4. What command should you use to create installation boot disks for Windows 2000?

_____

5. What command should you use to create an Emergency Repair Disk for Windows NT that includes a current copy of the user accounts database?

_____

EXERCISE 19-3

Installing the Recovery Console

Activity Time:

20 minutes

Objective:

To install the Windows XP Recovery Console as a startup option, and test the Recovery Console installation.

Setup:

The Windows XP Professional installation files are located in the \\2000srv\WinXP share on the classroom server.

Scenario:

One of your clients is an elementary school. In addition to keeping all the Windows 2000 computers at the school up and running, you're also responsible for managing the Windows XP computers. You want to be prepared for any emergency on the Windows XP computers. Having the Recovery Console installed before you encounter problems will make it easier for you to repair the computer in the event of a problem.

19

What You Do	How You Do It
1. **Install the Recovery Console as a startup option.**	a. **Restart the computer and choose Windows XP Professional from the boot menu.**
	b. **Log on as Admin#.**
	c. From the Start menu, **choose Run.**
	d. In the Open text box, **type \\2000srv\WinXP\ i386\Winnt32.exe#/cmdcons**
	e. **Click OK.**
	f. **Click Yes** to confirm that you want to install the Recovery Console.
	If your computer is connected to the Internet, Windows Setup will automatically connect to the Internet and download updated Windows XP Professional installation files from the Microsoft Web site.
	g. When the Recovery Console installation is complete, **click OK.**

2. **Test the Recovery Console installation.**

    a. **Shut down and restart the computer.**

    b. From the boot menu, **select Microsoft Windows Recovery Console.**

    c. When prompted, **enter** 2 (the number assigned to the Windows XP professional installation).

    d. When you're prompted for Administrator's password, **enter** `password`

    e. **Enter** `exit` to exit the Recovery Console and restart the computer.

    f. **Select Windows 2000 Professional from the boot menu.**

Review Questions

1. What software will you need to install the Recovery Console on a Windows XP computer?

2. What command do you use to install the Recovery Console?

3. You plan to install the Recovery Console on a computer that's configured to dual-boot between Windows 2000 and Windows XP. Which version of Windows' installation files should you use?

4. How can you verify that the Recovery Console is installed correctly?

5. True or False: When you access a Windows installation using the Recovery Console, you don't have to specify a user name or password.

19

EXERCISE 19-4

Backing Up Data in Windows 2000

Activity Time:

15 minutes

Objective:

To use the Windows Backup program to back up user data.

Data Files:

* D:\Data\Personnel

Setup:

Restart the computer. From the boot menu, choose Windows 2000.

Scenario:

One of your clients is concerned about the personnel records she keeps on her computer. She would like you to show her how she can make backup copies of the files to floppy disk. She stores all personnel records in files and folders within the D:\Data\Personnel folder.

What You Do	How You Do It

1. **Back up the D:\Data\Personnel folder** (including all files and folders within it).

    a. **Log on as Admin#.**

    b. **Insert a floppy disk into the floppy disk drive.**

    c. From the Start menu, **choose Programs→ Accessories→System Tools→Backup.**

    d. **Click Backup Wizard.**

    e. **Click Next.**

    f. **Select Back Up Selected Files, Drives, Or Network Data.**

Select what you want to back up:

    ○ Back up everything on my computer

    ● Back up selected files, drives, or network data

    ○ Only back up the System State data

    g. **Click Next.**

    h. Below What To Back Up, **expand Win2000-# and then the D drive.**

    i. **Expand the D:\Data folder.**

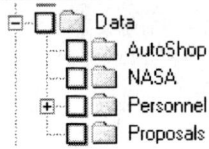

    j. **Check Personnel.**

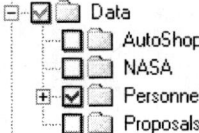

k. **Click Next.**

l. In the Backup Media Or File Name text box,
type *A:\personnel.bkf*

```
Backup media or file name:
A:\personnel.bkf
```

m. **Click Next.**

n. **Click Finish.**

---

2. **View the Backup Report to check for
any errors.**

a. When the backup completes, **click Report.**

b. **Verify that the backup completed and that
four files were backed up.**

```
Backup started on 1/16/2003 at 3:34 PM.
Backup completed on 1/16/2003 at 3:34 PM.
Directories: 4
Files: 4
Bytes: 8,139
Time:  4 seconds
```

c. **Close Notepad.**

d. **Click Close** to close the Backup Progress dialog
box.

e. **Close Backup.**

f. **Remove the floppy disk and label it.**

Review Questions

1. What happens to the Archive attribute of a file when Windows 2000 backs it up during a full backup?

   _____

2. What happens to the Archive attribute of a file when Windows 2000 backs it up during an incremental backup?

   _____

3. What permissions must you have to back up a file in Windows 2000?

   _____

   _____

4. How can you schedule a backup in Windows 2000?

   _____

5. List three types of backup media to which you can back up in Windows 2000.

   _____

   _____

19

EXERCISE 19-5

Backing Up the System State Data

Activity Time:

20 minutes

Objective:

To back up the System State Data on a Windows 2000 computer.

Setup:

You will need approximately 400 MB of free space on your C drive to complete the backup.

Scenario:

One of your clients uses his computer 100 percent of the time to do his job. His computer uses the Windows 2000 operating system. He is very concerned about a computer crash. He wants to make sure that you will be able to reconstruct his computer as quickly as possible in the event of an operating system failure.

1. Create a folder for storing the System State Data backup.	a. Open Windows Explorer.
	b. Select the C drive.
	c. Right-click the C drive and choose Properties.
	d. Verify that you have enough free disk space to store the System State Data backup.

■ Used space:	1,395,195,904 bytes	1.29 GB
▨ Free space:	751,271,936 bytes	716 MB

	e. Click Cancel to close the Properties dialog box.
	f. Choose File→New→Folder.
	g. Type *Backup* and press Enter.
	h. Close Windows Explorer.

19

2. **Back up the System State Data.**

    a.   From the Start menu, **choose Programs→ Accessories→System Tools→Backup.**

    b.   **Click Backup Wizard.**

    c.   **Click Next.**

    d.   **Select Only Back Up The System State Data.**

Select what you want to back up:

- ○ Back up everything on my computer
- ○ Back up selected files, drives, or network data
- ● Only back up the System State data

    e.   **Click Next.**

    f.   In the Backup Media Or File Name text box, **type *C:\Backup\SystemState.bkf***

    g.   **Click Next.**

    h.   **Click Finish.** You can see the amount of time and size of the backup in the Backup Progress dialog box.

Device:	System State		
Media name:	Media created 1/16/2003 at 3:44 PM		
Status:	Backing up files from disk...		
Progress:	■		
	Elapsed:		Estimated remaining:
Time:		2 sec.	1 min., 6 sec.
Processing:	System State\...OSOFT SHARED\VGX\vgx.dll		
	Processed:		Estimated:
Files:		44	1,633
Bytes:		6,573,201	224,216,729

i. When the backup is complete, **click Close.**

j. **Close Backup.**

Review Questions

1. What is system state data in Windows 2000?

   _____

   _____

2. How much space does a backup of system state data require?

   _____

19

Exercise 19-6

Backing Up a Registry Key with Registry Editor

Activity Time:

10 minutes

Objective:

To back up a Registry key by exporting it from Registry Editor.

Scenario:

After researching a problem one of your clients is experiencing in Windows 2000, you have determined that the only way you can repair the problem is by editing the Registry. You need to make a change to the HKEY_LOCAL_MACHINE\Software\Microsoft key. Before you make this change, you want to back up the Registry in case anything goes wrong during the repair.

What You Do	How You Do It
1. **Back up the Registry key.**	a. From the Start menu, **choose Run.**
	b. In the Open text box, **type** *regedit* **and press Enter.**
	c. In the left pane, **verify that My Computer is selected.**
	d. **Expand HKEY_LOCAL_MACHINE.**
	e. **Expand Software.**
	f. **Select the Microsoft key.**

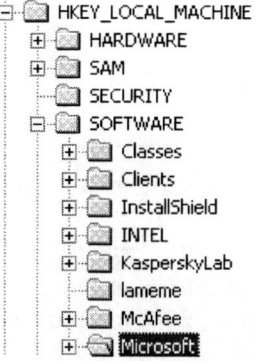

	g. **Choose Registry→Export Registry File.**
	h. From the Save In drop-down list, **select the C drive.**
	i. **Double-click the Backup folder.**
	j. In the File Name text box, **type** *regback*
	k. **Click Save** to back up the Registry.
	l. **Close Registry Editor.**

19

2. **Verify the Registry backup.**

    a. **Open Windows Explorer.**

    b. **Select the C:\Backup folder.**

    c. In the right pane, **verify that you see the RegBack.reg file.**

regback.reg

    d. **Close Windows Explorer.**

Review Questions

1. What utility can you use to back up the Registry in Windows 2000?

   _____

2. What utility can you use to back up the Registry in Windows NT?

   _____

3. A user reports that he is attempting to back up the Registry on his Windows NT computer but is unable to do so. What might be the problem?

   _____

   _____   _____

EXERCISE 19-7

Preparing an ASR Backup Set

Activity Time:

1 hour(s)

Objective:

To create an ASR backup set and ASR floppy disk to enable complete recovery of a Windows XP Professional computer.

Setup:

To complete this activity, you will need a blank, formatted floppy disk. You will also need either:

- approximately 2 GB of unallocated free space on your hard disk (not on your C drive); or
- a local backup device. A local backup device could be a second hard disk, a local CD-ROM burner, a compact-storage drive such as an Iomega Jaz drive, or a tape backup device, but not a network drive.

Setup:

To prepare for this activity:

1. Restart the computer and choose Windows XP Professional from the boot menu.
2. Log on as Admin#.
3. Use Computer Management to delete the G: partition.
4. Create a new 2 GB primary partition.
5. Format the new partition to use the NTFS file system.

Scenario:

One of your client's Windows XP computers is critical to the operation of her business. For this reason, she has asked you to minimize the amount of downtime she might incur in the event of a catastrophe.

19

What You Do	How You Do It
1. **Create the ASR backup set.**	a. **Run Backup** (from the Start menu, choose All Programs→Accessories→System Tools→ Backup).
	b. On the Welcome page, **click Advanced Mode.**
	c. **Click Automated System Recovery Wizard.**
	d. **Click Next.**
	e. In the Backup Media Or File Name text box, **type *G:\ASR.bkf***

Backup media or file name:

    G:\ASR.bkf

| | f. **Click Next.** |
| | g. **Click Finish.** The Backup Progress dialog box will show you the status of the backup. This process can take up to 30 minutes to complete. |

2. **Create the ASR floppy disk.**

 Make sure that the floppy disk you use is formatted. If it isn't, this step will fail and you will have to re-create the ASR backup set from the beginning.

a. When prompted, **insert a blank, formatted floppy disk into the floppy disk drive and click OK.**

 Insert a blank, 1.44 MB, formatted diskette in drive A:. Recovery information will be written to this diskette.

b. When the disk creation is complete, **click OK.**

 Remove the diskette, and label it as shown:

Windows Automated System Recovery Disk for ASR.blf created 1/23/2003 at 10:53 AM

Keep it in a safe place in case your system needs to be restored using Windows Automated System Recovery.

c. In the Backup Progress dialog box, **click Close.**

d. **Close Backup.**

3. **Store the ASR disks in a safe location.**

a. **Remove the floppy disk from the disk drive and label it.**

b. If you created the ASR backup set on removable media (such as a tape), **remove the media and label it.**

Review Questions

1. What do you need to perform an Automated System Recovery (ASR) in Windows XP?

2. You have just performed an ASR to recover a user's computer. The user reports that the computer does not have any of her data. What must you do?

3. What utility do you use to create an ASR floppy disk?

19

4. What Windows operating systems support ASR?

5. How much space does an ASR backup require?

_____

LAB 19-1

Preparing for Disaster Recovery

Activity Time:

2 hour(s), 30 minutes

Objective:

To perform standard disaster-recovery preparation measures for a computer that dual boots betwen Windows 2000 and Windows XP.

Setup:

You cannot complete this activity using the computers configured for the classroom. This activity requires:

- A client computer configured to dual-boot between Windows 2000 and Windows XP. This computer should have a 6 GB or larger hard disk.
- Three blank floppy disks.
- Access to the Windows XP Professional installation source files.

Prepare the client computer:

1. Perform a default installation of Windows 2000 Professional.

   - During the installation, create a C partition that is 2 GB in size and uses the NTFS file system.
   - Install Windows 2000 Professional on the C partition.
   - Install the course data files into the C:\Data folder.

2. After you have completed this installation, in Windows 2000 Professional, create two additional primary partitions that are each 2 GB in size. Format these partitions to use the NTFS file system.

3. Install Windows XP Professional on the second primary partition on the computer.

Scenario:

You have been asked to take whatever steps you can to prepare a client's computer for any disaster she might encounter. This client does custom programming, so she uses a computer configured to dual-boot between Windows 2000 and Windows XP; this configuration enables her to test the programs she writes in both operating systems. She stores all of the programs she creates in the C:\Data folder. Because time is money to your client, she is very concerned about preparing her computer so that she can quickly recover if disaster strikes. She would like you to store any backups you create in the partition on the computer that does not contain the Windows 2000 or Windows XP operating systems. She is planning to buy a tape backup drive this week, and will back up the contents of this partition when she has the tape drive.

19

When you have finished the lab, you can refer to the Preparing for Disaster Recovery Lab Results.txt file to check your work.

1. **Create a boot disk.**

2. **Create an emergency repair disk for Windows 2000.**

3. **Install the Windows XP Professional Recovery Console.**

4. **Back up the C:\Data folder to the empty data partition.**

5. **Back up the Windows XP System State Data.**

6. **Back up the Windows XP Registry.**

7. **Create an ASR Backup Set.**

CHAPTER 20

Recovering from Disaster

Activities included in this chapter:

- Exercise 20-1 Troubleshooting Application Problems
- Exercise 20-2 Troubleshooting Hard Disk Problems
- Exercise 20-3 Restoring Data
- Exercise 20-4 Restoring the Registry
- Exercise 20-5 Restoring System State Data
- Exercise 20-6 Recovering Boot Sector Files
- Exercise 20-7 Performing an Automated System Recovery
- Lab 20-1 Recovering from Disaster

Exercise 20-1

Troubleshooting Application Problems

Activity Time:

15 minutes

Objective:

To determine the proper troubleshooting approach to take in various application problem scenarios.

Scenario:

Your company's network consists of a mix of Windows 2000 Professional and Windows 98 clients. You have installed the company's applications on all client computers. As part of your job as an A+ technician, you're responsible for troubleshooting any problems users encounter with these applications. You have several technical support calls waiting for you.

---

1. A Windows 2000 user reports that he attempted to install a new application on his computer. During the installation, the power failed. When the user attempted to resume the installation, he received an error message stating that the application is already installed. But, the application won't run and the user is also unable to uninstall the application. After researching the problem on Microsoft's Help and Support Web site, you've determined that you must edit the user's Registry in order to completely remove the application from the computer. Once you've edited the Registry, the user will be able to complete the installation of the application.

   What utility should you use to edit the user's Registry?

   a) Registry Editor (regedt32.exe)

   b) Registry Editor (regedit.exe)

   c) System Configuration Editor (sysedit.exe)

   d) Microsoft Configuration Utility (msconfig.exe)

---

2. A user calls to tell you that when she received a low disk space error message, she attempted to free up disk space on her computer by deleting files. She's now unable to run any of the applications in Microsoft Office.

What's the most efficient way to solve this user's problem?

a) Identify which files she deleted and copy them from another computer to the user's computer.

b) Re-install Microsoft Office.

c) Determine which files the user deleted. Copy the files from the Microsoft Office installation CD-ROMs and expand them by using Expand.exe.

d) Remove Microsoft Office. Reboot the computer, and then re-install Microsoft Office.

3. One of your Windows 2000 users is experiencing intermittent problems with an application. The user is receiving the 'program performed an illegal operation" error message. You want to search the application publisher's Knowledge Base to see if you can find a solution for the problem.

What utility can you use to capture detailed information about the problem?

Review Questions

1. What types of problems can cause a General Protection Fault in an application?

2. What type of problem can cause an Illegal Operation message in an application?

3. What troubleshooting tools enable you to find information about an application error?

4. What step should you perform before clearing the Application log in Event Viewer?

5. Which Windows 2000 utility enables you to view a list of the applications that are currently running on the computer and close any applications that aren't responding?

20

6. What utility should you use if you need to manually transfer files from the Windows 2000 installation CD-ROM to replace corrupted versions on the hard disk?

_____

Exercise 20-2

Troubleshooting Hard Disk Problems

Activity Time:

25 minutes

Objective:

To determine the proper troubleshooting approach to take in various hard-disk problem scenarios.

Scenario:

As the in-house technician for a company, you're responsible for troubleshooting any problems users encounter with their Windows 2000 and Windows 98 computers. You've received four troubleshooting requests.

Troubleshooting Request #1

1. A user reports that he was exploring his Windows 2000 computer and opened Computer Management. He found some free space on his hard disk so he created and formatted a new partition. Now, his computer won't boot.

   What do you think is the problem? How should you fix it?

20

Troubleshooting Request #2

2. Another user reports that she is unable to boot her Windows 2000 computer. You attempt to boot her computer using a boot disk with no success. After referring to your documentation of the configuration of the user's computer, you know that the computer's hard disk is an IDE disk that contains only a single partition.

What should you try next? Why?

Troubleshooting Request #3

3. You've received a computer from a new employee, Dave. He complains that his computer was terribly slow and now he can't boot into Windows 98. You try to boot with an MS-DOS boot disk and can get MS-DOS to load from the floppy disk.

What can you eliminate as the problem?

4. **What should you try next to fix Dave's computer?**

Troubleshooting Request #4

5. Jane calls to say that her computer is slow to start up in Windows 98 and periodically the screen will go blue on her and she has to reboot. You receive Jane's computer and can boot into Windows 98, but it is very slow.

    What should you do to try to fix Jane's computer?

Review Questions

1. You suspect that a device driver you just installed is preventing Windows 2000 from booting successfully. What should you do?

2. You have created a new partition on a user's computer and now Windows 2000 won't boot. What might be the problem?

3. How do you boot a Windows 2000 computer to Safe Mode?

4. Why would you use the Safe Mode With Networking option?

5. A user reports that she is unable to boot her computer. You suspect that she deleted some of the Windows 2000 boot files. What should you do to fix the problem?

6. Which Windows 98 boot option enables you to boot the computer and load the drivers in Config.sys, Autoexec.bat, and Windows 98 one line at a time?

20

7. A user is receiving an error message stating that his Windows 98 computer's Registry is missing or corrupt. How should you repair the computer's Registry?

_____

Exercise 20-3

Restoring Data

Activity Time:

10 minutes

Objective:

To restore files from a backup and to verify the restored files.

Setup:

You have a backup set containing a backup of the D:\Data\Personnel folder on a floppy disk. The name of the backup file is personnel.bkf.

Setup:

Before you start this activity, complete the following steps:

1. Log on to Windows 2000 as Admin#.

2. Make sure you have a backup of D:\Data\Personnel on floppy disk.

3. In Windows Explorer, delete the D:\Data\Personnel folder.

4. Close Windows Explorer.

Scenario:

You have been hired as an A+ technician to perform system maintenance and management tasks for a client. You have configured each user's Windows 2000 computer to back up on a weekly basis. You want to test a backup you made to verify that you're getting valid backups.

What You Do	How You Do It
1. Restore the backup of the D:\Data\ Personnel folder.	a. Insert the floppy disk containing the backup into the floppy disk drive.
	b. Run Backup.
	c. Click Restore Wizard.
	d. Click Next.

20

e. Below What To Restore, **expand File and then the backup media.**

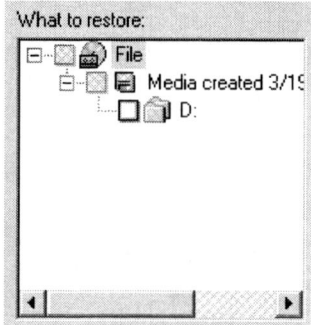

f. **Expand D.**

g. When prompted, in the Backup File Name text box, **verify that the correct path and backup file name is displayed.**

h. **Click OK.**

i. **Check the D:\Data\Personnel folder.**

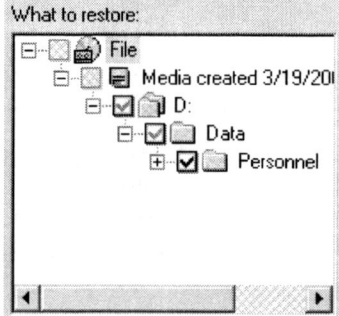

j. **Click Next.**

k. **Click Finish.**

l. **Click OK** to confirm that you have inserted the backup media.

m. **Click Close** to close the Restore Progress dialog box.

n. **Close Backup.**

2. **Verify that the D:\Data\Personnel folder restored successfully.**

a. In Windows Explorer, **verify that you see the D:\Data\Personnel folder.**

b. **Select the D:\Data\Personnel folder.**

c. **Verify that you see the Salary.doc file within it, along with a Reports folder.**

d. **Close Windows Explorer.**

Review Questions

1. What permissions must you have in order to restore files in Windows 2000?

    _____

    _____

    _____

2. What is the last step you should perform when restoring a file?

    _____

3. True or False: You must restore a file into the same folder from which it was backed up in Windows 2000.

    _____

20

EXERCISE 20-4

Restoring the Registry

Activity Time:

20 minutes

Objective:

To restore a Registry key from a backup, and to verify the restoration.

Setup:

You have backed up the HKEY_LOCAL_MACHINE\Software\Microsoft key within Registry Editor.

Scenario:

You have installed a new Microsoft application on a Windows 2000 computer that's causing other applications to hang. You've already tried restoring the Last Known Good configuration from the boot menu, but it didn't fix the problem. Fortunately, before you installed the new application, you backed up the HKEY_LOCAL_MACHINE\Software\Microsoft key by using Registry Editor. You now want to restore the backup.

What You Do	How You Do It

1. Restore the Registry backup.

a. **Restart the computer.**

b. When the boot menu is displayed, **press F8** to open the Advanced Options menu.

c. From the Windows Advanced Options Menu, **select Safe Mode and press Enter.**

d. From the operating system menu, **select Microsoft Windows 2000 Professional and press Enter.**

e. **Log on as Admin#.**

f. **Run Registry Editor** (from the Start menu, choose Run. In the Open text box, type regedit.exe and click OK).

g. **Click OK.**

h. In the left pane, **select HKEY_LOCAL_ MACHINE\Software\Microsoft.**

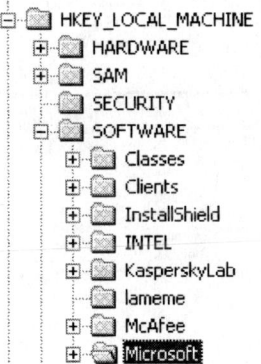

i. **Choose Registry→Import Registry File.**

j. **Open the C:\Backup folder.**

k. **Select the RegBack.reg file and click Open.**

20

		l.	When the import is complete, **click OK** to close the Registry Editor message box.
		m.	**Close Registry Editor.**
2.	**Verify that the computer boots successfully.**	a.	**Shut down and restart the computer.**
		b.	**Choose Windows 2000 Professional from the boot menu.**
		c.	**Log on as Admin#.**

Review Questions

1. What option do you choose in Registry Editor to restore a Registry Editor backup?

   _____

2. A user is experiencing a problem with his computer's Registry that is preventing his computer from booting normally. You want to restore the computer's Registry from a Registry Editor backup. What should you do first?

   _____

3. What permissions do you need to restore the Registry in Windows NT, Windows 2000, and Windows XP?

   _____

EXERCISE 20-5

Restoring System State Data

Activity Time:

20 minutes

Objective:

To restore the System State Data on a Windows 2000 computer.

Setup:

You have backed up the System State Data for Windows 2000 to C:\Backup\SystemState.bkf.

Scenario:

A programmer just installed a custom application he developed on one of your client's computers. The client has contacted you because he's now experiencing problems with his computer. You aren't sure what the custom application changed on the computer. Fortunately, you scheduled a System State Data backup to take place on a regular basis; the last backup occurred last night.

20

1. **Restore the System State Data.**

    a. **Open Backup.**

    b. **Click Restore Wizard.**

    c. **Click Next.**

    d. **Expand the media set and check System State.**

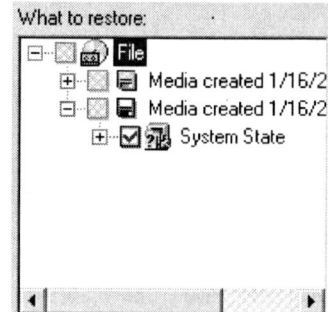

What to restore:

- File
    - Media created 1/16/2
    - Media created 1/16/2
        - System State

    e. **Click Next.**

    f. **Click Advanced.**

    g. On the Where To Restore page, **click Next** to accept the default of Original location.

    h. On the How To Restore page, **select Always Replace The File On Disk and click Next.**

    i. On the Advanced Restore Options page, **click Next.**

    j. **Click Finish.**

    k. **Browse to C:\Backup and double-click System State.bkf.**

    l. **Click OK.**

    m. When the restore is complete, **click Close.**

    n. When prompted, **click Yes** to restart the computer. The restart might take longer than usual.

    o. **Log on as Admin#.**

Review Questions

1. You have determined that you need to restore a user's backup of his Windows 2000 system state data. What should you do first?

2. How do you know that a restore of a computer's system state data succeeded?

20

EXERCISE 20-6

Recovering Boot Sector Files

Activity Time:

20 minutes

Objective:

To use Recovery Console to repair and restore boot files and the boot sector on a Windows XP Professional computer.

Setup:

You have installed the Windows XP Recovery Console as an option on the boot menu. The Windows XP installation is in E:\Windows.

Scenario:

One of your clients reports that he is unable to boot his Windows XP computer. You suspect that he used a utility that modified either his computer's boot sector or the master boot record. On a previous visit to the client's office, you installed the Recovery Console on all Windows XP computers.

What You Do	How You Do It
1. Repair the boot sector and master boot record on the computer.	a. Restart the computer and choose the Microsoft Windows Recovery Console from the boot menu.
	b. When prompted for the Windows installation you want to repair, **enter** 2
	c. For the Administrator's password, **enter** `password`
	d. At the E:\Windows prompt, **enter** `fixboot` to repair the boot sector.
	e. When prompted, **enter** `y` to confirm that you want to update the boot sector on the C drive. You should see a message stating that the boot sector was successfully written.
	f. **Enter** `fixmbr` to repair the computer's master boot record.
	g. When prompted, **enter** `y` to confirm that you want to write a new master boot record on the C drive. You should see a message stating that the master boot record was successfully written.
	h. **Enter** `exit` to restart the computer.
2. Verify that you can log on to Windows XP.	a. From the boot menu, **choose Windows XP Professional.**
	b. **Log on as Admin#.**

Review Questions

1. You have determined that you need to perform repairs on a Windows XP computer. The computer does not have the Recovery Console installed. What should you do?

_____

_____

20

2. What command should you use in the Recovery Console to repair the computer's master boot record?

_____

3. What command should you use in the Recovery Console to re-create the boot sector of a computer?

_____

4. You are attempting to repair a computer configured to dual-boot between Windows 2000 and Windows XP. You have determined that the computer is experiencing a problem that requires you to replace its boot files. How should you repair the computer?

_____

5. You need to perform an emergency repair on a Windows 2000 computer that does not have a bootable CD-ROM drive. What should you do?

_____

_____

EXERCISE 20-7

Performing an Automated System Recovery

Activity Time:

1 hour(s), 30 minutes

Objective:

To use an ASR floppy disk and ASR backup set to perform a complete recovery of a Windows XP Professional computer.

Setup:

You have created an ASR backup set and floppy.

Scenario:

You have been called in by a client to repair his Windows XP computer. You have tried just about everything to fix it, including re-writing the master boot record and boot sector information in the Recovery Console, restoring a backup of the Registry, and even restoring a System State Data backup. The computer still won't boot. When you initially installed the computer and configured the user's applications, you created an ASR backup set and floppy disk for just such an emergency.

20

1. **Initiate an ASR.**	a. **Insert the Windows XP Professional installation CD into your CD-ROM drive.**
	b. **Restart the computer.**
	c. **Press a key when prompted** to boot from the CD-ROM.
	d. When the Press [F2] To Run Automated System Recovery (ASR) message appears in the status bar, **press F2.**

 The ASR message appears only briefly in the status bar at the bottom of the screen (after the screen turns blue). You'll first see a message prompting you to press F6 to install third-party drivers; the next message is the ASR prompt. If you miss the ASR prompt, restart the computer and start over.

<table>
<tr><td>2.</td><td>**Complete the ASR.**</td><td>a.</td><td>When prompted, **insert the ASR boot floppy disk and press any key.** (If the ASR floppy disk is not recognized, restart the ASR by rebooting from the CD-ROM with the ASR floppy disk already in the drive.)</td></tr>
<tr><td></td><td></td><td>b.</td><td>When prompted, **press C** to confirm deletion of all the partitions on your disk so that ASR can re-create the disk as a basic disk. After configuring the disks, Windows Setup will automatically install the operating system. This phase will take about 45 minutes.</td></tr>
</table>

⚠ After the disks are scanned and configured, you might see a prompt that you need to restart because Setup has performed system maintenance. Restart the computer and initiate the ASR process again by pressing F2.

<table>
<tr><td></td><td></td><td>c.</td><td>When the Automated System Recovery Wizard appears, **click Next.**</td></tr>
<tr><td></td><td></td><td>d.</td><td>When prompted for the location of the backup set, **insert your backup media.**</td></tr>
<tr><td></td><td></td><td>e.</td><td>In the Automated System Recovery Wizard, **verify the location of the backup set and click Next.**</td></tr>
<tr><td></td><td></td><td>f.</td><td>**Click Finish** to close the Automated System Recovery Wizard. The system restoration should proceed automatically. The restoration will take about 30 minutes. When it completes, the computer will automatically restart.</td></tr>
<tr><td>3.</td><td>**Verify that Windows XP was successfully restored.**</td><td>a.</td><td>**Log on as Admin#.**</td></tr>
<tr><td></td><td></td><td>b.</td><td>**Use various administrative tools to verify your computer's configuration.** For example, use Computer Management to verify that all your user accounts are available. Check that the computer is a member of the class.com domain.</td></tr>
</table>

20

Review Questions

1. How do you start an Automated System Recovery (ASR)?

    _____

    _____

2. What key must you press to start an ASR?

    _____

3. How do you verify that the ASR worked correctly?

    _____

Lab 20-1

Recovering from Disaster

Activity Time:

1 hour(s)

Objective:

To research, document, and perform the appropriate disaster-recovery procedures for Windows 98 and Windows 2000 computers with system problems or data loss.

Data Files:

- Templates.bkf

Setup:

You cannot complete this activity using the computers configured for the classroom. You will need:

- A networked computer with a default installation of Windows 2000.
- A bootable Windows 2000 Professional installation CD-ROM.
- An Internet connection so that you can research error messages.
- Access to the Lab Data folder from the student data files.
- A current Emergency Repair Disk for this computer (optional).

Scenario:

You work for the Help Desk at AlphaBeta Company. After returning from lunch, you discover that you have three trouble tickets waiting for you.

 When you have finished the lab, you can refer to the Recovering from Disaster Lab Results.txt file to check your work.

Trouble Ticket #1

1. One of the users reports that she is getting a "Windows Protection Error" message when she attempts to shut down her computer in Windows 98. **Research the error at Microsoft's Support Web site (*support.microsoft.com*) and create a plan for solving the problem.**

20

Trouble Ticket #2

2. A user reports that when he turned on his Windows 2000 computer, he received the error message 'NTLDR is missing." **Research the error at Microsoft's Support Web site (*support.microsoft.com*) and create a plan for solving the problem.**

3. After researching the user's problem with the missing NTLDR file, you have determined that your best course of action is to repair the computer's boot files. **Perform an emergency repair.**

Trouble Ticket #3

4. A user tells you that she accidentally deleted the C:\Templates folder on her Windows 2000 computer. This folder contains files that are critical to her job. Because the files are so important to her, she backs them up regularly to a file named Template.bkf in the C:\Data folder. **Restore the backup file.**

CHAPTER 21

Installing Client Operating Systems

Activities included in this chapter:

- Exercise 21-1 Installing Windows 98 and Windows 2000 on a Single Computer
- Exercise 21-2 Upgrading Windows 98 to Windows 2000
- Exercise 21-3 Upgrading Windows 2000 to Windows XP
- Exercise 21-4 Troubleshoot Operating System Installations
- Exercise 21-5 Removing Operating System Components
- Lab 21-1 Installing Client Operating Systems

EXERCISE 21-1

Installing Windows 98 and Windows 2000 on a Single Computer

Activity Time:

4 hour(s)

Objective:

To install a computer to dual-boot between Windows 98 and Windows 2000, and to configure, test, and update the two operating system installations.

Setup:

You have created a Windows 98 Startup disk. You have the Windows 98 CD-ROM. The Windows 2000 Professional installation files are shared on \\2000srv\win2000.

Setup:

You will need two blank floppy disks to complete this activity.

Scenario:

Your client, Applications Developers, Inc., has asked you to install both Windows 98 and Windows 2000 on several computers. Applications Developers, Inc., is located in San Francisco. This company does custom programming, so Mike Jones (the president) wants to have Windows 98 and Windows 2000 available for programmers to test applications they develop. Because the computers will be used for testing purposes, Mike would like you to make sure that all the default configuration options are set in both Windows 98 and Windows 2000. These computers have existing operating systems, applications, and data files, so he has asked you to make sure to remove them before installing Windows 98 and Windows 2000.

Your client would like you to name each computer Win98-# and Win2000-# (in the appropriate operating systems), where # is a unique number. His existing workgroup is named AppDev. Each computer should have a user named Admin# for each operating system, where # is the same number assigned to the computer. The password for each user should be password. Mike's network has a DHCP server for configuring TCP/IP.

Mike has mentioned to you that the users will primarily work in Windows 2000. For this reason, he would like you to make as much disk space as possible available to the Windows 2000 operating system. He also would like you to make sure that the files the users create in Windows 2000 are secure.

What You Do	How You Do It
1. Remove all old operating systems and data from the computer.	a. Insert the Windows 98 Startup disk and turn on the computer.
	b. When prompted, choose Start Computer Without CD-ROM Support and press Enter.
	c. Enter `fdisk`
	d. Enter N twice to disable large disk support.
	e. Delete all partitions.

21

2. **Create and format a primary partition.**

   a.   In Fdisk, **enter** 1 to create a DOS partition.

   b.   **Enter** 1 to create a primary DOS partition.

   c.   **Enter** N to specify that you want to manually enter a size for your primary partition and manually mark it active.

   d.   **Enter** 2048 or the maximum allowed size to create the partition for the partition size.

   e.   **Press Esc.**

   f.   **Enter** 2 to mark a partition active.

   g.   **Enter** 1 to make the partition active.

   h.   **Press Esc** until you exit Fdisk.

   i.   **Press Ctrl+Alt+Delete** to restart the computer.

   j.   When prompted, **choose Start Computer With CD-ROM Support and press Enter.**

   k.   At the A: prompt, **enter** `format c: /s`

   l.   **Enter** Y to confirm that you want to format the C drive.

   m.   **Press Enter** to accept a blank volume label.

3. **Install Windows 98.**

a. **Insert the Windows 98 installation CD-ROM into the computer's CD-ROM drive.**

b. At the A prompt, **enter** `x:\setup` (where x is the letter of the computer's CD-ROM drive).

c. **Press Enter to continue.**

d. When ScanDisk completes, **press** `x` to exit.

e. **Click Continue.**

f. On the License Agreement page, **select I Accept The Agreement and click Next.**

g. **Enter the Windows 98 product key and click Next.**

h. On the Select Directory page, **verify that C:\WINDOWS is selected and click Next.**

i. On the Setup Options page, **verify that Typical is selected and click Next.**

j. In the User Name text box, **type** *Mike Jones*

k. In the Company Name text box, **type** *Application Developers, Inc.*

l. **Click Next.**

m. **Verify that Install The Most Common Components (Recommended) is selected and click Next.**

n. In the Computer Name text box, **type** *Win98-#*, where # is your assigned number.

o. In the Workgroup Name text box, **type** *AppDev* **and click Next.**

p. **Verify that United States is selected and click**

21

Next.

q.   **Click Next** to create a Windows 98 Startup disk.

r.   When prompted, **insert a blank floppy disk and click OK.**

s.   When the Startup disk creation is complete, **remove the floppy disk and label it. Click OK.**

t.   **Click Next.** Setup now copies the necessary Windows 98 files to the hard disk.

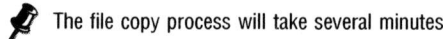 The file copy process will take several minutes.

u.   If neccessary, when the file copy is complete, **click Restart Now.**

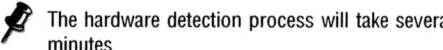 The hardware detection process will take several minutes.

v.   Setup now performs hardware detection. If neccessary, when the process is complete, **click Restart Now.**

w.   If neccessary, **click OK** to close the Network message box.

x.   **Click Close.**

y.   In the Date/Time Properties dialog box, **configure the appropriate date, time, and time zone for San Francisco.**

z.   **Click Close.**

aa. If neccessary, when the installation is complete, **click Restart Now.**

ab. In the User Name text box, **type *Admin#***

<table>
<tr><td></td><td>ac.</td><td>In the password text box, **type** *password* **and click OK.**</td></tr>
<tr><td></td><td>ad.</td><td>In the Confirm New Password text box, **type** *password* **and click OK** to log on.</td></tr>
<tr><td></td><td>ae.</td><td>**Uncheck Show This Screen Each Time Windows 98 Starts and close the window.**</td></tr>
</table>

---

4. **Configure an Internet connection.**

    a.   **Choose Start→Programs→Accessories→ Internet Tools→Internet Connection Wizard.**

    b.   **Select I Want To Set Up My Internet Connection Manually, Or I Want To Connect Through A Local Area Network (LAN).**

    c.   **Click Next.**

    d.   **Select the appropriate connection option.**

    e.   **Click Next.**

    f.   If you selected to connect to the Internet through a local area network (LAN), **configure the proxy server information as needed.**

    g.   **Click Next.**

    h.   **Select No** to skip configuring an Internet email account.

    i.   **Click Finish.**

21

5. **Verify that all hardware drivers installed correctly.**

a. In Device Manager, **view the status of all devices.** An exclamation point within a yellow circle indicates that the driver for a device is not working properly.

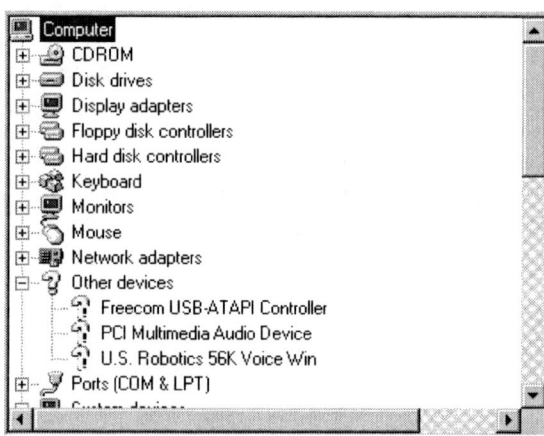

b. If necessary, **use Add/Remove Hardware** in Control Panel to install drivers for hardware devices or **connect to the hardware manufacturer's Web site** to download the appropriate drivers.

6. **Update Windows 98.**

a. From the Start menu, **choose Windows Update.**

b. **Click Yes** to install and run the Windows Update Control Package.

c. If necessary, **click Yes** again.

d. **Click Scan For Updates** to look for all updates to Windows 98.

Welcome to Windows Update

Get the latest updates available for your computer's operating system, software, and hardware.

Windows Update scans your computer and provides you with a selection of updates tailored just for you.

Scan for updates

e. **Click Review And Install Updates.**

f. **Click Yes** to continue.

g. **Follow the prompts to install the updates you want.**

h. If necessary, **restart the computer when prompted.**

i. **Log back on as Admin#.**

7. **Install Windows 2000 Professional.**

    a. In Windows 98, **access \\2000srv\win2000.**

    b. **Double-click winnt32.exe.**

       ⚠ Do not upgrade Windows 98.

    c. On the Welcome page, **verify that Install A New Copy Of Windows 2000 (Clean Install) is selected and click Next.**

    d. **Select I Accept This Agreement and click Next.**

    e. On the Select Special Options page, **click Advanced Options.**

       ⚠ Make sure that you specify that you want to choose the installation partition during setup.

    f. **Check I Want To Choose The Installation Partition During Setup and click OK.**

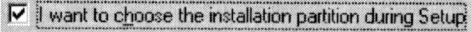

    g. **Click Next.**

    h. **Click Finish** to restart the computer.

    i. On the Welcome page, **press Enter.**

    j. **Highlight the unpartitioned space on the hard disk and press C** to create a new partition.

    k. **Press Enter** to accept the default partition size of all remaining free space on the hard disk.

    l. **Highlight the new partition and press Enter** to install Windows 2000 on this partition.

m. **Verify that Format The Partition Using The NTFS File System is selected and press Enter.**

n. **Press Enter** to restart the computer.

o. On the Welcome page, **click Next.**

p. On the Regional Settings page, **click Next** to accept the default locale and keyboard layout.

q. On the Personalize Your Software page, in the Name text box, **type** *Mike Jones*

    In the Organization text box, **type** *Application Developers, Inc.*

r. **Click Next.**

s. On the Computer Name And Administrator password page, in the Computer Name text box, **type** *WIN2000–#*, where # is your assigned number.

t. In the Administrator password text box, **type** *password*

    In the Confirm Password text box, **type** *password*

u. **Click Next.**

v. If Setup detected a modem, in the What Area Code (Or City Code) Are You In Now text box, **type** *415*

w. **Click Next.**

x. On the Date And Time Settings page, **configure the date, time, and time zone. Click Next.**

y. On the Networking Settings page, **verify that Typical Settings is selected and click Next.**

z. On the Workgroup Or Computer Domain page,

verify that **No, This Computer Is Not On A Network** is selected.

aa. In the Workgroup Or Computer Domain text box, **type** *APPDEV*

ab. **Click Next.** Setup now installs the Windows components.

 Setup now copies the necessary files to the hard disk. This process will take 15 or 20 minutes to complete.

ac. **Click Finish.** The computer restarts.

---

8. **Require users to log on to the computer.**

    a. **Select Windows 2000 Professional and press Enter.**

    b. **In the Network Identification Wizard, click Next.**

    c. **Select Users Must Enter A User Name And Password To Use This Computer.**

    d. **Click Next.**

    e. **Click Finish.**

    f. **Log on as Administrator with a password of password.**

    g. **Uncheck Show This Screen At Startup.**

    h. **Click Exit.**

---

9. **Configure an Internet connection.**

a. **Run the Internet Connection Wizard.**

b. **Specify that you want to configure the Internet connection manually and click Next.**

c. **Select the appropriate connection option.**

d. **Click Next.**

e. If you selected to connect to the Internet through a local area network (LAN), **configure the proxy server information as needed.**

f. **Click Next.**

g. **Select No** to skip configuring an Internet email account. **Click Next.**

h. If neccessary, **uncheck the To Connect To The Internet Immediately check box.**

i. **Click Finish.**

10. **Verify that all hardware drivers installed correctly.**

a. In Device Manager, **view the status of all devices.**

b. If necessary, **use Add/Remove Hardware** in Control Panel to install drivers for hardware devices, **or connect to the Manufacturer's Web site(s)** to download and install the appropriate drivers.

11. **Update Windows 2000.**

a. From the Start menu, **choose Windows Update.**

b. **Click Yes** to install and run the Windows Update Control Package.

c. If necessary, **click Yes** again.

d. **Click Scan For Updates** to look for all updates to Windows 2000.

Scan for updates

e. **Click Review And Install Updates.**

f. **Click Yes** to continue.

g. **Follow the prompts to install the updates you want.**

h. If necessary, **restart the computer when prompted.**

i. **Log back on as Administrator.**

12. Create Admin#.

    a. In Computer Management, **expand Local Users And Groups.**

    b. **Right-click Users and choose New User.**

    c. In the User Name text box, **type** *Admin#*

    d. In the Password text box, **type** *password*

    e. In the Confirm Password text box, **type** *password*

    f. **Uncheck User Must Change Password At Next Logon.**

    g. **Click Create.**

    h. **Click Close.**

    i. **Close Computer Management.**

Review Questions

1. You are planning to install both Windows 98 and Windows 2000 on the same computer. Which operating system must you install first?

_____

2. How do you start a Windows 98 installation?

_____

3. You are planning to install Windows 2000 on a computer that does not have a bootable CD-ROM. The computer does not yet have an operating system installed What should you do?

_____

4. Which installation option should you choose if you want to install Windows 98 with the necessary options for a laptop computer?

_____

5. You have configured a computer to dual-boot between Windows 2000 and Windows 98. How can you make Windows 98 the default operating system?

_____

_____

21

Exercise 21-2

Upgrading Windows 98 to Windows 2000

Activity Time:

1 hour(s), 30 minutes

Objective:

To upgrade an installation of Windows 98 to Windows 2000, and to verify and update the upgraded operating system.

Setup:

Before you can complete this activity, you will need to remove the dual-boot environment. Use the following steps to do so:

1. In Windows 98, use Windows Explorer to access the C:\Windows\Command folder.
2. Copy the sys.com file to your Windows 98 Startup disk.
3. Boot the computer with the Windows 98 Startup disk.
4. Overwrite the hard disk's Master Boot Record by entering `sys C:`.
5. Restart the computer to Windows 98.

 Do not delete the Windows 2000 partition.

Setup:

You will need a Windows 98 Startup disk to complete this activity. The Windows 2000 Professional installation files are in \\2000srv\win2000.

Scenario:

A client has asked you to upgrade her computer from Windows 98 to Windows 2000 Professional. She's interested in implementing the security features that are available in Windows 2000 and not Windows 98. She also wants to make sure that she won't have to re-install her applications or lose any of her data. The client also tells you that she has copied the Windows 98 installation files to C:\Win98 and backed up portions of Windows 98 to C:\Backup; she will no longer need these files.

What You Do	How You Do It
1. **Verify that the computer's hardware meets the minimum Windows 2000 Professional requirements.**	a. In Internet Explorer, **connect to** *www.microsoft.com/windows2000/ professional/evaluation/sysreqs/ default.asp.*
	b. **Review the minimum hardware requirements.**
	c. On the desktop, **right-click My Computer and choose Properties** to display information about the computer's processor and RAM. **Verify that the processor and RAM meet the minimum requirements.**
	d. **Click Cancel** to close the System Properties dialog box.
	e. **Use Windows Explorer** to verify that you have enough free disk space.
	f. **Close all open windows.**

2. **Upgrade Windows 98 to Windows 2000.**

    a. **Connect to \\2000srv\win2000.**

    b. **Double-click winnt32.exe.**

    c. If neccessary, **click Yes** to upgrade Windows 98.

    d. **Select Upgrade To Windows 2000 (Recommended) and click Next.**

    e. **Select I Accept This Agreement and click Next.**

    f. **Click Next** to skip connecting to the Windows Compatibility Web site to check the computer's hardware.

    g. **Select No, I Don't Have Any Upgrade Packs and click Next.**

    h. **Select Yes, Upgrade My Drive** to upgrade the hard disk to NTFS.

    i. **Click Next.**

    j. **Review the Upgrade Report for any problems.**

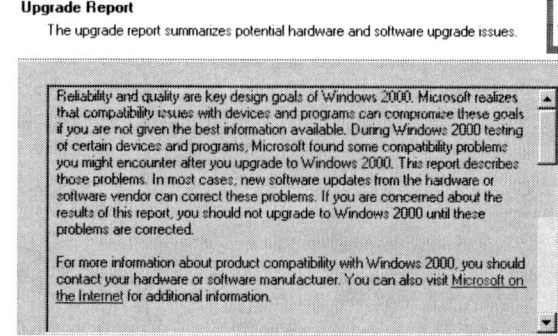

k. **Click Next.**

l. **Click Next** to begin the upgrade.

⚠ Do not boot from the Windows 2000 CD-ROM.

m. When prompted, **restart the computer.** Setup will now copy some of the Windows 2000 files to the hard disk.

n. When prompted, **press Enter** to restart the computer.

Setup will now convert the hard disk to NTFS. After the conversion, your computer will automatically restart. Setup will then continue with detecting hardware, installing the network components, and copying the rest of the Windows 2000 files. This process can take up to 30 minutes.

o. When the installation is complete, **click Restart Now.**

p. In the New Password Creation dialog box, in the Password text box, **type *password***

q. In the Confirm New Password text box, **type *password***

r. **Click OK.**

3. **Verify that all hardware drivers installed correctly.**

a. **Log on as Administrator with a password of password.**

b. **Uncheck Show This Screen At Startup and click Exit.**

21

c. In Device Manager, **view the status of all devices.**

d. If necessary, **use Add/Remove Hardware** in Control Panel to install drivers for hardware devices **or connect to the Manufacturer's Web site** to download and install the appropriate drivers.

4. **Update Windows 2000.**

    a. From the Start menu, **choose Windows Update.**

    b. **Click Yes** to install and run the Windows Update Control Package.

    c. If necessary, **click Yes** again.

    d. **Click Scan For Updates** to look for all updates to Windows 2000.

Scan for updates

    e. **Click Review And Install Updates.**

    f. **Click Yes** to continue.

    g. **Follow the prompts to install the updates you want.**

    h. If necessary, **restart the computer when prompted.**

    i. From the boot menu, **choose the first Windows 2000 Professional option** (the second Windows 2000 Professional option is the installation of Windows 2000 you completed in the previous activity).

    j. **Log back on as Administrator.**

5.	Delete any files the client no longer needs.	a.	**Open Windows Explorer.**
		b.	**Access C:\.**
		c.	**Right-click C:\Win98 and choose Delete** to delete the Windows 98 installation files.
		d.	**Click Yes** to confirm deleting the folder.
		e.	**Delete the C:\Backup folder.**
		f.	**Close Windows Explorer.**

Review Questions

1. To what operating system(s) can you upgrade a Windows 98 computer?

   _____

2. You have just upgraded a computer from Windows 98 to Windows 2000. How can you update Windows 2000 to make sure that you have the latest patches and fixes for the software?

   _____

3. After you have verified that the computer meets the minimum hardware requirements for an upgrade, what step should you perform next before upgrading the computer's operating system?

   _____

EXERCISE 21-3

Upgrading Windows 2000 to Windows XP

Activity Time:

1 hour(s), 30 minutes

Objective:

To upgrade an installation of Windows 2000 to Windows XP, and to verify and update the upgraded operating system.

Setup:

The Windows XP installation files are in \\2000srv\winxp.

Setup:

To complete this activity successfully, perform the following tasks:

1. Restart the computer.

2. From the boot menu, choose the second Windows 2000 Professional installation.

3. Log on as Administrator#.

Scenario:

One of your clients calls to tell you that he's just purchased Windows XP Professional. He's currently running Windows 2000 Professional on his computer.

21

What You Do	How You Do It
1. Verify that the computer's hardware meets the minimum Windows XP Professional requirements.	a. In Internet Explorer, **connect to** *www.microsoft.com/windowsxp/pro/ evaluation/sysreqs.asp.*
	b. **Review the minimum hardware requirements.**
	c. On the desktop, **right-click My Computer and choose Properties** to display information about the computer's processor and RAM. **Verify that the processor and RAM meet the minimum requirements.**
	d. **Click Cancel** to close the System Properties dialog box.
	e. **Use Windows Explorer** to verify that you have enough free disk space.
	f. **Close all open windows.**

2.	**Upgrade Windows 2000 to Windows XP.**	a.	In Windows 2000, **access \\2000srv\winxp\ i386.**
		b.	**Double-click winnt32.exe.**
		c.	**Click Install Windows XP.**
		d.	From the Installation Type drop-down list, **select Upgrade (Recommended) and click Next.**
		e.	**Select I Accept This Agreement and click Next.**
		f.	**Enter the Product Key and click Next.**
		g.	**Verify that Yes, Download The Updated Setup Files (Recommended) is selected and click Next** to connect to Microsoft's Web site and download updates for installing Windows XP. Your computer will automatically restart after downloading the updates.
			After copying files, Setup will automatically restart the computer again. Setup completes the upgrade, which can take from 30 to 45 minutes. Your computer will automatically restart again.
		h.	If necessary, in the Display Settings message box, **click OK. Click OK** again to confirm the adjusted display settings.
		i.	**Click Next.**
		j.	On the Ready To Register With Microsoft page, **select No and click Next.**
		k.	**Click Finish.**
3.	**Verify that all hardware drivers installed correctly.**	a.	**Log on to Windows XP as Administrator.**

21

b. In Device Manager, **view the status of all devices.**

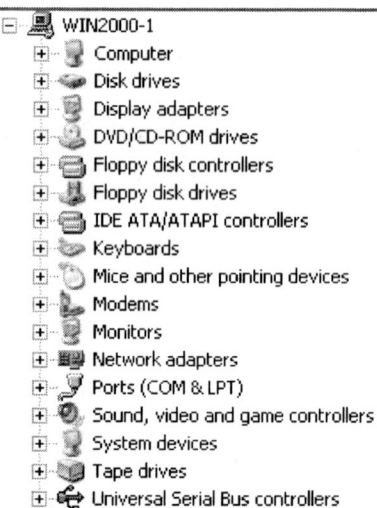

c. If necessary, **use Add Or Remove Hardware** in Control Panel to install drivers for hardware devices **or connect to the Manufacturer's Web site** to download and install the appropriate drivers.

4. **Update Windows XP.**

    a. From the Start menu, **choose Windows Update.**

    b. **Click Yes** to install and run the Windows Update Control Package.

    c. If necessary, **click Yes** again.

    d. **Click Scan For Updates** to look for all updates to Windows XP.

     Scan for updates

    e. **Click Review And Install Updates.**

    f. **Click Yes** to continue.

    g. **Follow the prompts to install the updates you want.**

    h. If necessary, **restart the computer when prompted.**

    i. **Log back on as Administrator.**

Review Questions

1. From which operating system(s) can you upgrade to Windows XP Professional?

2. What step should you perform first before attempting to upgrade a computer to Windows XP Professional?

21

3. What should you do if you upgrade a computer to Windows XP and then discover that the computer's modem doesn't work?

_____

_____

EXERCISE 21-4

Troubleshoot Operating System Installations

Activity Time:

15 minutes

Objective:

To determine the proper troubleshooting approach to take in various operating system installation problem scenarios.

Scenario:

As an A+ technician, you've been hired by a computer retailer to work in their Service department. As part of your job, you're expected to install and troubleshoot operating systems on a daily basis.

---

1. A customer bought the Windows XP Professional upgrade. He brought in his Windows 98 computer to the Service department to have the upgrade installed. One of the technicians reports that the installation is failing after Setup copies files to the hard disk and reboots the computer.

   What might be the problem? How should you fix it?

---

2. A customer brought in a computer on which she would like you to remove all existing data and install Windows 2000 Professional. You have deleted the partitions on the computer's hard disk. You insert the Windows 2000 CD-ROM but the computer won't boot from it.

   What should you do?

21

Review Questions

1. You are attempting to install Windows 2000 but the installation keeps failing. What might be the problem?

   _____

2. You are attempting to install Windows 2000 from CD-ROM, but Windows 2000 doesn't recognize the computer's CD-ROM drive. The computer does not have an operating system. What should you do?

   _____

3. You are attempting to install Windows 2000 from CD-ROM, but Windows 2000 doesn't recognize the computer's CD-ROM drive. The computer already has Windows 98 installed. What should you do?

   _____

   _____

EXERCISE 21-5

Removing Operating System Components

Activity Time:

10 minutes

Objective:

To remove the Games component from an installation of Windows XP Professional.

Scenario:

You recently installed Windows XP Professional on a client's computers. The owner of the company feels that users are spending too much time playing the games included with Windows XP.

What You Do	How You Do It
1. Remove the games from Windows XP.	a. In Control Panel, **click Add Or Remove Programs.**
	b. **Click Add/Remove Windows Components.**
	c. In the Components list, **select Accessories And Utilities and click Details.**
	d. **Uncheck Games and click OK.**

	e. **Click Next.**
	f. **Click Finish.**
	g. **Click Close** to close Add Or Remove Programs.
	h. **Close Control Panel.**

21

2. **Verify that the computer no longer has games.**

    a. From the Start menu, **choose All Programs→ Games.** There are no games available on the menu.

    b. **Close the Start menu.**

Review Questions

1. You have been asked to remove the games from a user's Windows 2000 computer. What should you do?

    _____

    _____

2. What permissions do you need to remove an operating system component?

    _____

3. You plan to install a Windows component on a Windows 2000 computer. What software might you need to complete this task?

    _____

LAB 21-1

Installing Client Operating Systems

Activity Time:

3 hour(s)

Objective:

To install a computer to dual boot between one of the following pairs of operating systems: Windows 98 and Windows 2000; Windows 98 and Windows XP; or Windows 2000 and Windows XP.

Setup:

You cannot complete this activity using the computers configured for the classroom. You will need:

- A computer that meets the minimum hardware requirements for the two operating systems you will install. This computer should have a hard disk that is 4 GB or larger.

- Access to the installation CD-ROMs for the operating systems you will install. If the drivers for your computers' hardware are not included on the installation CD-ROMs, you will also need access to the hardware drivers.

- Access to the Internet so that you can update the computer after completing the installations.

- A domain controller. Use the "For the Classroom Domain Controller" setup procedure from the Class Setup instructions to set up the domain controller.

Scenario:

One of your clients has asked you to configure a new computer on her network. She does custom programming, so she would like to have both her company's supported operating systems on the computer for testing purposes. After interviewing the client, you've determined that her network contains the following:

- A Windows 2000 Server domain named class.com, which contains the primary network user logon accounts.

- A Novell NetWare 3.12 server.

- A DHCP server to provide IP address leases.

 When you've finished the lab, you can refer to the Installing Client Operating Systems Lab Results.txt file to check your work.

21

1. **Install the two operating systems.**

_____

2. **Update both operating systems.**

_____

CHAPTER 22

Automating Client Operating System Installations

Activities included in this chapter:

- Exercise 22-1 Performing an Unattended Installation
- Exercise 22-2 Creating an Image of Windows 2000
- Exercise 22-3 Installing a Computer Image
- Lab 22-1 Automating Client Operating System Installations

EXERCISE 22-1

Performing an Unattended Installation

Activity Time:

2 hour(s)

Objective:

To create unattended installation files with Setup Manager, and perform and verify an unattended installation of Windows 2000 Professional.

Setup:

The Classroom Management Company is located in Rochester, New York. The client uses the 585 area code.

Setup:

Restart the computer to Windows 2000 Professional.

Scenario:

The network administrator at one of your clients, Classroom Management Company, has asked you to automate the installation of Windows 2000 Professional for her. She would like you to prepare an answer file that will enable anyone in the IT department to install Windows 2000 Professional on a computer without having to sit at the computer during the installation process. After reviewing the client's network environment, you have determined the following information:

- The client has an Active Directory domain named class.com. All Windows 2000 computers are members of this domain.

- The Admin1 domain user account with a password of password has sufficient permissions to add computers to a domain.

- Classroom Management Company uses DHCP servers to assign IP addresses to its clients.

- The network administrator is not concerned about the names of the computers. She says you can use whatever naming convention is the easiest when automating the installations.

- The network administrator wants all administrator accounts to have the same password.

- The Windows 2000 installation files have been shared on the company's Windows 2000 server at \\2000srv\win2000. The Windows 2000 Support Tools have been shared in \\2000srv\support.

- All of the computers the network administrator purchases have monitors and video cards that support true color (32 bit) and at least 800 x 600 screen resolution.

- All computers on the network print to the \\2000srv\netprint shared network printer.

- The network administrator would like you to save the files you create to automate installations on a floppy disk.

Your client would like you to test the unattended installation files you create to verify that they work.

What You Do	How You Do It
1. Install Setup Manager.	a. Log on as Administrator.
	b. In Windows Explorer, **create a folder named C:\Setup.**
	c. **Access \\2000srv\support.**
	d. **Double-click Deploy.cab.**
	e. **Copy the Setupmgr.exe and Setupmgx.dll files to C:\Setup.**

2. **Create the unattended installation files.**

    a. In Windows Explorer, **access the C:\Setup folder.**

    b. **Double-click setupmgr.exe.**

    c. **Click Next.**

    d. **Verify that Create A New Answer File is selected and click Next.**

    > Do you want to create a new answer file or modify an existing one?
    >
    > ⦿ Create a new answer file
    >
    > ○ Create an answer file that duplicates this computer's configuration
    >
    > ○ Modify an existing answer file

    e. **Verify that Windows 2000 Unattended Installation is selected and click Next.**

    > This answer file is for:
    >
    > ⦿ Windows 2000 Unattended Installation
    >
    > ○ Sysprep Install
    >
    > ○ Remote Installation Services

    f. **Verify that Windows 2000 Professional is selected and click Next.**

    g. On the User Interaction Level page, **select Fully Automated.**

    > Select the level of user interaction during Windows Setup:
    >
    > ○ Provide defaults
    >
    > ⦿ Fully automated

    h. **Click Next.**

    i. **Check I Accept The Terms Of The License Agreement and click Next.**

j. In the Name text box, **type *Network Adminis-trator***

k. In the Organization text box, **type *Classroom Management Company* and click Next.**

l. On the Computer Names page, **check Auto-matically Generate Computer Names Based On Organization Name.**

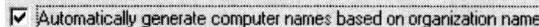

m. **Click Next.**

n. In the Password and Confirm Password text boxes, **type *password* and click Next.**

o. On the Display Settings page, from the Colors drop-down list, **select True Color (24 bit).**

p. From the Screen Area drop-down list, **select 800 x 600.**

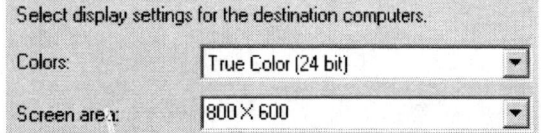

q. **Click Next.**

   📌 You can use Typical Settings because the client's network has a DHCP server.

r. On the Network Settings page, **verify that Typical Settings is selected and click Next.**

s. On the Workgroup Or Domain Page, **select Windows Server Domain.**

t. In the Domain text box, **type *class***

u. **Check Create A Computer Account In The Domain.**

v. In the User Name text box, **type** *Admin1*

w. In the Password and Confirm Password text boxes, **type** *password*

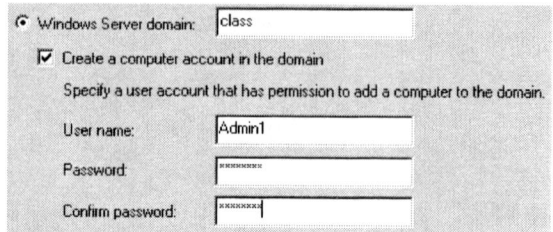

x. **Click Next.**

y. From the Time Zone drop-down list, **select (GMT–05:00) Eastern Time (US & Canada) and click Next.**

z. **Verify that Yes, Edit The Additional Settings is selected and click Next.**

aa. On the Telephony page, in the What Area (Or City) Code Are You In text box, **type *585* and click Next.**

ab. On the Regional Settings page, **click Next** to accept the default settings.

ac. On the Languages page, **click Next** to skip adding any additional language groups.

ad. On the Browser And Shell Settings page, **click Next** to accept the default settings.

ae. On the Installation Folder page, **click Next** to accept the default folder name of \Winnt.

af. On the Install Printers page, in the Network Printer Name text box, **type *2000srv*\\ *netprint* and click Add.**

Network printer name:
```
[                                    ]  [  Add  ]
```
Install these printers:
```
\\2000srv\netprint                      [ Remove ]
```

ag. **Click Next.**

ah. On the Run Once page, **click Next.**

ai. **Select No, This Answer File Will Be Used To Install From A CD.** You can choose this option even though you will be using a network share to install Windows 2000.

Do you want to create or modify a distribution folder?

○ Yes, create or modify a distribution folder

● No, this answer file will be used to install from a CD

aj. **Click Next.**

ak. **Insert a blank, formatted floppy disk into the floppy disk drive.**

al. On the Answer File Name page, in the Location And File Name text box, **enter A:\Unattend. txt and click Next.** Setup Manager also names the setup batch file unattend.bat by default.

Location and file name:
```
A:\Unattend.txt
```

am. **Click Finish.**

an. In Windows Explorer, **access the A drive.**

ao. **Right-click unattend.bat and choose Edit.**

ap. In the set SetupFiles = line, **change the path to set SetupFiles = \\2000srv\win2000.**

aq. **Change the line to run the winnt32 command to read \\2000srv\win2000\winnt32 /s:%SetupFiles% /unattend:%AnswerFile%**

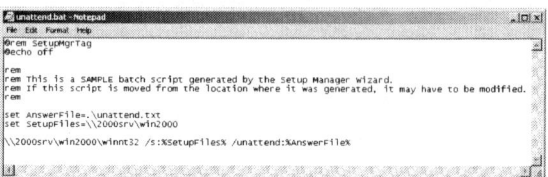

ar. **Save your changes and close Notepad.**

3. **Test the unattended installation.**

a. In Windows Explorer, **verify that you're accessing the A drive.**

b. **Double-click unattend.bat** to start the installation. **Remove the floppy disk when prompted.**

c. When the installation is complete, **log on as Administrator** to verify that the installation completed successfully.

d. **Check to see that the computer has the NetPrint network printer installed and that the display settings are set to 800 x 600 and true color (24 bit).**

Review Questions

1. You are planning to perform an unattended installation of Windows 2000. What utility can you use to create the unattended installation file?

2. What sections are required in a Windows 2000 unattended installation file?

_____

3. What is the syntax of the command you use to start an unattended installation from a Windows 2000 computer?

_____

4. You plan to perform an unattended installation by using the Windows 2000 CD-ROM. You have created an unattended installation file. What must you name this file, and where must you store it?

_____

5. You would like to use the utility for creating an unattended installation file, but it isn't on your Windows 2000 computer. How do you install this utility?

_____

_____

Exercise 22-2

Creating an Image of Windows 2000

Activity Time:

2 hour(s)

Objective:

To prepare a reference computer and use imaging software to create an installation image.

Scenario:

The network administrator at one of your clients, Classroom Management Company, has asked you to automate the installation of Windows 2000 for her. This company teaches training courses in Windows 2000 and would like an easy way to wipe out and re-install Windows 2000 on classroom computers when a course completes. To facilitate this goal, the network administrator would like you to create an image of one of the classroom computers. After reviewing the client's network environment, you have determined the following information:

- The client has an Active Directory domain named class.com. All Windows 2000 computers are members of this domain.

- The Admin1 domain user account with a password of password has sufficient permissions to add computers to a domain.

- Classroom Management Company uses DHCP servers to assign IP addresses to its clients.

- The network administrator wants all administrator accounts to have the same password.

- The Windows 2000 installation files have been shared on the company's Windows 2000 server at \\2000srv\win2000. This share contains both the \i386 folder and the \Support\ Tools folders.

- All computers use the Windows 2000 background as their wallpaper.

- All computers on the network print to the \\2000srv\netprint shared network printer.

- Each computer should be named Win2000–1. The network administrator will rename the computers whenever she installs the image.

- The network administrator does not want Norton Ghost or any system preparation tools included in the image. Because you won't be leaving Ghost on the computer, you don't need to register it.

Your client's network administrator has purchased Norton Ghost 2003 and copied its installation files to \\2000srv\ghost. In addition, she has created a share named \\2000srv\images on the server for storing cloned computer images for the network. She copied the Ghost executable files to \\2000srv\images.

The network administrator has already installed Windows 2000 Professional on the computer she wants you to clone. She would like you to install the latest Service Pack on this computer before you clone it.

What You Do	How You Do It
1. If necessary, **install the latest Windows 2000 Service Pack.**	a. **Open Internet Explorer.** If necessary, **configure the Internet connection.**
	b. In the Address text box in Internet Explorer, enter *www.microsoft.com/windows2000/ downloads/servicepacks*
	c. In the Service Packs list, **click the link for the most recent Service Pack.**
	d. **Click Download Windows 2000 SP#**, where # is the number of the most recent Service Pack.
	e. **Click Go.**
	f. **Click Yes.**
	g. Below Download, **click SP# Express Installation.**
	h. **Select Run This Program From Its Current Location and click OK.**
	i. **Click Yes.**
	j. **Follow the prompts to install the Service Pack.**
	k. When the Service Pack installation is complete, **click Finish.**

2. **Install Ghost.**

    a. **Log on as Administrator.**

    b. **Access the \\2000srv\ghost share.**

    c. **Double-click Ghost** to install Norton Ghost 2003.

    d. **Click Next.**

    e. **Select I Accept The Terms In The License Agreement and click Next.**

    f. If necessary, in the User Name and Organization text boxes, **enter the appropriate names.**

    g. **Click Next.**

    h. **Click Next** to accept the default installation folder.

    i. **Click Install.**

    j. If you're prompted to register the software, **click Skip and then click Yes.**

    k. **Click Next.**

    l. **Click Finish.**

A+ Certification Troubleshooting and Repair Lab Guide, Third Edition

3. **Create a Ghost boot disk.**

a. **Use Device Manager** to determine the driver for the computer's network card.

b. **Record the name of the network adapter driver:** _____

c. **Close Device Manager.**

d. From the Start menu, **choose Programs→ Norton Ghost 2003→Norton Ghost.**

e. In the left pane, **click Ghost Utilities.**

f. **Click Norton Ghost Boot Wizard.**

g. **Select Drive Mapping Boot Disk and click Next.**

h. In the Name list, **select the driver for the computer's network card.**

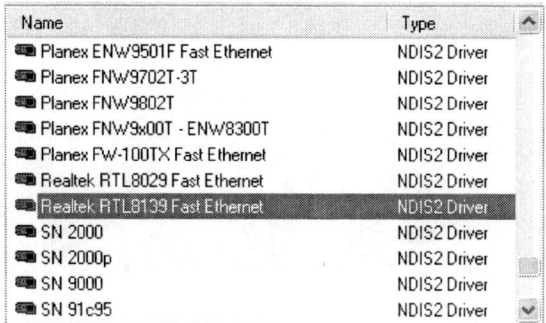

Name	Type
Planex ENW9501F Fast Ethernet	NDIS2 Driver
Planex FNW9702T-3T	NDIS2 Driver
Planex FNW9802T	NDIS2 Driver
Planex FNW9x00T - ENW8300T	NDIS2 Driver
Planex FW-100TX Fast Ethernet	NDIS2 Driver
Realtek RTL8029 Fast Ethernet	NDIS2 Driver
Realtek RTL8139 Fast Ethernet	NDIS2 Driver
SN 2000	NDIS2 Driver
SN 2000p	NDIS2 Driver
SN 9000	NDIS2 Driver
SN 91c95	NDIS2 Driver

i. **Click Next.**

j. On the DOS version page, **click Next.**

k. In the Client Computer Name text box, **type *computer#*** where # is your assigned number.

l. In the User Name text box, **type *Admin#***

m. In the Domain text box, **type** *class*

Client Computer Name:	computer1
User Name:	Admin1
Domain:	class

n. From the Drive Letter drop-down list, **select G:**

o. In the Maps To text box, **type \\\\2000srv** ***images***

Drive Letter:	G:
Maps To:	\\2000srv\images

p. **Click Next.**

q. **Verify that DHCP Will Assign The IP Settings is selected and click Next.**

⦿ DHCP will assign the IP settings
◯ The IP settings will be statically defined:

r. On the Destination Drive page, **click Next.**

s. **Click Next.**

t. **Click Start** to format the disk.

u. **Click OK** to begin the format.

v. **Click OK** when the format is complete.

w. **Click Close.**

x. When the boot disk is created, **click Finish.**

		y.	**Close Norton Ghost.**
		z.	**Remove the floppy disk and label it.**
4.	**Uninstall Norton Ghost.**	a.	In Control Panel, **double-click Add/Remove Programs.**
		b.	**Select Norton Ghost.**
		c.	**Click Remove.**
		d.	**Click Yes.**
		e.	**Close Add/Remove Programs and Control Panel.**

5. **Configure the necessary operating system settings.**

a. If neccessary, **create an administrative user named Admin# with a password of password.** You're going to use this account to configure the default user profile.

b. **Log on as Admin#.**

     If you don't disable this wizard, it will show up each time you download the computer image to a computer.

c. In the Getting Started With Windows 2000 window, **uncheck Show This Screen At Startup and click Exit.**

d. On the desktop, **right-click the background and choose Properties.**

e. In the Select A Background Picture list, **select Windows 2000.**

f. **Click OK** to save your changes.

g. If necessary, **click Yes** to enable Active Desktop.

h. In the Printers folder, **use the Add Printer wizard to install the \\2000srv\Netprint network printer.**

i. If necessary, **configure the computer as a member of the class.com domain** (right-click My Computer and select the Network Identification tab). **Restart the computer** when prompted.

6. **Update the default user profile.**

⚠ You must log on as an administrative user other than Admin# to copy the user profile.

a. **Log on to the local computer as administrator with a password of password.**

b. In Windows Explorer, **configure the Documents And Settings folder to display hidden files and folders** (access the C:\Documents And Settings folder. Choose Tools→Folder Options. Select the View tab, choose Show Hidden Files And Folders and click OK).

c. **Close Windows Explorer.**

d. **Right-click My Computer and choose Properties.**

e. **Select the User Profiles tab.**

f. In the Profiles Stored On This Computer list, **select Admin#.**

g. **Click Copy To.**

h. When you're prompted to log on to the domain, **click Cancel.**

i. **Click Browse.**

j. Below My Computer, **select the C:\Documents And Settings\Default User.**

k. **Click OK** to specify that you want to copy the Admin# user's profile to the Default User profile.

l. Below Permitted To Use, **click Change.**

m. When you're prompted to log on to the domain, **click Cancel.**

n. From the Look In drop-down list, **select your local computer.**

o. In the Name list, **double-click Everyone.**

p. **Click OK** to close the Copy To dialog box.

q. **Click Yes** to confirm that you want to copy the profile.

r. **Click OK** to close the System Properties dialog boxes.

7.   **Create the sysprep answer file.**

a.   In Windows Explorer, **create a folder named C:\Sysprep.**

b.   **Access \\2000srv\Support.**

c.   **Double-click Deploy.cab.**

d.   **Copy the all files to C:\Sysprep.**

e.   In Windows Explorer, **access the C:\Sysprep folder.**

f.   **Double-click setupmgr.exe.**

g.   **Click Next.**

h.   **Verify that Create A New Answer File is selected and click Next.**

i.   **Select Sysprep Install and click Next.**

j.   **Verify that Windows 2000 Professional is selected and click Next.**

k.   **Select Yes, Fully Automate The Installation and click Next.**

l.   In the Name text box, **type** *Network Administrator*

m.   In the Organization text box, **type** *Classroom Management Company* **and click Next.**

n.   In the Computer Name text box, **type** *Win2000–#*

o.   **Click Next.**

p.   In the Password and Confirm Password text boxes, **type** *password* **and click Next.**

q.   On the Display Settings page, **click Next to**

accept the default settings.

r. On the Network Settings page, **verify that Typical Settings is selected and click Next.**

s. On the Workgroup Or Domain Page, **select Windows Server Domain.**

t. In the Domain text box, **type** *class*

u. **Check Create A Computer Account In The Domain.**

v. In the User Name text box, **type** *Admin1*

w. In the Password and Confirm Password text boxes, **type** *password*

x. **Click Next.**

y. From the Time Zone drop-down list, **select (GMT-05:00) Eastern Time (US & Canada) and click Next.**

z. **Select No, Do Not Edit The Additional Settings and click Next.**

aa. **Verify that Yes, Create Or Modify The Sysprep Folder is selected and click Next.**

ab. On the Additional Commands page, **click Next.**

ac. On the OEM Branding page, **click Next.**

ad. On the Additional Files Or Folders page, **click Next.**

ae. On the OEM Duplicator String page, **click Next.**

af. On the Answer File Name page, **click Next** to accept the default answer file name of sysprep.inf.

8. **Prepare the computer for cloning.**

    a. In Windows Explorer, **access the C:\Sysprep folder.**

    b. In the C:\Sysprep folder, **double-click sysprep. exe.**

    c. **Close the C:\Sysprep folder.**

    d. In the Windows 2000 System Preparation Tool message box, **click OK.** Your computer will shut down when the system preparation is complete.

9. **Clone the computer.**

    a.   **Insert the Ghost boot disk and turn the computer on.**

    b.   When prompted, **press Enter** to log on as the user account you specified when you created the boot disk.

    c.   **Enter** *password*

    d.   **Enter** G:

    e.   **Enter** ghost

    f.   If necessary, **press Enter** to mark the computer's hard disks.

    g.   **Press Enter again.**

    h.   **Verify that Local is selected and press Enter.**

    i.   **Verify that Disk is selected and press Enter.**

    j.   **Select To Image and press Enter.**

    k.   On the Select Local Source Drive page, **press Enter.**

    l.   In the File Name text box, **type** *Adnıin#*

    m.   **Press Enter.**

    n.   **Verify that No is selected and press Enter.**

    o.   **Press Alt+Y to create the image.**

    p.   If neccessary, **press Enter** in the New Media dialog box.

    q.   When the image creation is complete, **press Enter** to continue.

r. **Press Q** to close Ghost.

s. **Press Y** to confirm you want to close Ghost.

Review Questions

1. You are planning to create an image of a computer that you will use to prepare Windows 2000 on 50 computers. You have installed all the user applications you want to include in the image. What should you do to make sure that these applications are accessible to any user that logs on to the computer after you've installed the image?

2. Which Windows 2000 utility enables you to prepare a computer you plan to image so that when you install the image on another computer, the computer runs a mini-setup routine the first time it boots?

3. Which utility do you use to create an image of a computer?

4. You are planning to create an image of a computer that you will use to prepare Windows 2000 on 50 computers. You have installed Windows 2000 on this computer. What should you do next?

5. You want to automate the mini-setup routine that runs when you install a computer image on another computer. What should you do?

EXERCISE 22-3

Installing a Computer Image

Activity Time:

45 minutes

Objective:
To install and verify a computer image on a target computer.

Scenario:
Your client, Classroom Management Company, has asked you to prepare their Windows 2000 classroom for class next week. You don't know how the computers are currently configured, but the client has an image of exactly how the computers must be configured for the class in the \\2000srv\images folder. The network administrator has installed Ghost in this share and provided you with a Ghost boot disk.

This image has the following settings:

- The computer is a member of the class.com Active Directory domain.
- It uses DHCP servers to obtain its IP address.
- The computer uses the Windows 2000 background as its wallpaper.
- It's configured to print to the \\2000srv\netprint shared network printer.

What You Do	How You Do It
1. Install the computer image.	a. **Shut down the computer.**
	b. **Insert the Ghost boot disk and turn on the computer.**
	c. When prompted, **press Enter** to log on as the user account you specified when you created the boot disk.
	d. **Enter** *password*
	e. **Enter** G:
	f. **Enter** ghost
	g. **Press Enter.**
	h. **Verify that Local is selected and press Enter.**
	i. **Verify that Disk is selected and press Enter.**
	j. **Select From Image and press Enter.**
	k. **Use the arrow keys to highlight the Admin#. GHO image file and press Alt+O.**
	l. On the Select Local Destination Drive page, **press Enter.**
	m. **Press Alt+O.**
	n. **Press Alt+Y to install the image.**
	o. **Press Enter** to restart the computer.
	p. **Remove the boot disk.**

2. **Verify the computer installation.**

    a. The mini-setup process now runs. When the process is complete, **log on locally as Admin#.**

    b. **Verify that the desktop wallpaper is Windows 2000.**

    c. **Make sure that the computer is configured to print to the \\2000srv\netprint network printer.**

    d. **Verify that the computer is a member of the class.com domain.**

    e. **Verify that the computer is configured to obtain its IP address from a DHCP server.**

Review Questions

1. What do you need to install a computer image on a computer?

_____

_____

2. True or False: You can change the size of a computer's partitions when you install an image file.

_____

3. How can you verify that the computer image installed successfully?

_____

_____

Lab 22-1

Automating Client Operating System Installations

Activity Time:

2 hour(s)

Objective:

To perform an unattended installation of either Windows 2000 Professional or Windows XP Professional.

Setup:

You cannot complete this activity using the computers configured for the classroom. You will need:

- A computer that meets the minimum hardware requirements for the operating system you will install.

- A computer on which to create the unattended answer file. This can be the same computer on which you will perform the new installation, as long as the computer currently has an operating system.

- Access to the installation CD-ROM for the operating system you will install.

- If the drivers for your computer's hardware are not included on the installation CD-ROMs, you will also need access to the hardware drivers.

- Access to the Internet, so that you can update the computer after completing the installation.

Scenario:

Your client would like you to install his new operating system on 50 new computers he has purchased. Because some of the computers have different hardware, you can't use Ghost to install the computers. These computers will all be members of the Research workgroup. The network is TCP/IP-based and clients obtain IP addresses from a DHCP server. Your client would like you to install the operating system in as little time as possible.

 When you have finished the lab, you can refer to the Automating Client Operating System Installations Lab Results.txt file to check your work.

1. **Perform an unattended installation of the operating system.**

---

2. **Update the operating system.**

Follow-up

In this course, you installed, removed, upgraded, maintained, and troubleshot computer hardware. You also performed operating systems management tasks in the Windows 98, Windows 2000, Windows NT, and Windows XP operating systems. Mastering the skills in this course will enable you to respond to any hardware or operating system technical support calls you encounter. By combining the class experience with review, study, and hands-on experience, you'll also be prepared to demonstrate your knowledge on the A+ certification examinations.

GLOSSARY

8008

Introduced by Intel in 1972, the 8008 was the first microprocessor to be supported by a high-level language compiler.

abacus

An early calculating instrument that uses sliding beads in columns that are divided in two by a center bar.

AC

(alternating current) Electrical current that flows in two directions at variable voltages.

adapter card

Add-on boards or cards that provide special functions for customizing or extending a computer's capability.

AGP

(Accelerated Graphics Port) A bus architecture based on PCI and designed specifically to speed up 3D graphics.

ampere

Unit of measure for current. Also known as amps.

Analytical Engine

Charles Babbage's vision of a mechanical calculator that would follow programmed instructions to perform any mathematical operations. The engine could store results for use later, and look up values in tables and call on standard subroutines.

answer file

A setup file that provides the answers needed by the Windows Setup program during an unattended installation.

APIPA

(Automatic Private IP Addressing) The private IP address range from 169.254.0.1 to 169.254.255.254 used by Microsoft to provide temporary IP connectivity between Windows computers that are part of a single network segment and are not connected to the Internet.

application software

High-level programs that are written to run on specific operating systems and that provide specific functionality such as word processing, graphics creation, or database management.

ASR

(Automated System Recovery) A process that uses backup data and the Windows XP Professional installation source files to rebuild a failed computer.

asynchronous

A bit synchronization transmission technique that uses start and stop bits.

AT commands

The modem command set developed by the Hayes company for use on its modems and now used on most modems.

ATA

(Advanced Technology Attachment) The official ANSI term for IDE drives.

ATAPI

(AT Attachment Packet Interface) An extension to EIDE that enables support for CD-ROM, CD-R, CD-RW, DVD-ROM, DVD-R, and tape drives.

Autoexec.bat

A file used by the MS-DOS operating system to automatically load software whenever the computer boots.

backside bus

A bus connecting the CPU to L2 cache. It runs faster than the frontside bus. It connects the two chips at the same clock rate as the CPU itself as opposed to the frontside bus which runs at only a fraction of the CPU clock speed.

bank

Multiple rows of DRAM in a single system that can be accessed simultaneously.

basic disk

A physical hard disk that is divided logically into partitions. A basic hard disk can contain a maximum of four partitions, of which, a maximum of one can be extended.

binary number system

A numbering system based on two discrete states.

BIOS
(Basic Input Output System) Low-level software that acts as the interface between the hardware and the operating system in a computer.

bit
A single binary digit having a value of 0 or 1.

boolean
An expression where the results are either true or false. The expression uses AND, OR, and NOT functions to compare values.

boot partition
The hard disk partition that contains the \Windows or \Winnt folder.

boot sector
The reserved area on a hard disk or floppy disk where the information for booting the computer is stored.

boot sequence
The portion of the Windows 2000/NT/XP startup process where the computer physically starts up and the system hardware is initialized.

Bootsect.dos
A Windows 2000/NT/XP boot file that loads a non-Windows 2000, Windows XP, or Windows NT operating system on a dual-boot computer.

buffers
A configuration setting that enables you to specify how much memory is reserved for transferring temporary information between a non-Windows application in RAM and I/O devices.

built-in groups
The security groups created automatically when you install Windows 2000, Windows XP, or Window NT.

built-in user accounts
The user accounts created automatically when you install Windows 2000, Windows XP, or Windows NT.

bus
The collection of wires that connect an interface card and the microprocessor, and the rules that describe how data should be transferred through the connection. Examples include ISA, EISA, and PCI.

bus master
Takes control of the bus away from the CPU to transfer data directly to RAM or other devices.

bus topology
A physical topology where a single main cable called the bus or backbone carries all network data. Nodes connect directly to the bus.

byte
A group of 8 bits.

card services
Assigns resources of PC Cards and detects when a card is inserted or removed.

CardBus
A bus mastering technology used on PC Cards.

CAT5
(Category 5) A type of cabling that consists of four twisted-pairs of copper wire terminated by RJ-45 connectors. Can be used for Token Ring, 1000BaseT, 100BaseT, and 10BaseT networking.

channel
A communication path between components.

charge
The difference between the number of electrons and protons associated with a body.

chipset
The set of chips on the system board that support the CPU and other basic functions.

CIS
(Card Information Structure) A PC Card feature that passes information about the PC Card to the computer so that the card can be automatically configured for use.

client
A computer on a network that makes use of the resources managed by a server.

client-server network
A network where one or more computers act primarily as providers of network resources (servers), and one or more computers act primarily as consumers of network resources (clients).

cluster

The smallest unit of disk space used when the operating system writes to the hard disk.

CMOS

(Complimentary Metal Oxide Semiconductor) Pronounced see-moss. The most widely used type of integrated circuit for digital processors and memories. Virtually everything is configured through CMOS today.

CMOS RAM

(Complementary Metal Oxide Semiconductor RAM) A special type of memory that stores information about the computer's setup.

coaxial cable

A high-capacity cable used in communications and video, commonly called coax. It contains an insulated solid or stranded wire surrounded by a solid or braided metallic shield, wrapped in a plastic cover.

Command.com

An MS-DOS operating system file that provides the command line interface. Also called the command interpreter and the DOS shell.

computer image

An exact duplicate copy of a computer hard disk's information.

Config.sys

A file used by the MS-DOS operating system to perform tasks such as load device drivers, configuring the operating system environment, and optimizing memory management.

conventional memory

The first 640 KB of RAM in the computer. MS-DOS uses this portion of memory whenever you run an application such as the MS-DOS Edit program. If you run a DOS application within Windows, Windows uses some of the computer's memory to simulate conventional memory.

corona

An assembly within a laser printer that contains a wire (the corona wire) which is responsible for charging the paper.

CPU

(Central Processing Unit) The main chip on the system board, the CPU performs software instructions and mathematical and logical equations.

CPU cache

A type of high-speed RAM that is added directly to a processor to improve computing speed. Often referred to as onboard cache, primary cache, or L1 (Level 1) cache. Compare with L2 cache and RAM.

CRT

(Cathode Ray Tube) Displays images using phosphorous dots with a scanned electron beam.

current

The amount of electricity moving through a conductive material such as a wire. Current is measured in amps.

cylinder

The aggregate of all tracks that reside in the same location on every disk surface. On multiple-platter disks, the cylinder is the sum total of every track with the same track number on every surface. On a floppy disk, a cylinder comprises the top and corresponding bottom track.

data

The configuration information stored within a Registry value.

data bus

The connection between the CPU, memory, and peripheral devices.

DC

(direct current) Electrical current that flows in only one direction and at a constant voltage.

decimal number system

A numbering system based on 10 discrete states.

default gateway

An IP address used to identify a TCP/IP-based router that provides access to a remote network. When you configure a computer's default gateway, the computer forwards any communications for remote networks to the IP address of the default gateway.

degauss

Remove magnetism from a device.

device conflict
A conflict between devices that have been assigned the same resources.

device driver
Software that enables the operating system and a peripheral device to communicate with each other.

DHCP
(Dynamic Host Configuration Protocol) A protocol which enables a Windows NT or Windows 2000 server to dynamically assign IP addresses to clients.

dial-up connection
An outbound connection that uses WAN transmission media such as modems and phone lines to connect a client on one physical network to a Remote Access Server (RAS) on a remote network.

DIMM
(Dual In-line Memory Module) A group of memory chips that transfer information 64 bits at a time.

diode
An electronic component that acts like a one-way valve. Diodes are often used to change Alternating Current (AC) to Direct Current (DC), as temperature or light sensors, and as light emitters.

dip switch
Switches on hardware used to configure hardware settings. These are usually rocker switches (like light switches) to turn on or off.

dissipative material
A conductive material with high resistance that dissipates a charge slowly.

DMA
(Direct Memory Access) Specialized circuitry or a dedicated microprocessor that transfers data from adapters to memory without using the CPU.

DNS
(Domain Name System) A static, distributed, hierarchical database system used to map computer (host) names to IP addresses.

domain
A Microsoft network model that an administrator implements by grouping computers together for the purpose of sharing a centralized user account database. Sharing this user account database enables users to use these accounts to log on at any computer in the domain.

domain controller
A server that stores the user account database for the domain and is responsible for authenticating users when they log on to the domain.

dot-matrix printer
A printer that forms images out of dots on paper. Dot patterns are created by a set of pins that strike an inked ribbon.

DRAM
(Dynamic RAM) A type of RAM that needs to be refreshed.

drive controller
The circuitry that enables the drive and the CPU to communicate with each other.

drive interface
The collection of electrical and logical connections between a hard drive and a PC.

driver
Software that enables the operating system and a peripheral device to communicate with each other. Also referred to as device driver.

dynamic disk
A physical hard disk that is divided logically into volumes. A dynamic disk can contain an unlimited number of volumes.

ECC
(Error Correction Code) A type of memory that corrects errors on the fly.

ECP
(Extended Capability Port) Newer-generation parallel port standard that provides roughly 10 times faster throughput than the Centronics standard. Used by newer-generation printers and scanners.

EDO RAM

(Extended Data Output RAM) A type of DRAM that enables a memory address to hold data for multiple reads.

EDSAC

(Electronic Delay Storage Automatic Computer) A well-engineered machine built by Maurice Wilkes and colleagues at the University of Cambridge Mathematics Lab in 1949 and was a productive tool for mathematicians.

EDVAC

(Electronic Discrete Variable Automatic Computer) The first computer to use stored programs.

EEPROM

(Electrically Erasable Programmable Read-Only Memory) A memory chip that is programmed and erased electrically. When the EEPROM is programmed, it acts like a regular ROM chip.

EISA bus

(Extended Industry Standard Architecture bus) A PC bus standard that extends the 16-bit ISA bus (AT bus) to 32 bits and provides bus mastering.

electrical energy

The total amount of electrical power delivered in a given time period.

electrical potential

The potential energy stored in an electrically-charged body.

emm386.exe

A driver that must be loaded before DOS can access expanded memory. You load this driver by modifying the computer's config.sys file and adding the line `device = c:\dos\emm386.exe`. You can also use the emm386.exe driver to make the upper memory area accessible for storing TSRs by adding (or modifying) the line in config.sys to read `device = c:\dos\emm386.exe noems`.

EMS

(expanded RAM) The first technology that enabled computers and MS-DOS to access more than 1 MB of memory; this goal was accomplished by installing an expansion card in the computer with additional memory chips. MS-DOS accessed expanded RAM by swapping it in and out of the upper memory area, 64 KB at a time. This type of memory is also referred to as EMS, which is short for"expanded memory specification."

encryption

The process of using an encryption key to translate data into a coded version that cannot be read without access to the required decryption key.

ENIAC

(Electronic Numerical Integrator And Computer) Developed for the U.S. Army by J. Presper Eckert and John Mauchly at the University of Pennsylvania in Philadelphia. ENIAC was programmed by plugging in cords and setting thousands of switches to direct how 18,000 vacuum tubes would perform 5,000 calculations per second.

EPP

(Enhanced Parallel Port) Newer-generation parallel port standard that offers roughly 10 times faster throughput than the Centronics standard. Used mostly by non-printer peripherals such as CD-ROM drives and network adapters.

EPROM

(Erasable Programmable Read-Only Memory) A re-usable memory chip that is programmed electrically and erased by exposure to ultraviolet light. When the EPROM is programmed, it acts like a regular ROM chip.

ERD

(emergency repair disk) A disk that contains information about the current configuration of the operating system and that can be used to repair problems with the operating system.

ESD

(electrostatic discharge) Sparks (electrons) that jump from an electrically charged object to an approaching conductive object.

extended partition
A partition used simply for storing data. You cannot use an extended partition to boot a computer.

fastIrDA
Infrared standard that uses a transfer speed of 4 Mbps.

FAT32
A file system that provides support for disks larger than 2 GB on Windows 95 OSR2, Windows 98, and Windows ME systems.

files
A configuration setting that enables you to specify how much memory is reserved for the number of files opened by a DOS application.

FireWire
A high-speed serial bus developed by Apple and Texas Instruments that allows for the connection of up to 63 devices.

firmware
Software stored in memory chips that retains data whether or not power to the computer is on.

Flash memory
A special type of EEPROM that can be erased and written to in blocks instead of in bytes. When the flash memory is programmed, it acts like a regular ROM chip.

flash memory cards
A removable solid-state mass storage device that resides on a small card.

Flash ROM
Memory that stores data similarly to EEPROM, but uses a super-voltage charge to erase a block of data. Can only be erased and rewritten a few times.

form factor
The size and shape of a given component. Often used in terms of motherboard and drive characteristics.

FPM RAM
(Fast Page Mode RAM) Used in older 32-pin SIMMs.

fragmentation
The degree to which the pieces that make up files are spread across the hard disk.

frame type
Specifies the format in which the computer sends data and expects to receive data. Two computers must be using not only the NWLink IPX/SPX protocol but also the same frame type in order to communicate across a network.

full duplex
The ability to send and receive data simultaneously.

fusing assembly
A component in a laser printer that uses two rollers to heat toner particles, melting them into the paper.

geosynchronous
Maintains an orbit with a fixed relationship to Earth.

gigabyte
A means of measuring file or disk size, equivalent to 1,024 MB. Abbreviated as GB.

ground
Any conducting body with a potential of zero; usually, the earth itself or something connected to the earth.

group policy object
A collection of settings, applied within the Active Directory, that are used primarily to restrict users' actions on computers within an Active Directory domain.

GUI
(Graphical User Interface) A means of communicating with an operating system by using a mouse or other device to work with pictorial screen elements, instead of typing text commands at the keyboard.

Hal.dll
A Windows 2000/NT/XP driver that isolates the computer's hardware and device drivers from the operating system so that the same operating system can be used on a variety of hardware.

half duplex
The ability to send data in one direction at a time.

hazardous materials
Any materials that must be handled in a special way in order to prevent injury to people or damage to the environment.

heat sink

A device attached to a processor that addresses the problem of overheating processors. Cool air is blown by a fan onto the device's main elements, keeping the air around the processor cool.

hexadecimal number system

A numbering system based on 16 discrete states.

high memory area

The first 64 KB of RAM immediately after the first megabyte of RAM in the computer (this is the memory between 1024 KB and 1088 KB). In DOS, you can use the high memory area to store a single terminate-and-stay-resident (TSR) program, a device driver, or DOS itself. Windows does not simulate the high memory area when you run a non-Windows application.

himem.sys

A driver that must be loaded before DOS can access extended memory. You load this driver by modifying the computer's config.sys file and adding the line `device = c:\dos\himem.sys`.

hoax

Tricks users into believing there is a malicious code threat to their systems

hotswap

To change out a device without needing to power down the PC during installation or removal of the device.

HTML

(HyperText Markup Language) The authoring language used to create documents on the Web. HTML defines the structure and layout of a Web document as it should present itself in a Web browser.

hub

A central connecting device in a network that joins communication lines together in a star configuration.

HVD

(High Voltage Differential Signaling) A SCSI device that uses two wires, one for data and one for the inverse of data. These devices use high voltage and can't be used on a single-ended SCSI chain.

hybrid topology

A physical topology that uses two or more of the basic physical topologies, such as bus, ring, star, and mesh.

I/O address

A three-digit hexadecimal number (3F8, 278, and so on) used to identify and signal a peripheral device such as a parallel port, serial port, or sound card.

IDE

(Integrated Drive Electronics) A drive interface that provides inexpensive, high-speed data transfer between the IDE drive and the other components of the computer.

IEEE

(Institute of Electrical and Electronic Engineers) Pronounced "I-triple-E." An organization of scientists, engineers, and students of electronics and related fields whose technical and standards committees develop, publish, and revise computing and telecommunications standards.

inductance

Inductance is a circuit or device in which a change in the current generates an electromotive force.

infrared

Technology that uses a beam of light to transmit data, rather than cables, using line-of-sight technology.

inkjet printer

A printer that forms images by spraying ink on the paper.

instruction set

The collection of commands used by a CPU to perform calculations and other computing operations.

integrated circuit

An electronic component consisting of several transistors and resistors, connected together on a semiconductor chip.

interface card

A means of connecting devices to the system board so that they can communicate with the microprocessor.

interrupt

A signal that gets the attention of the CPU and is usually generated when I/O is required.

Io.sys

An MS-DOS operating system file that enables the operating system to access the computer's hardware.

IP address

Four numbers that uniquely identify a computer on the network. This address is typically shown in the format 192.168.200.200. A portion of the IP address is used to identify the network on which the computer resides (similar to the street name in a mailing address); the remaining portion of the IP address is used to identify the computer itself (similar to the house number portion of a mailing address.)

IRQ

(Interrupt Request Line) A hardware interrupt on a PC. The interrupt lets the CPU know that the device needs attention from the CPU.

ISA bus

(Industry Standard Architecture bus) An expansion bus commonly used in PCs.

jumper

A small plug placed over pins (or removed from pins) to configure hardware settings. Metal contacts inside the plug complete an electrical circuit to specify the settings for the hardware.

key

A folder that appears in the left pane of the Registry Editor window. A key can contain other keys (also called subkeys) and values.

kilobyte

A means of measuring file or disk size, equivalent to 1,024 bytes. Abbreviated as KB.

L1 cache

See primary cache.

L2 cache

See secondary cache.

L2TP

(Layer Two Tunneling Protocol) An Internet standard VPN protocol for connecting a variety of VPN servers, including RRAS servers running L2TP.

L3 cache

Memory on the motherboard between the processor and RAM when there's a built-in L2 cache on the processor.

laser printer

A type of printer that produces images on paper by using a laser beam and an electrophotographic drum. Produces high-quality output.

latency

The time between when a message is sent and received by the other party.

LCD

(Liquid Crystal Display) A monitor constructed of a liquid crystal solution between two sheets of polarized material.

Li-Ion

Portable computer lithium battery with a long life.

Lithium Polymer

Portable computer battery using a jelly-like material.

load

Power consumption of a device. A load is calculated with inductance, capacitance, and other electrical characteristics.

load phases

The portion of the Windows 2000/NT/XP startup process where the operating system is loaded.

LVD

(Low Voltage Differential Signaling) A SCSI device that uses two wires, one for data and one for the inverse of data. These devices use a low voltage and can be used on a single-ended SCSI chain.

magnetic core memory

Memory that stores binary data (0 or 1) in the orientation of magnetic charges in ferrite cores about one-sixteenth-inch in diameter.

malicious code attack

A type of software-based attack where an attacker inserts malicious code into a user's system to disrupt or disable the operating system or an application.

Mark I

A programmable, electromechanical calculator that combined 78 adding machines to perform three calculations per second. It was designed by Howard Aiken, built by IBM, and installed at Harvard in 1944.

math coprocessor

A mathematical circuit that performs high-speed floating point operations. It is generally built into the CPU chip. In older PCs, such as the 386SX and 486SX, the math coprocessor was an optional and separate chip.

MBR

(Master Boot Record) Contains the instructions for finding and loading the computer's operating system.

media

In a network, the transmission media that links computers together in a network. Usually a cable, but could be a wireless medium. In drives, the storage object on which data is stored.

megabyte

A means of measuring file or disk size, equivalent to 1,024 KB. Abbreviated as MB.

memory

Internal storage areas of the computer.

memory address

An area of computer memory assigned to a device.

memory bank

The collection of memory expansion slots in a computer.

memory package

A circuit board design that holds the memory chips that are plugged into the memory expansion slots on the motherboard.

mesh topology

A physical topology in which each node has a direct connection to all other nodes on the network, providing dedicated, permanent point-to-point communication paths.

microprocessor

A complete central processing unit on a single chip, the microprocessor controls the operation of all the other computer components.

MIDI

(Musical Instrument Digital Interface) An interface that allows you to connect and control electronic musical devices such as electric keyboards (pianos), synthesizers, drum kits, and guitars.

MNP

(Microcom Networking Protocol) Five modem standards offering different levels of error correction and detection.

motherboard

The main circuit board in a personal computer. Also referred to as a system board.

Msdos.sys

An MS-DOS operating system file that enables the computer to access disks.

MSDS

(Material Safety Data Sheets) Technical bulletins designed to give users and emergency personnel information about the proper procedures of the storage and handling of a hazardous substance.

multimeter

Electronic test equipment that can perform multiple tasks, usually including measurement of voltage, current, and resistance.

Napier's Bones

A set of rectangular rods with numbers etched on them that let users do multiplication by adding the numbers on properly positioned rods. Precursor of the slide rule.

NetBEUI

A small network protocol, developed by Microsoft, that enables computers to communicate over a network. You can use NetBEUI in place of a network protocol such as TCP/IP as long as the computers on the network do not need to access the Internet.

network adapter

A printed circuit board that plugs into both the clients and servers and controls the exchange of data between them. Also referred to as network boards, network cards, and Network Interface Cards (NICs).

network client

A software component you install that enables a computer to access shared files and printers on another computer across the network. For example, if you want a Windows 2000 computer to access shared files on a Novell NetWare 4.12 server, you must install the Client Service For NetWare on the Windows 2000 computer first.

network protocol
A special electronic language that enables network computers to communicate.

network-attached printer
A printer with an installed network card that is connected directly to the network cabling that you connect to by specifying its IP address.

nibble
A group of 4 bits. An 8-bit byte is written as 2 nibbles to make it easier to read.

NiCad
Portable computer battery made of nickel and cadmium with a three to four hour life.

NiMH
Environmentally friendly battery for portable computers.

node
Any of the devices that can be accessed on the network. This includes devices such as servers, clients, and printers.

non-routable
Refers to network protocols that cannot send data across routers.

Ntbootdd.sys
A Windows 2000/NT/XP boot file that initializes support for SCSI hard disks on which the BIOS is disabled.

Ntdetect.com
A Windows 2000/NT/XP boot file that performs hardware detection on the computer.

Ntldr
A Windows 2000/NT/XP boot file that loads the operating system.

Ntoskrnl.exe
A Windows 2000/NT/XP boot file that loads the basic Windows 2000, Windows NT, or Windows XP operating system.

NWLink IPX/SPX
Microsoft's version of Novell NetWare's proprietary network protocol, IPX/SPX. This protocol enables computers to communicate over a network (including across routers). The NWLink IPX/SPX protocol does not, however, enables computers to communicate on the Internet.

ohm
Unit of measure for resistance.

online UPS
A UPS that supplies power from a battery at all times. The battery is charged from the regular electrical supply.

operands
The values being compared in a logical or mathematical operation.

OS
(Operating System) A type of system software that provides the basic interface between the user and the computer components.

outbound connection
A network connection that connects clients on one physical network to resources on a remote network.

paging file
The file used by Windows to implement virtual memory. This file is also known as a swap file.

palmtop
Another name for a PDA.

parity
An error-checking method that uses a ninth bit or parity bit to validate the contents of memory.

partition
An area of hard disk that is treated logically as a single unit of storage.

Pascaline machine
A calculating machine that could add and subtract, developed in 1642 by Blaise Pascal.

path
An environment variable that enables you to specify the folders in which you want the operating system to search for executable files.

PC

(Personal Computer) Stand-alone, single-user desktop, or smaller, computers that can function independently. PC used to refer to any personal computer, but now refers to personal computers that follow the original design by IBM, use Intel or compatible chips, and usually have some version of Windows as an operating system. PCs are sometimes called IBM compatibles.

PC Card

The credit-card-sized devices which are used in portable instead of desktop expansion cards.

PCI bus

(Peripheral Component Interconnect bus) A peripheral bus commonly used in PCs that provides a high-speed data path between the CPU and peripheral devices.

PCMCIA

(Personal Computer Memory Card International Association) An association of organizations that establishes standards for PC Cards.

PDA

(Personal Digital Assistant) A very small computer that can be held in one hand. Often used to keep an electronic calendar and address book, get email, send faxes, and take notes on the go.

peer-to-peer network

A network where all computers connected to the network can act as a provider (server) or consumer (client) of network resources.

peripheral

Any computing device that is connected to the CPU and main memory.

PGA

(Pin Grid Array) A type of CPU packaging design on which pins are distributed evenly in parallel rows on the entire bottom of a square chip.

physical topology

The layout of networked computers in physical relationship to each other.

pixel

The smallest discrete element on a video display.

plenum

An air-handling space which is part of the heating and cooling system in a building and is often a convenient place to run cables.

plenum cable

Cable made of special materials in the insulation layers that make it fire resistant. When it burns, it produces a minimal amount of smoke and chemical fumes.

Plug and Play

A method in which the operating system automatically configures adapter settings. Also written as PnP.

port

A hardware connection interface on a computer system that enables devices to be connected to the system.

potential difference

A measurement of the difference in electrical potential energy between two different objects. Also called voltage.

potential energy

Energy that is stored in a body as a result of the position or condition of the body.

PPP

(Point-to-Point Protocol) A remote access protocol used to transmit data across phone lines.

PPTP

(Point-to-Point Tunneling Protocol) A Microsoft proprietary VPN protocol for connecting to Microsoft Routing and Remote Access Service (RRAS) servers running PPP.

primary cache

A type of high-speed RAM that is added directly to a processor to improve computing speed. Often referred to as onboard cache, CPU cache, or L1 (Level 1) cache. Compare with L2 cache and RAM.

primary network logon types

A configuration setting that determines how Windows 98 will attempt to log users on to the computer.

primary partition

A partition that can be used to boot the computer.

print driver
A software component you install in Windows to configure the operating system to communicate with a specific printer.

print spooler
The print process component that receives the job from the print driver and stores it until it can be produced on the printer.

processor
Another way to refer to the microprocessor, or CPU.

PROM
(Programmable Read-Only Memory) A memory chip that can be programmed once. After it's programmed, it acts like a regular ROM chip.

proprietary
A design that is unique to a specific manufacturer. The design has not been shared so there are no competing product lines making a component, so you are forced to purchase it directly from the manufacturer.

PS/2 interface
A round 6-pin port used to connect keyboards and mice to PCs.

RAM
(Random Access Memory) RAM chips are integrated circuit chips that act as the computer's primary temporary storage place for data.

RAM chip
An integrated circuit that acts as the computer's primary temporary storage place for data. RAM stands for Random Access Memory.

RAMDAC
(Random Access Memory Digital-Analog Converter) Component on the video card that reads the bytes of video data in the card's memory and converts the digital data in memory to continuous analog signals that tell the monitor what to display.

RDRAM
(Rambus Dynamic RAM) A new memory architecture by Rambus, Inc. that supports speeds up to 800 MHz.

Recovery Console
A command-line utility for repairing a computer.

register
A special high-speed storage area located within a processor.

Registry
A database of system and application configuration information.

remote connection
A network connection that connects clients on one physical network to resources on a remote network.

remote-access connection
A network connection that connects clients on one physical network to resources on a remote network.

resistance
Opposition to the flow of electrons.

resistor
An electronic component that resists the flow of electric current in an electronic circuit.

RIMM
(Rambus Inline Memory Module) A memory module for RDRAM. Supports from one to 16 direct RDRAM devices in a Rambus channel. Used primarily as main memory on a system board.

ring topology
A physical topology where all nodes are connected in a continuous loop, and nodes relay information around the loop in a round-robin manner.

riser card
A board that's plugged into the motherboard, it "rises" above the motherboard and is used to connect modems, audio cards, and network cards to the system.

ROM
(Read-Only Memory) A special type of memory that is permanent. It stores programs necessary to boot the computer and to diagnose problems.

SAM
(Sequential Access Memory) Used for memory where data can be stored in sequential order such as memory buffers.

SCSI

(Small Computer System Interface) A drive controller that provides high-performance data transfer between the SCSI device and the other components of the computer. Pronounced scuzzy.

SDRAM

(Synchronous DRAM) Memory that has a clock that is coordinated with the system clock to synchronize the memory chip's input and output signals.

SECC

(Single Edge Contact Cartridge) Type of CPU packaging that refers to a design where the processor is located on a circuit board that is inserted into a slot on the system board.

secondary cache

A type of high-speed RAM that is placed between the processor and conventional RAM to improve computing speed. Often referred to as L2 (Level 2) cache. Compare with CPU cache and RAM.

sector

The smallest unit of storage read or written on a disk.

semiconductor

A solid-state substance that can be electrically altered to act as either a conductor or an insulator.

server

A computer on a network that manages resources for other computers on the network.

share-level security

Enables you to set a password on each individual shared resource.

SIMM

(Single In-line Memory Module) A group of memory chips that transfer information 32 bits at a time.

single-ended device

SCSI device that uses a single wire for each bit of data.

SLIP

(Serial Line Internet Protocol) A remote access protocol used to transmit data across serial lines.

slowIrDA

Infrared standard that uses a transfer speed of 9.6 Kbps.

socket services

Device driver software for a PC Card.

SODIMM

(Small Outline Dual Inline Memory Module) A memory module standard used in some notebook and iMac systems.

soldered

A means of securing electronic components to a circuit board by using a combination of lead, tin, and silver (solder) and a tool called a soldering iron.

sound card

An internal card used to convert digital signals to sound waves. Includes several external ports for connecting electronic musical instruments, game controllers, speakers, and microphones. Usually also includes internal connections for playback of audio CDs.

SPGA

(Staggered Pin Grid Array) This CPU packaging design staggers pins so that more pins will fit on the same amount of surface.

spools

The process of storing a print job on a hard disk; this print job is then later sent to the printer.

SRAM

(Static RAM) A type of RAM that doesn't need to be refreshed.

Standby UPS

SUPSs are UPSs that supply power from a battery when power problems are detected. Also referred to as a Standby Power Supply (SPS).

star topology

A physical topology where all nodes individually connect to a central device such as a hub.

static IP address

An IP address that is configured manually, not using DHCP. Static IP addresses are not meant to change frequently.

Stepped Reckoner

A mechanical calculator developed by Gottfried von Leibniz that improved Pascal's design to include multiplication and division.

STP

(shielded twisted-pair) Twisted-pair cable that is wrapped in a metal sheath. This reduces the possibility of problems caused by electrical interference.

subnet mask

Four numbers used to distinguish the network portion of the IP address from that of the computer portion. For example, if a computer's IP address is 192.168.200.200 and the subnet mask is 255.255.255.0, this means that the network portion of the address is 192.168.200, and the computer portion is the remaining byte (200).

synchronous

Transmission of a bit stream of data where the transmitter and receiver are synchronized.

System

The Windows 2000/NT/XP Registry file that contains the system configuration information and a list of the device drivers to be loaded during the boot process.

system board

The main circuit board in a personal computer. Also referred to as a motherboard

system partition

The hard disk partition that contains the files necessary for booting the Windows 2000, Windows NT, or Windows XP operating system.

system policy

A collection of settings used to restrict users' actions on computers within a Windows NT domain. These settings are applied through the use of a system policy file on the domain controllers.

system software

Low-level programs that provide the most basic functionality, such as operating systems.

system state data

The Windows 2000 or Windows XP boot files, Registry, COM+ object registrations, and all files installed during the installation of Windows 2000 or Windows XP that have the .sys, .dll, .ttf, .fon, .ocx, and .exe extension.

System.ini

A Windows initialization (.ini) file that's used to configure specific parameters used by DOS and Windows 9x.

TCP/IP

(Transmission Control Protocol/Internet Protocol) A suite of protocols that enables computers to communicate across a network and over the Internet. This protocol suite consists of many different protocols, most notably, TCP and IP. In addition, it includes SNMP for sending email and HTTP for connecting to and downloading Web pages.

thermal compound

Used to attach a heat sink to a CPU. Manufactured to provide maximum heat transfer from the CPU to the heat sink.

throughput

The amount of data that can be processed from input through to output within a given time period.

toner

An electrically charged dry ink substance used in laser printers.

track

A storage channel on a disk or tape. On disks, tracks are concentric circles (hard and floppy disks) or spirals (CDs and video disks). On tapes, they are parallel lines.

transceiver

A device that has the circuitry to enable it to be both a transmitter and a receiver.

transistor

A device containing semiconductor material that can amplify a signal or open and close a circuit. In computers, transistors function as an electronic switch.

triboelectric generation

Using friction to create a static charge.

Trojan Horse

A piece of malicious code that masquerades as a harmless file.

TSR program

(terminate-and-stay-resident program) An MS-DOS program that remains in memory after you initially run it. A TSR stays in memory until you reboot the computer. You typically run TSR programs only on computers that are using MS-DOS as the operating system.

twisted-pair cable

A thin-diameter wire (22 to 26 gauge) commonly used for telephone and network cabling. The wires are twisted around each other to minimize interference from other twisted pairs in the cable.

Ultra DMA

A newer faster drive technology for data transfers on IDE drives. Also called Ultra ATA and Fast ATA-2. Provides for transfer speeds of up to 100 MBps.

UMB

(upper memory blocks) Blocks of memory that are not in use within the upper memory area.

UNIVAC

(Universal Automatic Computer) Completed in 1951 by Eckert and Mauchly for the U.S. Bureau of the Census. It was the first commercial computer in the United States and could handle both numerical and alphabetical information.

upper memory area

The 384 KB of RAM between 640 KB and 1 MB in a computer. This segment of RAM is reserved in MS-DOS for use by the computer's hardware devices. If you run a DOS application within Windows, Windows simulates the upper memory area for the application.

UPS

(Uninterruptible Power Supply) A battery-operated device that is intended to save computer components from damage due to power problems such as power failures, spikes, and sags.

USB

(Universal Serial Bus) A hardware interface for connecting up to 127 USB peripherals.

user-level security

Enables you to specify which users and groups have access to each individual shared resource.

UTP

(unshielded twisted-pair) Twisted-pair cable that has two unshielded wires twisted around each other. This type of cabling is inexpensive, but electrical interference can be a problem.

vacuum tube

A sealed glass or metal container that controls a flow of electrons through a vacuum.

value

An entry in the Registry database that contains configuration information. A value consists of three parts: a name, data type, and the data stored in the value.

video output device

A computer peripheral that enables users to view information on a computer system.

Virtual Device Driver

A type of device driver used in Windows 9x. You sometimes see virtual device drivers referred to as VxDs because their associated files have the extension .vxd.

virus

A piece of malicious code that spreads from one computer to another by attaching itself to other files.

volt

Unit of measurement for voltage.

voltage

Electric potential or potential difference, expressed in volts.

VPN connection

(Virtual Private Network connection) An outbound connection that uses existing local or outbound connection objects to connect a client on one physical network, through a private connection over a public network, to a VPN server on a remote network.

VRAM

(Video RAM) These chips have two access paths to a single memory address to improve performance. One path is used for reads, the other for writes.

VRM

(Voltage Regulator Module) A module on the system board that regulates the voltage that's passed to the CPU.

watt

Energy per second delivered by electric current. Unit of measurement for power.

Win.com

A file used by Windows 9x to start the operating system.

Win.ini

A Windows 9x initialization (.ini) file used to set environment parameters for older applications that were written for Windows 3.1.

Windows 9x share permission

A collection of defined rights that allow access to a shared resource.

WINS

(Windows Internet Naming System) A Windows NT or Windows 2000 service used to enable clients to obtain the IP address for a given computer name.

workgroup

A Microsoft network model that simply groups computers together for ease of finding shared resources such as folders and printers. A workgroup does not share a centralized user account database.

worm

A piece of malicious code that spreads from one computer to another on its own, not by attaching itself to another file.

WRAM

(Windows RAM) Developed by Samsung Electronics, this type of RAM is optimized for display adapters.

XIP

(Execute In Place) A PC Card feature that enables operating system and application code stored on the PC Card to run directly from the PC Card rather than executing in RAM.

XMS

(extended RAM) All of the memory in the computer after the first 1,088 KB. This segment of memory is also referred to as XMS, which is short for "extended memory specification."

ZIF socket

(Zero Insertion Force socket) A type of processor socket that uses a lever to tighten or loosen the pin connections between the processor chip and the socket.

Zinc Air

Portable computer battery that uses a carbon membrane that absorbs oxygen.

zoned-bit recording

A method of creating sectors on a hard disk so that there are more sectors on the outer tracks than on inner tracks.

ZV

(Zoomed Video) A connection between a PC Card and the host system that allows the card to write video data directly to the VGA controller.